ROAD SAFETY

Data Collection, Analysis, Monitoring, and Countermeasure Evaluations with Cases

M. Ohidul Haque

University Press of America,® Inc.
Lanham · Boulder · New York · Toronto · Plymouth, UK

Copyright © 2009 by
University Press of America,® Inc.
4501 Forbes Boulevard
Suite 200
Lanham, Maryland 20706
UPA Acquisitions Department (301) 459-3366

Estover Road
Plymouth PL6 7PY
United Kingdom

All rights reserved
Printed in the United States of America
British Library Cataloging in Publication Information Available

Library of Congress Control Number: 2008937874
ISBN-13: 978-0-7618-4039-8 (paperback : alk. paper)
ISBN-10: 0-7618-4039-7 (paperback : alk. paper)
eISBN-13: 978-0-7618-4434-1
eISBN-10: 0-7618-4434-1

∞™ The paper used in this publication meets the minimum
requirements of American National Standard for Information
Sciences—Permanence of Paper for Printed Library Materials,
ANSI Z39.48—1984

DEDICATED TO MY PARENTS

CONTENTS

		Page
CHAPTER 1:	INTRODUCTION	1
CHAPTER 2:	ACCIDENT STATISTICS FOR THE SHIRE OF MELTON	21
CHAPTER 3:	A REVIEW OF SERIOUS ROAD CASUALTY DATA	27
CHAPTER 4:	ESTIMATION OF SAMPLE SIZE FOR THE COMPARISON OF ACCIDENT RISKS BASED ON AN EXPOSURE SURVEY	37
CHAPTER 5:	DEVELOPING ROAD SAFETY COUNTERMEASURE INITIATIVES USING ROAD FATALITY DATA	45
CHAPTER 6:	A SHORT-TERM ACCIDENT MONITORING SYSTEM: A CASE STUDY FOR VICTORIA	53
CHAPTER 7:	EVALUATION OF SOME MAJOR STATEWIDE POLICE INITIATIVES	67
CHAPTER 8	METHODS OF EVALUATION OF IMPLEMENTED ROAD SAFETY LAWS	73
CHAPTER 9:	EVALUATION OF IMPLEMENTED ROAD SAFETY COUNTERMEASURES USING INTERVENTION TIME SERIES ANALYSIS	89
CHAPTER 10:	DETAILED ANALYSES OF THE VICTORIAN ZERO BAC LEGISLATION ON SERIOUS CASUALTY ACCIDENTS	105
CHAPTER 11:	EVALUATION OF THE DEMERIT POINTS SYSTEM IN DETERRING TRAFFIC OFFENSES	131

CHAPTER 12:	UNEMPLOYMENT AND ROAD FATALITIES	145
CHAPTER 13:	COST OF ROAD ACCIDENTS	161
CHAPTER 14:	RISK ANALYSIS IN ROAD SAFETY	175
CHAPTER 15	CONCLUSIONS	183
APPENDICES		189
BIBLIOGRAPHY		215

LIST OF TABLES

Page

Table 2.1:	Distribution of population for Melton and Victoria by broad age groups, June 1988	23
Table 2.2:	Distribution of serious casualties for drivers and motorcyclist by broad age groups	25
Table 3.1:	Road casualty hospital admission data	34
Table 5.1:	Persons killed by road user type (preliminary figures for 1990)	47
Table 5.2:	Number of fatalities in Victoria by age group and road user type	51
Table 6.1:	Accidents reported in the Melbourne Statistical Division	60
Table 6.2:	Comparison of forecasting models for tow-truck allocation data	62
Table 6.3:	Monthly report of number of vehicles involved in accidents and towed away within Melbourne metropolitan areas	65
Table 7.1:	Persons killed and seriously injured due to road accidents for Friday before, during and after Easter holidays: 1986–1990	68
Table 7.2:	Persons killed and seriously injured due to road accidents, Friday to Monday period before, during and after Queen's birthday holidays: 1986–1990	68
Table 7.3:	Persons killed and seriously injured of equivalent times, before during and after targeting commercial vehicles: 1986–1990	70
Table 7.4:	Evaluation of project 100	70
Table 8.1:	Drivers involved in serious casualty accidents, July 1984 – December 1984 (six months post-legislation)	85
Table 8.2:	Effects of the Zero BAC law in the first six months post legislation	86
Table 9.1:	Best models for two series considered on the basis of Akaike's information criterion and Portmanteau test	97
Table 9.2:	Estimated parameters for intervention models	98

Table 9.3:	Persons involved in motorcycle casualty accidents, estimate of intervention effect, July 1983 – December 1984	98
Table 9.4:	Estimated intervention coefficients fitted to the serious casualty accident data	101
Table 9.5:	Estimates of the intervention effects of serious casualty accidents, 24 October – 31 December 1984	101
Table 10.1:	Drivers of cars and car-derivatives involved in serious casualty accidents by license type, 1980–1984	110
Table 10.2:	Effects of the Zero BAC law in the first six months post legislation	114
Table 10.3:	Effects of the Zero BAC law in the second six months post legislation	115
Table 10.4:	Effects of the Zero BAC law in the first twelve months post legislation	117
Table 10.5:	Effects of the Zero BAC law in the first eighteen months post legislation	118
Table 10.6:	Drivers involved in serious casualty accidents during July 1984 – December 1985 (18 months post-legislation)	123
Table 10.7:	Power analysis for the test for an effect of the Zero BAC legislation	124
Table 11.1	Distribution of time intervals between second and third detected traffic offenses	136
Table 11.2:	Drivers experience and estimated mean time Intervals (in days) between first and second offenses for DIP and MRB drivers	138
Table 11.3:	Estimates of the average time intervals (in days) between second and third offenses of the DIP and MRB drivers	140
Table 11.4:	Test for the unconditional mean time intervals between first and second, and second and third offenses at various driving experience levels for all drivers	141
Table 12.1:	Estimated regression coefficients for various road safety and socio-economic variables	151
Table 13.1:	Cost matrix by accident type and injury severity levels	169
Table 13.2:	Total number of accidents including total and average cost of accident types and injury severity levels in MSD and rest of Victoria	171

Table 8B1:	Drivers involved in serious casualty accidents during July 1984 – December 1984 (6 months post-legislation)	202
Table 8B2:	Drivers involved in serious casualty accidents during (six month pre- and post- legislation periods)	203
Table 10A.1:	Drivers involved in serious casualty accidents During July 1984 – December 1985 (18 months Post-legislation): Intervention Method	205
Table 10A.2:	Drivers involved in serious casualty accidents During July 1984 – December 1985 (18 months Post-legislation period): Pre-post Method	206
Table 10A.3:	Drivers involved in serious casualty accidents During July 1984 – December 1984 (6 months Post-legislation): Intervention Method	206
Table 10A.4:	Drivers involved in serious casualty accidents During July 1984 – December 1984 (6 months Post-legislation): Pre-post Method	207
Table 12A.1:	Fatalities involving trucks, Victoria, 1980–1990	211
Table 12A.2(a):	Pair-wise correlations of various variables for Long-term fatality model	212
Table 12A.2(b):	Pair-wise correlation of various variable for short-term fatality model	213

LIST OF FIGURES

Figure 1.1:	Road fatality, vehicle registration and population in Victoria, 1970–2000	13
Figure 1.2:	Serious road casualty, vehicle registration and Population in Victoria, 1970–2000	14
Figure 1.3:	Fatalities per 100,000 population and Vehicles in Victoria, 1970–2000	15
Figure 1.4:	Serious road casualty per 100,000 population and vehicles in Victoria, 1970–2000	16
Figure 2.1:	Percentage distribution of population by broad age groups, Melton Vs. Victoria, June 1988	24
Figure 2.2:	Percentage distribution of population by age groups, Melton Vs. Victoria, June 1988	24
Figure 3.1:	Hospital admission	29
Figure 3.2:	Hospital admissions, Melbourne	31
Figure 3.3:	Hospital admission, rest of Victoria	32
Figure 5.1:	Total road fatalities, 1990 vs. six-year trend	48
Figure 5.2:	Vehicle occupant fatalities, cumulative 1990 vs. six year trend	48
Figure 5.3:	Pedestrian fatalities, cumulative 1990 vs. six year trend	49
Figure 5.4:	Motorcyclist and pillion fatalities, cumulative 1990 vs. six year trend	49
Figure 5.5:	Bicycle fatalities, cumulative 1990 vs. six year trend	50
Figure 5.6:	Fatalities from truck accidents, cumulative 1990 vs. six year trend	50
Figure 6.1:	Patterns of monthly road accidents, April 1983 to December 1986	61
Figure 6.2:	12 month moving totals of road accidents	61
Figure 6.3:	Short-term accident pattern forecast of tow-truck allocations	63
Figure 6.4:	Short-term accident pattern, 1987 forecast of tow-truck allocations	64
Figure 6.5:	Cumulative tow-truck allocations	64

Figure 8.1:	Number of serious casualty accidents for target and control group drivers at alcohol times in Victoria, 1977–1985	79
Figure 9.1:	Serious casualty accidents, estimates based on ARIMA and intervention models	94
Figure 9.2:	The nature of the RBT campaign	99
Figure 9.3:	Motorcycle riders in casualty accident's category: Learners, Regions: MSD, post-intervention period only	102
Figure 9.4:	Motorcycle riders in casualty accident's category: Standard, region: MSD, post intervention period only	102
Figure 10.1:	Time series analysis, 12 month moving totals of serious casualty accidents for target group drivers	120
Figure 10.2:	Time series analysis, 12-month moving totals of serious casualty accidents for control group (standard license) drivers	121
Figure 10.3	Drivers killed or hospitalised in Victoria by age for whom their blood alcohol is known	121
Figure 10.4:	Drivers killed or hospitalized in Victoria by license type for whom their blood alcohol is known	122
Figure 10.5:	Car learner permits issues per month	127
Figure 10.6:	Car probationary licences issues per month	127
Figure 10.7:	First year car P licences current 12 months, cumulative total of new issues	127
Figure 10.8:	Number of preliminary breath tests in Victoria	128
Figure 11.1:	Histogram of all drivers in time intervals (days) between second and third offences	135
Figure 11.2:	Unconditional average time interval between offences and experiences for all drivers	142
Figure 12.1:	Fit of the Victorian long-term road fatality Model, 1960–90	157
Figure 12.2:	Fit of the Victorian short-term road fatality model, with the seasonally adjusted monthly data, 1985–1990	158
Figure 14.1:	Construction of decision rule to control α and β risk, large sample, one-sided upper tail test	178
Figure 5A.1:	Victorian road fatalities, monthly data, moving 12 month average	196
Figure 5A.2:	Speed offences, Victorian police data, total Victoria: 1986–1990	197

Figure 5A.3:	Random breath testing, monthly data, total Victoria: 1984–1990	197
Figure 5A.4:	Random breath tests, 12 months Moving average: 1984–1990	198

PREFACE

Road safety is a major issue in almost all countries in the world, particularly in developed countries. The number of motor vehicles and people has increased significantly over the past couple of decades, while money spent for the development of roads and safety network has not increased significantly. As a result, road accidents have increased dramatically over the past couple of decades. Road accident is an indirect measure of road safety. Its frequency gives an index of 'un-safety' on the road. Therefore to reduce road accidents, and in particular to reduce road casualties, is a major concern to all road safety administrators and governments. It is a very sensitive issue too. Road safety depends on many factors such as road users, vehicles, roads, the environment and people.

This book is mainly concerned with road safety data collection, analysis, monitoring and countermeasure evaluations with reference to Victoria, a state in Australia, which is one of the champions in road safety in the world. Some of the road safety techniques, which are described in this book can be applied in many countries of the world, and probably can save many road casualties.

Occurrence of road accidents, its effects and countermeasure initiatives and evaluation techniques are briefly discussed in Chapter 1. A brief history of road accidents, various countermeasure initiatives and its effects with reference to Victoria are also provided in Chapter 1. Chapter 2 provides an account of road accident information for a small local geographical area in Victoria. A review of serious road casualty data by various sources is presented in Chapter 3. Chapter 4 deals with the estimation of the sample size for the comparison of accident risks based on an exposure survey. A short-term accident monitoring system, which can provide a timely and accurate picture of any changes in level rather than level *per se* of road accident, is presented in Chapter 5, where an example of a monthly preliminary fatal data monitoring system is provided. A short-term road accident monitoring system is further developed in Chapter 6, using tow-truck allocation data, an appropriate timely available large accident data set. Chapter 7 deals with the evaluations of some major road safety police initiatives in Victoria. Chapter 8 provides some methods of evaluation of implemented road safety legislations, which are illustrated with an example. Chapter 9 deals with the evaluation of two road safety countermeasure programs: the Motorcycle Rider Training and Licensing Scheme, and the 1983 Random Breath Testing Campaign, using the techniques of intervention time series analyses with the SAS computer software. A detailed analysis of the effect of the Victorian Zero BAC Legislation on serious casualties for the first 18 months post legislation period is provided in Chapter 10. A statistical model for the evaluation of the effectiveness of the Demerit Point System in reducing traffic offences is presented in Chapter 11. Chapter 12 attempts to analyse the casual relationship between economic activities and road fatalities, incorporating some major implemented road safety legislation. Some methodological issues on how to estimate the cost of road accidents are surveyed, and an appropriate method of estimating the cost of road accident is presented in Chapter 13, while Chapter 14 provides some methodological issues on 'risk analysis in road safety'. The gist of our studies including some concluding remarks and limitations is presented in the final chapter of the book.

This is a research book on road safety issues, which can be widely used in various, developed, developing and under developed countries in the world. Various governments, road safety administrators and researchers can find this book very useful. Also some of the statistical and econometric techniques which are developed and used in this book can also be used to collect data, monitor, analyse and evaluate many programs in the fields of social science, health, engineering and humanities.

M. O. HAQUE

ACKNOWLEDGEMENTS

I wish to express my gratitude to the Road Traffic Authority of Victoria, and Victoria University, where I spent more than eight years to prepare this book, which is heavily drawn from my road safety research, while working as the Head of the Evaluation and Statistical Services Section. I am grateful to Ms Margarita Kumnick of CSES of Victoria University, who helped me to put the material into the publisher's format. I am highly indebted to Sunshine Foundation, and Philanthropy Australia, who provided financial assistance from the Estate of A. M White and Fred P Archer Charitable Trusts without which it would not have been possible to complete and/or publish this valuable and important book for the well-being of all people.

At this stage, I gratefully acknowledge the help and assistance of Mr Jeff Potter, Manager, Road User Behaviour, Road Safety Department, VicRoads, who approved the use of my works while I worked in VicRoads for my Road Safety book. I am also grateful to the publishers of Journal of Safety Research, Communications in Statistics: Methods and Applications, International Journal of Transport Economics and Evaluation Review, for their permission to use my articles and notes already published in these journals.

Finally, I wish to express my gratitude to my wife Rowshan, and my three children, Tariq, Sadira and Mahera; and our daughter-in-law Lima. I missed them in many enjoyable moments due to the heavy workload in preparing this book.

CHAPTER 1

INTRODUCTION

In this chapter, readers will find out what is contained in this book. A short description of road safety issues and its analyses based on statistical methods are provided in this introductory chapter. This is because the book is concerned with road safety data collection, analysis, monitoring and counter evaluations, which evolve from statistical theory. It also presents a brief review on Victorian road casualty history, and provides some important road safety countermeasures introduced in Victoria, which successfully reduced Victorian road toll to one of the lowest from one of the highest road casualty states. A broad outline and contributions of the book are also presented here along with some limitations and conclusions.

1.1 Introduction

A brief review of what is contained in this book is provided in this introductory chapter. The book is concerned with road safety data collection, analysis, monitoring and countermeasure evaluations, using Victorian (a state in Australia) road accident data. Victoria is generally considered as one of the champions in road safety in Australia. It is here in Victoria where the seatbelt legislation was introduced first in the world to avoid road casualties. More importantly, Victoria has a sound and accurate accident database, which can be used to show how to collect accurate road accident data, and how to monitor these data to identify any emerging trends so that remedial actions can be taken well in advance to reduce road accident casualties. This book also presents many examples of implemented road safety countermeasure evaluations based on highly sophisticated modern evaluation techniques. The nature of the book is partly theoretical and partly empirical. As the book is concerned with road safety, it is better to discuss some basic concepts of road safety, which are presented in this introductory section. Some methodological aspects regarding road safety data collection, analysis and countermeasure evaluations are provided in Section 2. A brief history of road safety in Victoria is provided in Section 3. An outline of the contributions of the book is given in Section 4. While, some concluding remarks and limitations of the studies presented in the book are provided in the final section.

1.1.1 Basic Concepts of Road Safety Issues

Road safety refers to the term 'how safe we are on the roads'. To answer this question we really look for 'road accident numbers'. The road accident number provides an indirect measure of road safety, because it indicates how safe or unsafe we are on our roads. The higher the road accident numbers, the lower the road safety and vice versa. Therefore, collecting and analysing road accident data are the main tasks of road safety, which are the main subject matters of this book.

An accident is a sudden event with sad consequences. A 'traffic accident' can happen only if several traffic participants try to occupy a specified space at the same time, and/or try to occupy a space, which is already occupied by other traffic participants and or objects (movable or fixed). There are several factors responsible for road accidents: **human** (includes drivers, motorcyclists, pillions, pedestrians, and public in general, that investigates according to age and gender breakdown); **vehicles** (types of motor vehicles, such as cars, trucks, buses, etc., that investigates the damage of the various locations of the vehicle); **roads** (design and condition of the roads, covering the location and the type of roads where the accidents happen); and **environment** (which covers a broad range of factors, such as weather, soil conditions, time of the day, day of the week, month of the year and even the political and economic conditions may be incorporated in this area, dry or weight conditions of roads, and busy locations such as schools, shopping centres and business centres, etc.). Accidents happen probably due to bad adjustments among these factors. Also, an increase in the number of vehicles on the roads is directly proportional to a greater number of license holders including the 'dangerous' ones, which consequently raises the accident numbers.

An individual's tendency to be involved in an accident can happen either due to the laws of chance and/or an inherent capacity to have accidents. But, it is impossible to separate those who have some knowledge and measurable human weakness, from those brought about the chance factor. The fact is that each road user differs, and identifying some and putting them in a special category is not realistic. There is a very high variation of accident involvements in each types of road users and hence, defining 'accident proneness' is just a relative term. However, there is a common perception that some groups are more accident prone than others. For example, it is generally believed that young male drivers are involved in accidents more than other drivers. This could probably happen

INTRODUCTION

due to lack of driving experience along with an age factor, which contributes significantly to accident proneness of young male drivers.

Accidents can be derived from the concepts of: (i) non-assignable causes, and (ii) assignable causes. Non-assignable causes refer to random occurrences, i.e., accidents which occur due to a 'chance situation'. However, it would be incorrect to suggest that all accidents are the results of a 'chance situation'. Accidents can happen due to carelessness, bad road design and condition of vehicles, and many other factors, which refer to assignable causes. Accidents occurring due to these latter factors can be identified and are possible to avoid or at least be reduced by improving the designs of roads and vehicles, and driving skills. As a result, the statistical hypothesis and the like as follows could be tested in order to verify some road safety concepts that could be used to improve the road safety situation.

- Drivers displaying aggressive behaviour while driving are, as a result, more liable to have accidents.

- Certain combinations of aggregation and anxiety are dangerous in motoring.

- Social status (marital, socio-economic, etc.) of a driver within a certain group has an influence on his/her accident contribution (high or low) to that group.

- Driving with great knowledge of the 'mechanics' of their vehicles results in safer motorists who use greater caution while driving.

Hence, the objectives of this book are as follows:

- to gain adequate knowledge on how to collect accurate, complete and reliable road accident data;

- to understand and develop a road accident monitoring system;

- to get an account of recent theoretical and empirical research, development and evaluation of road safety countermeasure initiatives; and

- to show the value of the statistical techniques in analysing road accident data, and the need for further development in and exchange of information about relevant statistical methodology.

1.2 Methodological Discussion on Road Accident Data Collection and Countermeasure Evaluation

1.2.1 Data

The aim of all road safety workers is to improve the safety on public roads. To achieve this objective both accident reductions and injury preventions are needed. Information about road accidents and how they occur is therefore necessary to record in road accident data. But, collecting accurate and complete road accident data is not an easy task, and it is one of the major challenges to all road safety organizations and investigators. This is because the definition of road accident data varies from one country to another, and it even differs from one organization to another within one country. Therefore, the difficulties of any road accident investigation are really the collection of correct and complete data, and their classification into different accident types. In this respect, a responsible police officer's interpretation of the accident record is widely accepted in almost all countries in the world. However, this police accident data are not immune to criticism. Hence, it seems that the major problem in the area of road safety is concerned with good data rather than analysis.

This raises two vital questions: (i) what information should be collected and recorded for road safety; and (ii) how should it be analysed? There is no easy answer for these questions. This is because most often policy makers and researchers have no clear idea about the problems. For example, are the road safety measures aimed at decreasing the number of accidents in relation to the traffic volume? Are they aimed at reducing accident severity? Are they trying to minimize the economic costs? In reality, they do not know the variables they need for analysis and/or the constraints, which are associated with such projects. The police accident data can be used to analyse various traffic safety investigations, but to shed light on road safety problems, one should have more detailed information about the relationship between accidents reported to the police and the whole accident population, which could be collected accurately through sample surveys. For example, an accident risk based exposure survey is a vital ingredient in the study of accident rates, because: (i) it provides a measure of exposure for those who are directly related to the risk of having accidents; (ii) it gives sufficient accident information for any category of drivers; (iii) it is inexpensive, and easily and quickly be used to analyse accident data; and (iv) it can be incorporated with other mass accident data which have already been collected.

In terms of road accident data collection, perhaps there is a need for public relations work to promote more understanding of our data collection techniques. On the other hand we must emphasize the need for co-operation among various road accident data collection agencies to solve the problems of data gathering and classification. Finally, we believe that data collected and published by various organisations could be improved and could be used to analyse accident data more appropriately. In this book we will discuss extensively how to collect accurate and complete road accident data, which will be used to analyse and to evaluate various implemented road safety countermeasures that will help to reduce future road accidents.

There are many studies on road accident data analysis in various countries in the world among which Margie, et al. (2004), Mohan (2004), Karlstrom (2005), Brude (2005), Jacobs (1996, 2000), Mackay (2003), Nantulya (2002), World Health Organisation (2004), Hossain (2006), Tanaboribbon et al. (2005), Trinca (1988), Australian Transport Council (2000) and Heidi (2006) are important.

1.2.2 Statistical Models of Road Accidents

If mean and variance of annual (monthly) accident data are the same, then a Poisson density function would be appropriate, which is given below:

$$f(A) = \frac{e^{-m} m^A}{A!}; A = 0, 1, 2, \ldots \infty \tag{1.1}$$

where A is the number of accidents, and m is the mean and variance of accident variable A.

However, if the variance is greater than the mean of the distribution then another distribution called Negative Binomial Distribution is usually considered to be a good approximation, which is given below:

$$f(A) = {}^{(A+k-1)}C_{(k-1)} \; P^k Q^A; \quad A = 0, 1, 2, \ldots, \text{ and } k > 0 \tag{1.2}$$

where C stands for combination, $Q = (1 - P)$ and $f(A)$ is the probability of having A number of accidents in exactly $(A+k)$ derives with k accident free derives in an indefinite series of binomial trials. Clearly the last derive must be an accident-free derive and its probability is P. Among the $(A + k - 1)$ derives, there must be $(k - 1)$ accident free derives and the probability of this is ${}^{(A+k-1)}C_{(k-1)}$ $P^{(k-1)} Q^A$. Multiplying the two probabilities we obtain the probability function given above in equation (1.2).1 It is possible to build a table in which one may determine directly the probability that on a certain day a certain number of accidents might happen.

It should be noted that the generating process is of stochastic nature, i.e., random, and therefore there is no reason to believe that in the years to come the phenomenon will acquire equal values at intervals situated at the same point of time. Therefore it is not justifiable to make 'a priori' indications of special or predetermined days, provided that no change is foreseen in the traffic characteristics, which might give real cause for a higher number of accidents.

In this study, a further development is undertaken in determining the probability of the intervals of time when no accident occurs, which could be obtained from the following differential equation.

$$\dot{P_o}(t) = -\lambda P_o(t) \tag{1.3}$$

Integrating the above equation (1.3), we obtain the following:

$$P_o(t) = K e^{-\lambda t}; \text{ where } K = 1, \text{ since } P_o(o) = 1. \tag{1.4}$$

Where $P_o(t)$ corresponds to the hypothesis that in the time t, the process has the state zero (o), meaning no accident has occurred. Thus, one can find out the probability of no accident happening at a certain interval of time say, 5 hours.

Furthermore, a model which specifies the mean incidence as a product of two factors, one pertaining to the road class: 'the risk on that part of the road network'; the other one to the day considered: 'the danger of that day'. In that case multiplicative Poisson law can also be used to find the probability:

$$P[A_{it}] = e^{-m_{it}} \frac{m_{it}^{A_{it}}}{A_{it}!}; \quad A = 0, 1, 2, \infty \tag{1.5}$$

where A_{it} denotes the number of accidents on the road class i at the tth day, while the mean incidence:

$$m_{it} = \psi_i \eta_t \tag{1.6}$$

This model implies that for any day the total number of accidents is scattered among the various road classes according to a multinomial distribution, the parameters of which depend solely upon the relative risks of the road classes, i.e., of the ψ_i's, thus being independent of the particular danger of the day, η_t .2

Experimental speed limits may produce a general reduction of the incidence of accidents, and require valid comparisons of total numbers of accidents at different times. No method of comparison for different periods at present seems to be available, but a comparison of 'similar days' in different years properly defined, e.g. as the 'Last Thursday' of each year, would seem possible.

If the multiplicative Poisson law could be applied for comparing two years on different days, the partitioning of the total number on two similar days into the two years should follow a binomial distribution with a fixed parameter. Actually the random variation turns out to be somewhat larger. In that case a negative binomial model appears to be appropriate with the property that for the comparison of two years any two 'similar days' may be used. Statistically speaking the outcome will depend on the year parameters only, not on the particular days. The mathematical formulation of the model is given as follows:

$$P[A_{xt}] = (-1)^{A_{xt}} \binom{-\alpha_x}{C_{A_{xt}}} \left(\frac{\eta_t}{1+\eta_t}\right)^A \times (1+\eta_t)^{-\alpha_x} \qquad (1.7)$$

where C stands for 'combination', A_{xt} denotes the number of accidents on the tth day of year x, and α_x is a year parameter and η_t is the day parameter. The said comparison rests upon the fact that the conditional probability of A_{xt} for a given total $A_{ot} = A_{xt} + A_{yt}$ over two years is a hyper-geometric distribution which is independent of the day parameter.3

Factor analysis is another method to investigate road accidents. The advantage of this method is finding essential factors of road accidents from the voluminous data. Once some important factors of road accidents are identified, road safety countermeasure initiatives targeting those factors can be taken to reduce road accidents. Nancy (2004), Ludwig (1985), Trinca (1988), O'Neill, et al. (2002), Gelman et al. (2003), Jacobs et al. (2000), Royal Thai Police (2004) and Traffic Safety of Japan (2005) have also used other models for recording accident data analysis.

1.2.3 A Model for Forecasting Traffic Accidents

The following model is set up on the basis of expressing accidents as a function of flow:

$$d = a \cdot N^P \qquad (1.8)$$

where d is accident/kilometer/year and N is average daily traffic (ADT), and the different road classes are characterised by different values of the parameters 'a and p', which can be estimated by the ordinary least squares (OLS) method, after taking logs on both sides of equation (1.8).

A model of the random variation within each section of the network had to be set up by assuming a Poisson law, which is the most straightforward assumption. An F-test can be formulated for the geographical differences once the model is established.

The value of P varies from about 0.6 (accidents grow considerably slower than traffic) to about 1.2 (more rapid growth of accident than traffic). By testing the value of a, one can find whether there is any significant difference between local area and the rest of the country with respect to parameter values.

1.2.4 Road Safety Countermeasure Evaluation Methods

1.2.4.1 Basic Statistical Evaluation Method

To evaluate the possible effects of implemented road safety countermeasures, the variation of the number of accidents of any particular type is necessary. The random part of this variation is assumed to follow a Poisson process, which provides a clear understanding about this variation. For example, if the average level of accident, is say 100 per week, then it allows for variation: $100 \pm 2\sqrt{(100)}$, i.e., 80 to 120 with 95% level of confidence without requiring any other explanation than randomness.

1.2.4.2 The Conventional Pre-post Method

The traditional pre-post method is usually used to measure the effectiveness of a certain countermeasure initiative by comparing the accident numbers within certain post legislation period (say 12 months after intervention) with the number of accidents of the same time period just before the intervention. Such comparison is quite suitable to evaluate the improvement of road safety after road construction and road engineering of certain section of roads. For example, it permits a successful determination of the effect of speed limits, etc., on individual stretches of motorways. With this method the influence of road construction measures on road safety as well as the arrangements of motorway junctions or the effect of improvement of road pavement can easily be found.

In studying the effectiveness of a road safety measure, accidents are counted in periods before and after the measure and one has to decide whether the change in the number of accidents is greater than one would expect if the measure had no real effect, taking into account the variations, which would occur in the number of accidents on a particular road or area even if conditions remained constant (according to the Poisson Distribution).

The interpretation of the accident data should take into account the effect of changes in traffic flow and weather; if from independent data one would expect accidents to increase (even if the measure had no effect) by a factor C (the control ratio), then the appropriate criteria is:

$$\chi^2 = \frac{(a-bC)^2}{(a+b)C} \tag{1.9}$$

where a and b denote the number of accidents after and before intervention. Here, we can test the following hypothesis.

Null hypothesis: H_0: There is no difference of accidents between the pre and post road safety intervention.

Alternative hypothesis: H_1: There is significant difference of accidents between the pre and post road safety intervention.

If the calculated value of χ^2 exceeds the critical value at 5% level of significance (3.841), we reject the null hypothesis, meaning that there is a significant change in accident numbers during the pre- and post-intervention period. However if the calculated value of χ^2 is less than 3.841, then we cannot reject the null hypothesis, meaning that there is no significant change in accident numbers between the pre- and post-legislation period. In that case, to find a real change, more data need to be collected from the same trial under the same conditions.

1.2.4.3 The Intervention Time Series Analysis

The pre-post method is appropriate to measure the road safety countermeasure evaluation only if no emerging trend is observed during the pre-legislation period. This is because if any downward (say) trend is observed during the pre-legislation period, then it is likely to continue to reduce the number of accidents even after the intervention, and there is no way of knowing whether the reduction of accident is due to the effect of intervention or due to trend effect. In that situation, intervention time series analysis is the appropriate method to evaluate the effectiveness of any implemented road safety countermeasure initiatives.

The modern time series forecasting technique was originally developed by Box and Jenkins (1970), and later modified by Box and Tiao (1975) to measure the effect of certain implemented legislation. Here, the idea is to identify a trend, based on past data, and then forecast for the future on the assumption that past trends would continue into the future. A road safety countermeasure can act as an intervention to the established trend, and hence any differences emerging between the actual and forecast values can be taken as the effect of intervention. We can test the intervention co-efficient to see whether there is any significant change in the post intervention period due to the implementation of the road safety measures [see Glass *et al.* (1975), Box and Tiao (1975) and Wiorkowski and Heckard (1977) for more details about the evaluation of implemented road safety countermeasures, using intervention time series analysis].

1.2.4.4 The Accident Relative Risk (RR) Method

The accident relative risk (RR) method based on exposure survey data can also be used to measure the effectiveness of implemented road safety countermeasure legislation and educational programs to test for a decrease in risk (shift from responsible to non-responsible accidents) in the target group as compared to the rest of population. It is based on the assumption that the frequency of involvement of any driver-vehicle combination as the 'non-responsible' combination in collision accidents is a measure of the exposure of the combination to (collision) accident risk. This assumption effectively provides the researchers with an induced control group with which to compare the responsible (accident) population. In the case of collision accidents, this control group is pair-wise matched with the accident population over all environmental conditions, thereby controlling for all such factors. To decide which driver vehicle combination was responsible and which was not, the police officer's interpretation of the accident was taken as correct and was recorded.

The RR defined for the *ith* driver vehicle category is given as follows:

$$RR_i = \frac{\text{frequency of occurence of the ith category in the responsible population}}{\text{frequency of occurence of ith category in the Non-responsible population}}$$

For any category i, RR_i can be considered as the risk of category i, relative to the average driver-vehicle combination. Note that for the whole accident population RR is unity. Also the ratio $\{RR_i/RR_j\}$ gives the comparative risk of the *ith* category to the *jth* category in the same population.

1.2.4.5 The Regression Method

A multiple regression equation for finding and representing quantitative relationships between various road safety factors can be used to evaluate road safety countermeasures. For example, a statistical relationship between accident frequency and road geometry is established. With these methods, the various types of motorway junctions could be evaluated with regard to their degree of safety, permitting a classification of road geometry elements and their use.

The theme of multiple regressions is very pervasive, and the method used in accident studies is not different from that of most social science research. As far as the choice of model is concerned, it is desirable to have an a priori model for regression analysis. But in a situation, with little or no a priori knowledge, the choice of a model becomes essentially finding what fits the data best. Most authors attach importance to a model which fits the data well rather than which is most convenient. In this respect, a multiplicative Poisson model would seem a priori to be the best model, and the Poisson assumption is likely to be quite good. It is suggested that a model assuming a Poisson distribution of accidents and a linear function or a log linear function should be used. A logistic transformation is defined by the following: Logit [$\log P / (1 - P)$]. If P is very small, one is left with essentially the logarithm of the number of accidents or the rate. The SAS or LIMDEP programs can be used to estimate such models.[4]

Number of road accidents can be expressed in a linear fashion with trend as one of the independent variables, and can be written as follows:

INTRODUCTION

$$Y = \beta_0 + \beta_1 X_1 + \beta_2 X_2 + \ldots + \beta_k X_k + \ldots + \beta_n X_n + \varepsilon \qquad (1.10)$$

where Y is the number of road casualties (fatalities, SCAs, pedestrian casualties, 4-wheeled casualties, etc.), and X_1, X_2, ... X_k, ... X_n, etc., are various independent variables, such as unemployment, fuel sales, seat-belt legislation, trend variable, etc., and β_1, β_2, ..., β_k .. β_n are parameters to be estimated. The least square estimation (LSE) method can be used to estimate these parameters, using any standard regression computer package.

Interpretation of the estimated regression coefficient is straightforward. For example the estimated value of β_1 gives the change in accident number (Y) for one unit change in X_1, provided other things remain constant. The other estimated regression coefficients can be interpreted in the same way. In other words, from the regression coefficients, one could find that an extra casualty per month or year could result from 200 extra motor vehicles, or 4,000 extra people in the city, or 300 extra bicyclists in the area, etc. Note that the positive value of the estimated regression coefficient indicates that there will be an increase in road accidents due to a specified factor, while a negative regression coefficient indicates a decrease in road accidents due to a specified independent variable. The test of significance for each of the regression coefficients can be done, using the usual t-statistic provided by most computer software's output.

It is expected that the safety benefit is higher resulting from the post-intervention period compared to the pre-intervention period. We feel the results are encouraging and may justify undertaking more detailed studies for road safety investment purposes. Of course the result depends on the availability and accuracy of the data and on the nature of the hypothesis on which it rests.

1.3 Road Safety in Victoria

Victoria is one of six states in Australia.5 It has a tragic road safety history, where road accidents resulted in 955 deaths in 1966 and climbed to a peak of 1061 road fatalities and 9,489 serious injuries with a population of 3.44 millions in 1970, probably one of the highest in the world.6 But, subsequently, in 2000 the number of road fatalities and serious injuries fell down to 407 and 6,364 respectively in Victoria. More importantly, it is seen from figures 1.1 and 1.2 that the numbers of people and vehicle registrations have increased significantly, while the numbers of road fatalities and serious road casualties have decreased significantly since 1970 in Victoria. Some people prefer to see the number of road fatalities and casualties per 100,000 population and vehicles, which are presented in figures 1.3 and 1.4 respectively, indicating that the number of fatalities and serious casualties have decreased. On the whole, it is clear from figures 1.1 to 1.4, that the numbers of road fatalities and serious casualties have decreased significantly in Victoria since 1970, despite a significant increase in population and vehicle registration. There is no doubt that Victoria has made significant progressive improvements in road safety during 1970 to 2000. It is therefore the subject matter of this book to discuss how Victoria has achieved such significant road safety improvement, which will help other countries to adopt such techniques to reduce their road tolls.

Indeed many factors contributed to achieve Victoria's recent impressive road safety records. But most notably, the following countermeasures appeared to have reduced the number of road casualty significantly in Victoria (see Appendix 1A for more important implemented legislations).

- wearing seat belt legislation;
- reduced speed limit;
- drink-driving countermeasures: random breath testing, higher penalties and media publicity;
- better driving, learning and educational programs;
- better road design and construction (including making more freeways);
- better vehicle design;
- use of red light and speed cameras; and
- awareness of road safety consciousness among road users.

In addition to the above factors, many other road safety techniques are used to reduce the road toll in Victoria. For example, better designing and showing art effects and signs on the roads and on boards have helped to reduce road accidents. Putting false signs up such as 'Red Light Camera Ahead', 'Speed Camera', etc. and also massive media publicity for avoiding drugs, alcohol and other frightening advertisements including picturing dying persons resulting from road accidents might have had some effect in reducing the road toll. In this sense, road safety techniques can be seen as an art, which could also reduce road casualties.

In fact, many road safety countermeasures were adopted to reduce Victorian road toll. The initial road safety countermeasures were described in Road Safety in Victoria (1982), and the subsequent countermeasures can be found in Social Development Committee (2000). Some important road safety countermeasures introduced in Victoria are presented in Appendix 1A.

To make a significant improvement in road safety, the first job is to identify the causes of road accidents. Most road accidents happen due to multiple causes. In this respect Treat (1977) indicated that 93% of road accidents happen due to error of human factors, 34% accident happens due to environmental factors and only 13% happens due to vehicle factors. Note that these percentages exceed 100% due to multiple causes.

In 1982, Parliament of Victoria (1982) stated that 60% of road casualty accidents could be avoided through road safety countermeasures and remedies: 25% from drivers, 20% from vehicles and 15% from better road design and construction.

Figure 1.1: Road Fatality, Vehicle Registration and Population in Victoria, 1970-2000

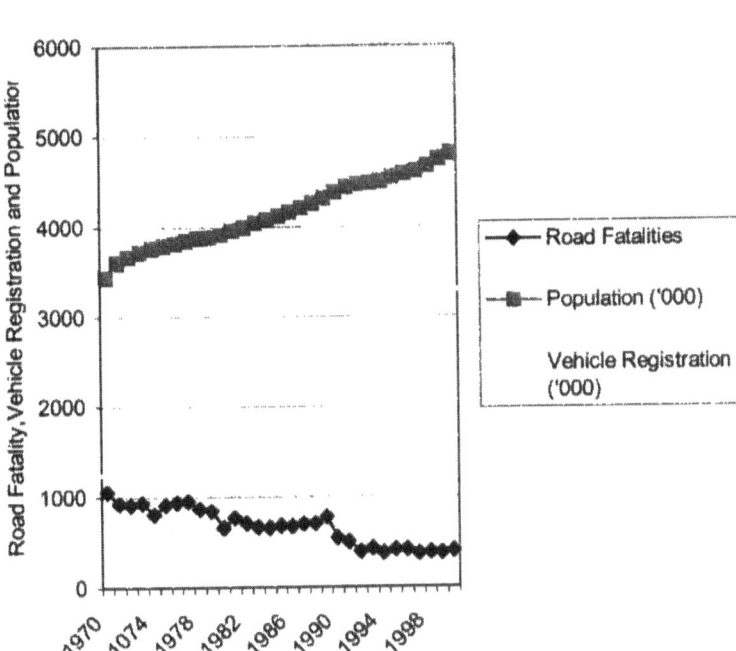

Source: Table 15: Road accident information, 1960 onwards supplied by VicRoads, based on Australian Bureau of Statistics (fatality data: 1960–1982; vehicle registration: 1996–99); rest of the data are taken from VicRoads data files; population figures are taken from ABS Catalogue No. 4101.0.

1.4 Outline and Contributions of this Book

This book is mainly concerned with road safety data collection, analysis, monitoring and countermeasure evaluation, using Victorian road accident data. The collection of road accident data is not an easy task, because of varying degrees in reporting, and the recording system, as well as variations in traffic rules, patterns and behaviour of road users from state to state and from one country to another. We usually collect two types of road accident data: time series data and cross sectional data. Time series data provide some very useful information on trends for any particular region, state or country. More importantly, a widely used regression model can be used to analyse the effect of various implemented road safety countermeasures. It also helps to find the causes of road accidents, which can then be targeted to reduce the road tolls. A 'secular trend' term can be used in a regression model to measure the effects of the gradual improvements

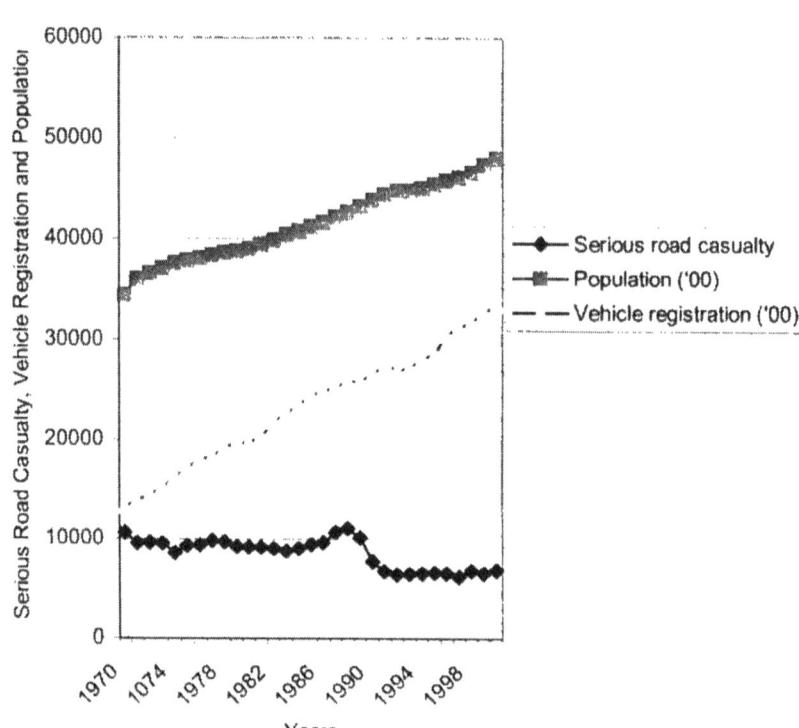

Figure 1.2: Serious Road Casualty*, Vehicle Registration and Population in Victoria, 1970-2000

* Serious casualty is as the sum of fatal, and people admitted to hospital"

Source: Table 15: Road accident information, 1960 onwards supplied by VicRoads, based on Australian Bureau of Statistics (fatality data: 1960–1982; vehicle registration: 1996–99); rest of the data are taken from VicRoads data files; population figures are taken from ABS Catalogue No. 4101.0.

INTRODUCTION

Figure 1.3: Fatalities Per 100,000 Population and Vehicles in Victoria, 1970-2000

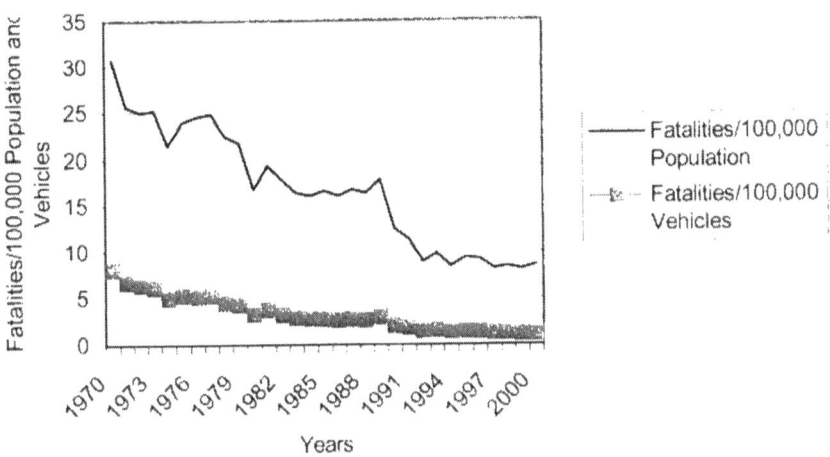

Source: Table 15: Road accident information, 1960 onwards supplied by VicRoads based on Australian Bureau of Statistics (fatality data: 1960–1982; Vehicle registration: 1996–99); rest of the data are taken from VicRoads data files; population figures are taken from ABS Catalogue No. 4101.0.

in road safety that has occurred in most countries since 1970. On the other hand, traffic survey data, particularly traffic exposure survey data, are designed to investigate traffic crash causes, types and travel pattern of various road users according to their age, sex, occupational status and other socio-economic characteristics, as well as vehicle type, location and timing of the day and day of the week, etc. Rapid economic and technological development during the last couple of decades might have implications for interpreting changes in pattern of road accidents. Analysing road accident data by various alternative methods is quite valid and relevant for various developing, developed and underdeveloped countries in the world. This is because the nature of road accident data in most countries remains more or less same. Thus, the analyses of road casualty data by various alternative methods presented in this book can be relevant and used in all developing, developed and underdeveloped countries in the world.

Another dimension of this book is to learn how to monitor road casualty data. Monitoring road casualty data, particularly short-term monitoring is an

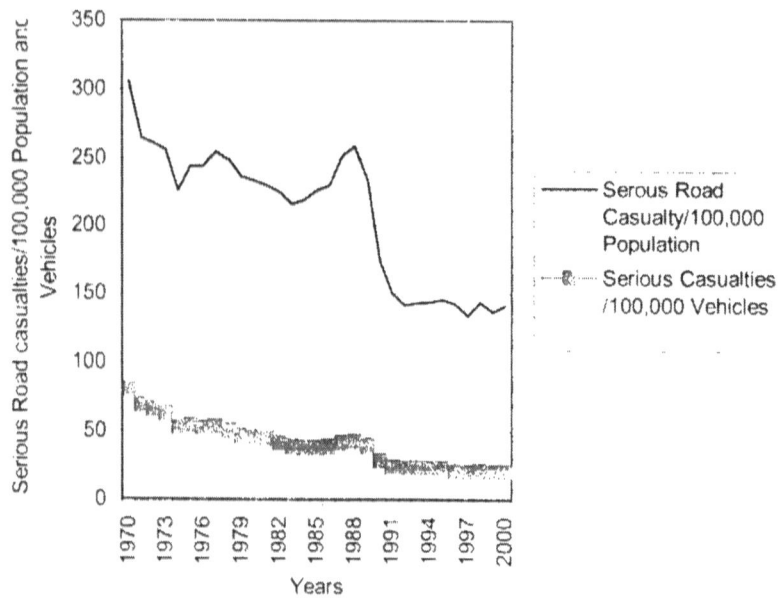

Figure 1.4: Serious Road Casualty per 100,000 Population and Vehicles in Victoria, 1970-2000

Source: Table 1.5: Road accident information, 1960 onwards supplied by VicRoads based on Australian Bureau of Statistics (fatality data: 1960–1982; Vehicle registration: 1996–99); rest of the data are taken from VicRoads data files; population figures are taken from ABS Catalogue No. 4101.0.

important aspect of road safety. This is because it helps to identify the emerging trend resulting from wide ranging changing situations, which can then be analysed and precautionary measures can be taken well in advance to avoid anticipated road casualties. The normal practice is to monitor road accidents by plotting the actual data against the forecasted values bounded by upper and lower limits with certain level of confidence. For example if it turns out that the actual two or three consecutive accident data points exceed the upper limit of the confidence limit, then we have to understand that there is something wrong in the process of road safety and as a result the road casualty data tend to increase. We then have to investigate the causes of such increasing trend immediately, and remedial action can be taken to reduce road casualty so that it can be reduced to the control limits. Similarly, if two or three consecutive points fall below the lower limit of the confidence interval, this indicates that something is working very well to reduce road toll. This can then be investigated and adopted quickly to reduce more road casualties in the future.

INTRODUCTION

This book also deals with the evaluation of implemented road safety countermeasure evaluations using two main methods: the pre-post method and the intervention time series method. These methods are usually used to measure the increase in road accidents due to the implementation of a certain road safety measure. The time series method is more appropriate to measure the actual gain resulting from an implemented road safety countermeasure. This is because it takes into account the effect of the pre-legislation trend effect. More importantly, we can test the effect of the implemented road safety countermeasures, using the standard statistical testing procedures. Besides these two evaluation methods, other statistical techniques can also be used to evaluate road safety countermeasures.

In addition to the above road accident data collection, analysis, monitoring and countermeasure evaluations, we also present a framework to estimate the cost of road accidents. Several accident cost categories have been separately estimated and combined to obtain the total road accident cost. Studies of road accident cost can help to allocate resources more efficiently to programs that reduce the accidents and severity of accidents. It also helps to raise public awareness of the economic and social impact of road accidents. More importantly, road accident cost estimates help to assess the benefits of various road safety programs. This book also attempts to establish the casual relationship between economic activities and road accidents. In this context it is shown here that there is a negative relationship between unemployment and road accidents. On the whole, this book presents a number of techniques showing how to collect accurate and complete road accident and casualty data, and how to analyse, monitor and evaluate implemented road safety countermeasure legislations. All these can be used to understand the accurate road safety situation. Following the lessons learned from our analyses, it is anticipated that other countries will benefit from this book to reduce the number of road accidents and severity of road casualties. The summary of each chapter of the book is given below.

Chapter 2 deals with the study of road accidents in a small geographical area, which contains a higher proportion of younger people compared to the state average. It shows that there is no significant difference of road casualties between a small geographical region (Shire of Melton) and rest of Victoria, which contradicts the popular belief that younger drivers are involved more in serious road casualties compared to the rest of the driving population. A review of serious road casualty data obtained from various sources is presented in Chapter 3. It shows that serious road casualty data collected by various agencies not only vary in magnitude but also vary in direction. Determination of sample size is an integral part of collecting road accident data based on transport exposure survey, which is presented in Chapter 4, dealing with the comparison of accident risks. Thus, by collecting an appropriate amount of information based on exposure survey, one could also get a good knowledge of the road safety situation.

Chapter 5 presents the monthly road fatality number and compares this number with the previous year, and the average of five years of the same month. It also plots current year's monthly actual and estimated road fatality numbers, and 95% confidence limits are also drawn against the estimated numbers to see whether current fatality numbers lie within tolerable limits. These are used as tools of the road safety monitoring system in Victoria to inform the current overall road safety situation to the government and society. Using road fatality data to know the overall road safety situation seems appropriate, but it represents only a small fraction of the overall road casualty situation. For that reason, the technique of a short-term accident monitoring system is developed and presented in Chapter 6, using a large accident data set. Victorian tow-truck allocation data seems appropriate and is used for this purpose. A short-term accident monitoring system provides a timely accurate picture of any change in level rather than level *per se* of road safety. It helps to measure the current road accident situation to see if it goes beyond the tolerable limits.

A short-term accident monitoring system helps to identify certain road users/vehicle types, times of day or days in a week or certain events in a year, where accident rates are historically high. Based on the results of a monitoring system, the Victorian police (main law enforcement agency) took some major state-wide initiatives to reduce the road toll by showing their presence frequently on the road and/or strictly following road safety laws at certain events such as Easter holidays. Preliminary evaluations of some of these state-wide police initiatives are presented in Chapter 7. Chapter 8 provides some methods of evaluation of implemented road safety legislations, giving an empirical illustration to measure the preliminary effect of the Victorian Zero BAC legislation. Chapter 9 presents two implemented road safety countermeasure evaluations related to: (i) the motorcycle rider training and licensing scheme; and (ii) the other with the evaluation of the 1983 Random Breath Testing campaign, using the techniques of intervention time series analyses. Detailed six-monthly sequential post-legislation analyses of Victorian Zero BAC legislation from July 1984 to December 1985 are presented in Chapter 10. This analysis shows that there was a small insignificant decrease of accidents for target group drivers at the post-legislation period. This could happen due to lack of publicity of the legislation, and the statistical power of the test was also poor. Evaluation of the demerit points system (DPS) in deterring traffic offences is presented in Chapter 11. A statistical model for the evaluation of the DPS system in reducing traffic offences is developed based on the exponential distribution. It is found that the DPS was responsible for most of the deterrent effect reflected in the increased mean time until the third offence subsequent to the first and second offence was detected in less than three years apart.

The effect of unemployment on road accidents is examined and presented in Chapter 12. It is shown in this chapter that the effect of unemployment has a negative association with road fatalities. It also provides evidences of the effectiveness of some major road safety initiatives in Victoria such as seatbelt wearing in motor vehicles and a package of drink driving reduction measures. More importantly, the progressive road safety initiatives and other effects over the years other than seatbelt and drink driving measures are estimated through the trend effect.

Chapter 13 discusses the methods of estimating the cost of road accidents. It recommends estimating the cost of road accidents, using the ex-post method encompassing the 'intangible cost, and economic value of life'. It also provides a framework for estimating the cost of road accidents including social costs. Chapter 14 provides some basic concepts of risk analysis in road safety. It aims to show how quantitative decision-making approaches can be used to choose the best option among various alternatives at the time of strict budget constraints. While some concluding remarks and limitations of the book are presented in the final section.

1.5 Conclusions and Limitations

This chapter briefly discusses the major issues of road safety data collection, analysis, monitoring and countermeasure evaluations. This is because road safety data collection, analysis, monitoring and countermeasure evaluations based on various alternative methods are presented in this book, which mainly evolve from the theory of statistics. Major contributions of this book are also presented in this introductory chapter. The methods of road safety data collection, analysis, monitoring and countermeasure evaluations presented in this book are highly relevant at present when various countries are disparately trying to reduce the road toll in the event of emerging economic growth. Road safety data collection methods presented in this book can provide an accurate picture of the road safety of a nation. The road safety monitoring system developed in this book would assist to detect an emerging trend of road accidents, which would help to take precautionary measures to reduce the road toll well in advance. Various methods of road safety countermeasure evaluations presented in this book would help to measure the effect of an implemented road safety countermeasure. More importantly, we have used a sophisticated intervention time series analysis, which will measure the actual effect of an implemented road safety countermeasure. This method allows us to test the significance of the coefficient of intervention variable to see whether there is any effect in any particular road safety countermeasure due to the implementation of such legislation, but is not diluted with any other countermeasures including the chance factor. It is thus hoped that the materials presented in this book would help to collect accurate and complete road safety data, and assist in monitoring road accident data to detect the emerging trends, so that precautionary measures can be taken to reduce road casualties well in advance. This book also helps to use the restricted road safety budget more efficiently by detecting the actual effect of the implemented road safety countermeasures, using the appropriate methods of evaluation presented here.

To get a clear understanding how to collect and monitor road safety information from traditional road accident data is always problematic. More importantly, accident data collection from one state to another state or country differs, not only because of varying degrees in reporting and recording accurately, but also because traffic rules, patterns and behavior of road users differ considerably from one country to another. Thus, data collection, analysis and monitoring methods presented in this book may not be automatically applied to other states and countries. However, the major themes of the techniques remain same and can be used with little adjustment according to local traffic rules, road user behaviour and environmental circumstances. More importantly, we have evaluated some specific road safety countermeasure legislation, using the pre-post and univariate intervention time series data analysis techniques, which ignore other relevant road users, vehicles, environmental, geographical, socio-economic and important variables, which together might have a significant effect in estimating the benefit for the implementation of road safety countermeasure legislation. The road safety data collection, analysis, monitoring and countermeasure evaluations presented in this book, are based on a variety of Victorian road accident data collected during the 1980s, which are dated. But, it is still valid and relevant, because most of the road accident data collection, monitoring and countermeasure evaluations techniques remain the same in analysing road accident data. It can thus be argued that some of the road accident data collection, analysis, monitoring and evaluation techniques presented in this book are still widely used and are more relevant even today, more than any other time when various countries of the world are facing the challenge to reduce the road toll at a time of economic growth. This is reflected in the studies of Ralin (1994), Mohan (2002), Hazet et al. (2006), Ghaffar et al. (2004), Romania Factbook (2005), Nantylya et al. (2002), Wegman et al. (2006) and Victor (1980).

Notes

1 Note that after some mathematical manipulations we can rewrite the negative binomial distribution as follows: $P(A) = {}^{-k}C_A P^k (-Q)^A$, $A = 0, 1, 2, \ldots$. This distribution is called Pascal's distribution with two parameters P and k. If $k = 1$ it reduces to the geometric distribution. It should also be noted that the Poisson distribution can be shown as the limiting case of negative binomial distribution.

2 Detailed theory can be found in Rasch (1960, 1969).

3 For derivation see Rasch (1969).

4 Declining road accidents can be expressed in a linear fashion with trend as a factor with a negative coefficient.

5 There are two territories in Australia: Northern Territory and Australian Capital Territory (ACT).

6 In 1966, the World Health Organisation (WHO) found that Australia was higher than any figures available from other countries. Also, Australia had higher ratios of number of registered motor vehicles to population and urban population to total population. It is shown that the proportion of fatalities with respect to total population is positively correlated with the proportion of urban population and hence explains Australia's higher fatality rates. It was found that in 1966 motor vehicle occupant deaths per 10^8 miles of travel for Australia was 5.77 compared to 4.34 in the USA.

CHAPTER 2

ACCIDENT STATISTICS FOR THE SHIRE OF MELTON

This chapter deals with the study of road accidents in a small geographical area, which contains a higher proportion of young people compared to the state average. It reviews the population and road accidents for the shire of Melton in Victoria, and evolved from the request of Mr. David Cunningham, Melton's representative to the Victorian (State) Lower House, who wanted to know his community's involvement in road accidents compared to the state average. Melton has a significantly high proportion of young and middle-aged (aged 0—24) people compared to the state average. In order to provide this information, we have analysed the 1988 local government area population and serious road casualties for Melton. However, serious casualties for drivers' and motorcyclists' show that there is no significant difference between Melton and the average of Victoria for various age groups. This contradicts the popular belief that young drivers are involved more in serious road casualty accidents than other drivers. Thus by reading this chapter, the readers will be able to learn techniques on how to compare the incidence of road accidents in a small geographical area with the national/state average figures.[1]

2.1 Introduction

Accurate and complete road accident data for small geographical areas are important in developing an overall road safety strategy for a country. This is important because some areas contain higher proportion of accident prone drivers such as young people, with some physiologically more risky than others, etc., with some exceptions. State laws are generally biased towards young drivers and sometimes make many harsh unnecessary driving rules, which make them disadvantaged. For this reason, research and accident data analysis for small geographical areas are important in assessing the actual situation of road accidents. In this respect the representative for the Shire of Melton to the State

Lower House, Mr David Cunningham claimed that his community was over represented by young people, while their involvement in road accidents was not over represented compared to the state average [also, see Anderson (1993)]. This is somewhat contradictory with the general perception that young people living in disadvantaged areas are expected to be involved in road accidents at a higher rate compared to the overall population, which can be seen from Mayhew *et al.* (1986) and Scottish Executive (2004). This study has been undertaken to verify his perception for the Melton community.

The objectives of the present study are to examine whether:

(i) the proportion of young people (aged 0—24 years) for Melton is higher than the Victorian state proportion; and

(ii) the proportion of serious road casualties for young people in Melton is lower than the Victorian state proportion.

The standard statistical technique was used to test these hypotheses, and it indicates that Melton has a significantly higher member of young people compared to the state average, while their involvement in road accidents is not significantly different from the state average.[2]

2.2 Data

The 1988 estimated residential population supplied by the Australian Bureau of Statistics is used for this study. This is because it is the only normal year for which the estimated residential population by age in statistical local area is available. The 1988 mid-year population figures are used as the representative population of the year for Melton and Victoria.

Accident data are taken from the VicRoads accident data system. Number of persons killed or injured by age group is only available for local government area by accident location, but not by home address. Hence, it is not possible to provide information on all serious casualties for Melton residents. However, the casualty series for 'number of drivers and motorcyclists' killed or injured by age group and home address is available for the same people for the shire of Melton and is used for the present analysis for Victorian drivers and motorcyclists, which account for about 50% of all serious casualties. It is also noted that approximately 80% of serious casualty accidents occur within 10 kms from their homes. Thus, this study would give some indication of involvement in serious road casualties for the Melton community.[3]

2.3 Methods

The following hypotheses are to be tested:

(i)   the proportion of young people (aged 24 years or less) for Melton could be expected to be higher than the state proportion; and

(ii)   the proportion of drivers and motorcyclists killed or seriously injured for Melton among people aged 18—24 years could be expected to be higher than the state average.

After estimating the proportion of respective population and casualties, these hypotheses were tested through a standard statistical test of difference for two proportions, using the formulas provided in Appendix 4A.

2.4 Analysis and Results

2.4.1 Distribution of Population for Melton and Victoria

Distributions of population by age groups for Melton and Victoria are presented in Table 2.1. This table also presents the percentage distribution of population by broad age groups. It shows that Melton has a higher proportion of young people (aged 0—24 years) compared to the state proportion. This table also shows that Melton has a higher proportion of middle aged people (25—49 years) than the state average, while it has significantly lower proportion of elderly people compared to the whole of Victoria (see also Figure 2.1).

More detailed percentage distributions of population by age groups for Melton and Victoria are presented in Figure 2.2. This figure shows that Melton has a lower percentage of high-risk population (aged 18—24 years) than the whole of Victoria. This kind of percentage distribution of population usually arises from new housing estates [see Haque (1988)] in urban areas.

Table 2.1:   Distribution of Population for Melton and Victoria by Broad Age Groups, June 1988

Age groups	Population		Percentage distribution of population	
	Melton	Victoria	Melton	Victoria
0—24	15349	1645780	48.04	38.62
25—49	13642	1557186	42.69	36.54
50+	2963	1058979	9.27	24.84
Total	31954	4261945	100	100

Source: Estimated residential population by age and sex in statistical local areas in Victoria, ABS Catalogue No. 3207.2.

2.4.2 Distribution of Accident Involvement (Per 1,000 Population) for Melton and Victoria

The numbers of drivers and motorcyclists killed or seriously injured by broad age groups for the Shire of Melton and Victoria are presented in Table 2.2.

This table also gives serious casualty rates of drivers and motorcyclists killed per 1000 population for Melton and Victoria. It shows that there is no statistical difference in serious casualties for drivers and motorcyclists between those who live in Melton compared to the state average.

Figure 2.1: Percentage Distribution of Population by Broad Age Groups, Melton Vs. Victoria, June 1988

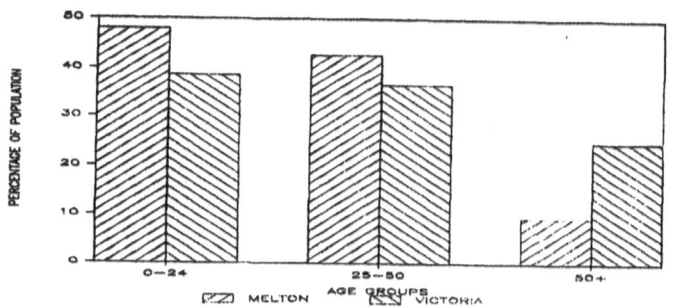

Source: Estimated residential population by age and sex in statistical local areas in Victoria, ABS Catalogue No. 3207.2.

Figure 2.2: Percentage Distribution of Population by Age Groups: Melton Vs. Victoria, June 1988

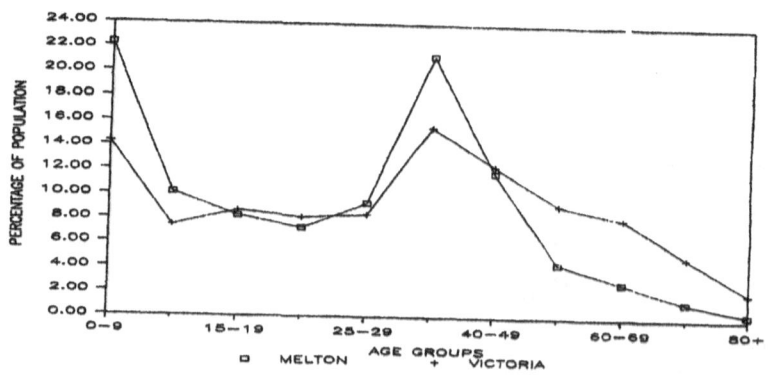

Source: Estimated residential population by age and sex in statistical local areas in Victoria, ABS Catalogue No. 3207.2.

ACCIDENT STATISTICS FOR THE SHIRE OF MELTON

Table 2.2: Distribution of Serious Casualties for Drivers and Motorcyclist by Broad Age Groups for Melton and Victoria

Age Groups	Population		Serious Casualties		Serious Casualty Rate Per 1000 Population		Comments
	Melton	Victoria	Melton	Victoria	Melton	Victoria	
18-24	3275	481673	13	2059	3.97	4.28	NS
20-49	13642	1557186	26	2596	1.91	1.67	NS
50+	2963	1058979	1	942	–	–	–

** NS stands for non-significance, which means that the difference might occur due to chance variation and/or non-sampling error; and ' – ' means figures are not avaiable.

Source: Estimated residential population by age and sex in statistical local areas in Victoria, ABS Catalogue No. 3207.2.

2.5 Problems and Future Options

2.5.1 Problems

A number of problems have arisen involving small area population estimates and accident involvements in a small local government area such as Melton. For this reason, the population estimate figures supplied by the Australian Bureau of Statistics have been readjusted for various desired age groups, which may not be correct compared to the actual population size of the group. Moreover, only one year's population data are used for the study, which may not be stable over the years in a relatively new suburb.

All accident data and home addresses are not available for a local government area. As such, accidents happening in a local government area for drivers and motorcyclists cannot give the full information for serious casualties for Melton. Moreover, other information such as number of drivers, exposure or other economic variables are not available for local government areas, particularly for Melton. As such, any findings from this study should be treated with caution. Moreover, only one year's serious casualty data for drivers and motorcyclists is not of great help for any definite conclusion, although it may give some indication about the likely outcome of a comprehensive study.

2.5.2 Possible Improvements

(1) The Australian Bureau of Statistics should provide yearly population figures by age groups and local government areas.

(2) Accident injury data by age groups and residential address should be recorded. The information required could be provided in the following ways:

(a) Sample survey methodology could be used in "high risk" local government areas.

(b) Residence and telephone surveys can provide further information for accident involvement in a local government area. This is very helpful particularly for the non-reported accident data series, such as bicycle accidents.

2.6 Conclusions and Recommendations

The following conclusions emerge from this study:

- The Shire of Melton has a significantly higher proportion of young (aged 0-24) and middle age people compared to the state average.

- However, more detailed analysis shows that Melton has fewer people in the high risk 18—24 population group compared to the whole of Victoria.

- The distribution of serious casualties for 'drivers and motorcyclists' by broad age groups, show that there is no significant difference between Melton and Victoria for various age groups.

These conclusions should be treated cautiously, as this analysis is based on only one year's data on serious casualties for drivers and motorcyclists. A detailed further study for Melton community's involvement in road accidents could be made, using several years population, accident and other economic data with more sophisticated statistical technique would be interesting and left for further investigation.

Notes

1 Such analysis of road accidents of a small geographical area has been undertaken by many authors among which Gururaj *et al.* (2000), Razzak *et al.* (1998), Romão *et al.* (2003), Andrews *et al.* (1999) and Quazi *et al.* (2005) are important.

2 A test for comparison of two sample proportions is presented in Appendix 4A.

3 Speeding is the one of the major causes of serious road casualties, which can be reduced by deriving the cars at an optimum speed on local residential streets indicated by Cameron (2000), Engel (1992), Carsten, Tight, Southwell and Plows (1989), and Institute for Public Policy Research and Imperical College (2002).

CHAPTER 3

A REVIEW OF SERIOUS ROAD CASUALTY DATA

A serious road casualty is defined as a person who is killed or injured and admitted to hospital as a result of a road accident. This chapter reports the availability and accuracy of various sources of hospital admission data. These data are now independently collected in Victoria by various organisations for their own purposes. This study shows that data collected by these organisations not only vary widely in magnitude but also vary in direction, which are shown through their trends. The Hospital Morbidity File (HMF) data is recommended as the most reliable source of hospital admission data. The HMF data together with the readily available fatality data can be used to monitor trends in serious road casualties in Victoria.

3.1 Introduction

A serious road casualty is defined as a person who is killed or injured and admitted to hospital as a result of a road accident. This chapter is concerned with a review of sources of hospital admission data, because there are a number of data sets that deal with this data.

Hospital admission is a larger data set than fatality data (updated daily). Road fatality data presents an important but only one aspect of the overall road casualty picture. The use of hospital admission data together with the readily available data on fatalities would make statistical tests more powerful and enable small effects of road safety measures to be detected.

For this reason, considerable effort has been made by VicRoads to collect accurate serious casualty data. Renewed attention was given to this data during the development of the joint Road Traffic Authority (RTA) and Road Construction Authority (RCA) Road Safety Strategy for 1989—93, in which it was proposed to obtain monthly hospital admission data to monitor the change of serious casualty trends.

Information on serious road casualty data is collected regularly by a number of independent organisations viz., (i) Victoria Police (VicRoads data system), (ii) Transport Accident Commission (TAC) Hospital Claim Data System, and (iii) the Hospital Morbidity File (HMF) data from the Department of Health. A detailed description of these data systems can be found in Haque and Le (1988, pp. 235-237).

Hospital admission data are collected and recorded by various organizations for a number of purposes and hence they differ slightly. For example, the Hospital Morbidity File (HMF) does not include information from private hospitals and public long-term hospitals, while the TAC excludes victims who do not claim compensation directly from them (for example, those who are eligible for WorkCare payments, those who are ineligible because the accident was not reported to the police, and those people who do not lodge a compensation claim).

The main purpose of this study is to identify the most accurate and complete hospital admission data series, which can be updated quickly enough to monitor road trauma trends and to provide a basis for developing road safety countermeasure initiatives. This can be achieved by examining the size and direction of trends for different hospital admission data series.

3.2 Data

The HMF, Police and TAC provide data on hospital admissions from road accidents. We are primarily interested in obtaining the most accurate and complete data series on hospital admissions. There would be no problem in using any one of these sources if each of them is accurate and complete, and if they coincide. Table 3.1 and Figure 3.1 clearly show that they do not coincide. The question can therefore be raised, 'which is the most complete and accurate hospital admission data series?'

3.2.1 Police-reported Hospital Admission Data

In Victoria, by law, all road casualty accidents (which include those involving hospital admissions) must be reported to the police. In some cases the police go to the scene and wait until the victim is put in an ambulance. The police should then fill in the Police Accident Report Form and then later verify with the hospital that the person was actually admitted. However, it has been suggested that while in country areas almost all cases are checked, this be not done to the same extent in the Melbourne Metropolitan Area.

Figure 3.1: Hospital Admissions

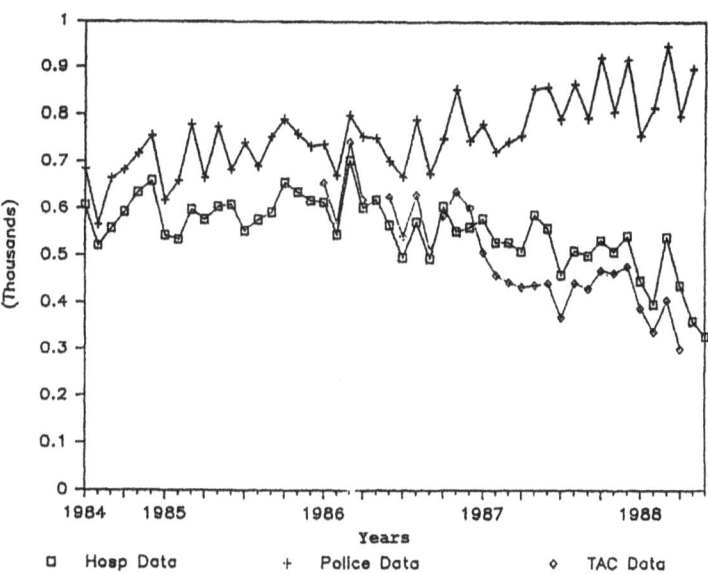

Source: Hospital data is taken from the Road Accident Data File of the Department of Health of Victoria;
Police data is taken from the Road Traffic Accident Data File of the Road Traffic Authority of Victoria;
TAC data is taken from the Road Accident Data File of the Traffic Accident Commission of Victoria.

3.2.2 Comparison of Police Data with HMF Data

The medical record administrator of the Health Department, Ms Robyn Bailey, estimated that the HMF contains more than 95% of the total hospital admissions of road accident victims. The HMF and police data for Melbourne and rest of Victoria are presented in figures 3.2 and 3.3 respectively. It should be noted that the HMF data are based on place of hospitals, while the police data are based on place of accidents. It is assumed, however, that most seriously injured road victims are taken to the nearest hospital with very few road victims from a country area being transferred to a metropolitan hospital before being recorded at the country hospital. This is a reasonable assumption, which could be researched by comparing the place of accident with the place of hospital on police accident reports.

Figure 3.2 shows that the police monthly total for hospital admissions is significantly higher (not only in magnitude but also in direction of their trends) than the HMF total in the Melbourne Metropolitan area. This confirms the suggestion that the police do not contact the hospitals and hence include victims who are treated at hospital but not necessarily admitted.

Figure 3.3 shows that there is more consistency between the police and HMF data for the rest of Victoria, although the discrepancies cannot be totally explained by the likely magnitude of admissions to hospital, which do not contribute to the HMF.

3.2.3 The TAC Data

Before 1987, the Motor Accident Board (MAB) paid no-fault compensation to all road victims in the form of hospital, medical, funeral and ambulance expenses including a certain proportion of loss of earnings, even if the accident was not reported to the police.

The new Transport Accident Act was introduced in January 1987. Under this Act, a transport accident claims for compensation will be paid to the road accident victim (including those who are admitted to hospital) within four weeks if the accident is reported to the police. In order to provide compensation to the road accident victim in time, TAC collects police traffic accident report forms daily. The hospital admission data can be taken directly from this system.

However, it is understood that even though the TAC provides a relatively up to date source of information, the data collected is incomplete and discontinuous. People who have a road accident traveling to or from work or during work time (including lunch breaks) are excluded from the database because they are compensated through WorkCare. From January 1987, the Transport Accident Act also excluded victims whose road accident was not reported to the police. There is no record kept of the missing data although the WorkCare component could be estimated.

3.2.4 Hospital Morbidity File (HMF)

The HMF is administered by the Department of Health in Victoria. The coverage of this data system is given in Appendix 3A.

All public hospitals, which admit emergency road trauma victims, have contributed to the scheme since June 1984. However, psychiatric, repatriation and private hospitals, and nursing homes are not normally included in this data set; the only exceptions being acute emergency patients admitted to public rehabilitation and extended care facilities. The HMF covers only those road accident victims who were actually formally admitted to the public hospital and normally would have spent at least one night in the hospital. Duplication is generally avoided by not registering people as acute emergency cases in any of their subsequent admissions. The exception could be if the patient was transferred within a few hours, say from a country hospital to a metropolitan hospital.1

Figure 3.2: Hospital Admissions, Melbourne

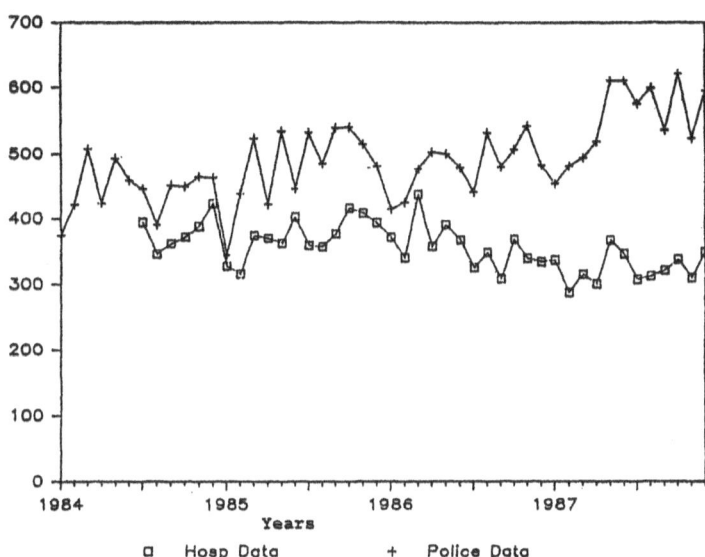

Source: Hospital data is taken from the Road Accident Data File of the Department of Health of Victoria;
Police data is taken from the Road Traffic Accident Data File of the Road Traffic Authority of Victoria.

Information such as age, sex and hospital location is available within four weeks, whereas 80—90% of other information such as road user type is not available in this timeframe. Diagnostic information is entered after the patient is discharged from hospital and this may take up to four months.

Public hospitals update the HMF on the same date of every month. Thus it should be possible to obtain a monthly total of all road victims admitted to a public hospital within the previous four weeks. Examination of the hospital reporting showed that in every month, approximately ten hospitals failed to meet the monthly deadline. These were not the same ten hospitals but each missing one could be contacted and the information could be added manually.

The monthly total of the HMF data was compared with the TAC and the police data (Figure 3.1). The graph suggests that the data missing from the HMF and the TAC do not constitute a bias. The assumption is that the HMF contains 95% of the total road casualty hospital admissions and can be checked using the police-reported 'hospital admissions' and examining the hospital codes to sort them into the various hospitals say public, private, repatriation, psychiatric, etc.

Figure 3.3 Hospital Admissions, Rest of Victoria

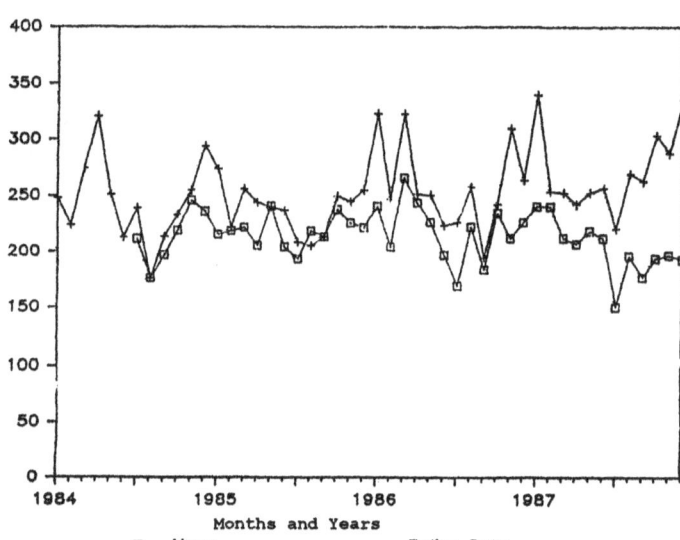

Source: Hospital data is taken from the Road Accident Data File of the Department of Health of Victoria;
Police data is taken from the Road Traffic Accident Data File of the Road Traffic Authority of Victoria.

3.3   Some Observations

None of the available data sets contain complete and accurate data on hospital admissions. They are presented in Table 3.1 and Figure 3.1. One noticeable feature of these data is that the police monthly total is consistently higher than the HMF and TAC data. The difference varies between 80% and 100% when police data are compared with HMF data. More importantly, this difference has increased with time. For example, the police data was 22% higher than the HMF in 1985, whilst the corresponding figure was about 55% in 1987.

The monthly TAC totals are slightly higher than the HMF throughout 1986, but after January 1987, when the reporting of accidents to the police became a criterion for an acceptable TAC claim, the monthly figure dropped below that of the HMF. There are good reasons to expect such behaviour for the TAC data. The higher figures for the TAC data prior to January 1987 can be explained by the fact that prior to that time hospital bills were paid for all hospitalised road accident victims even though the accident was not reported to the police. In contrast, from January 1987 hospital bills were only paid if the accident was reported to the police. Moreover, TAC excludes those road accident victims who are covered by WorkCare payments, and who do not claim compensation from them. Thus, one could expect a better agreement between the HMF and TAC data once the latter is corrected for different factors.

The most important observation from Figure 3.1, however, is the upward trend for the police data, and a downward trend for both the HMF and TAC data. Figure 3.1 clearly indicates that the police data is significantly higher than both the HMF and TAC data, particularly from the beginning of 1986.

3.4 Conclusions

The "hospital admission" data provided by the police is more likely to be casualty data, that is persons injured and taken to hospital, but not necessarily admitted to hospital.

The TAC data is a good indicator for hospital admission, but this data cannot be used for the evaluation of road safety measures because of its limited coverage. The HMF data is the only reliable source of hospital admission data, which can be used for monitoring the trends in serious road casualties in Victoria. This data can be used for developing road safety initiatives to reduce overall road casualties.

3.5 Recommendation

The HMF data should be used to monitor the trends of serious road accident casualties in Victoria. The police 'hospital admission' data can still be used as an indicator of road casualties, which covers persons injured and taken to hospital.

3.6 Further Investigations Needed

1. A review should be carried out of police-reported 'hospital admissions' and the specific hospitals to which the road trauma victims were taken, to establish the proportions taken to:

    (a) public acute hospitals (i.e., hospitals covered by the HMF)
    (b) public long-term hospitals
    (c) private hospitals

2. A hospital-by-hospital comparison could be done of police-reported hospital admissions and numbers recorded in the HMF data file, for a specific period, to establish hospital-related factors influencing the false recording of 'hospital admission' by the police, such as:

    (a) location of hospital
    (b) admission policies

(c) road user type, age, sex
(d) length of stay in hospital

Table 3.1: Road Casualty Hospital Admission Data

		Hospital Data	Police Data	TAC Data
1984	JUL	607	684	
	AUG	522	567	
	SEP	559	665	
	OCT	592	682	
	NOV	635	719	
	DEC	659	756	
1985	JAN	544	618	
	FEB	535	660	
	MAR	597	780	
	APR	577	666	
	MAY	604	775	
	JUN	608	683	
	JUL	554	742	
	AUG	577	691	
	SEP	592	754	
	OCT	655	791	
	NOV	635	760	
	DEC	617	735	
1986	JAN	613	738	654
	FEB	546	672	569
	MAR	703	799	742
	APR	602	755	619
	MAY	618	751	621
	JUN	566	702	624
	JUL	496	668	542
	AUG	572	790	628
	SEP	494	675	510
	OCT	604	750	584
	NOV	553	852	636
	DEC	562	746	600

Table 3.1. (continued)

1987	JAN	579	781	508
	FEB	530	723	459
	MAR	529	744	444
	APR	510	757	434
	MAY	587	854	438
	JUN	560	858	442
	JUL	460	792	370
	AUG	511	864	442
	SEP	501	794	431
	OCT	534	922	469
	NOV	510	807	469
	DEC	544	917	478
1988	JAN	447	757	389
	FEB	397	814	338
	MAR	541	948	406
	APR	437	797	301
	MAY	361	896	
	JUN	328		

Source: Hospital data is taken from the Road Accident Data File of the Department of Health of Victoria,
Police data is taken from the Road Traffic Accident Data File of the Road Traffic Authority of Victoria,
TAC data is taken from the Road Accident Data File of the Traffic Accident Commission of Victoria.

3. A review of police-reported accident data received since January 1987 should be undertaken to establish whether multiple reports of the same accidents appear in the data file or whether such reports have been rationalised by the police prior to data entry.

4. A review of police-reported 'place of accident' and 'place of hospital' to which the road accident victims were taken should be investigated, to establish the proportion taken to the nearest hospital, such as:

    (a) MSD hospitals
    (b) country hospitals

5. A thorough study should be undertaken to know the degree of overlapping and accuracy of the three data systems:

(a) police reported "hospital admissions"
(b) hospital Morbidity File
(c) accepted TAC claims resulting from hospital admissions.

The investigation listed above should be carried out by drawing a sample of 1000 cases from each of systems (a), (b) and (c), and then matching them with cases appearing in each of the other two systems. This is expected to be a longer-term but more definitive study to gain a fuller understanding of the three data systems.

None of these proposed investigations should influence or delay the adoption of the primary recommendation of this review. The investigations are most relevant to gaining a better understanding of the nature of police-reported hospital admission data in particular, as well as the other two sources of hospital admission data.

Notes

1 Hospital based data were previously used by Maheshwari and Mohan (1989), OECD Road Transport Research (2005), Ponboon (2005), Ruengsorn et al. (2003), Tanaboriboon et al. (1999), Karim (1995), Elvik and Myson (1999), Sidi and Kaharo (2001), Kobusingye and Lett (2000), Hossain (2006) and many others.

CHAPTER 4

ESTIMATION OF SAMPLE SIZE FOR THE COMPARISON OF ACCIDENT RISKS BASED ON AN EXPOSURE SURVEY

This chapter provides statistical formulas to estimate sample size for the comparison of accident risks based on an exposure survey. It is demonstrated here how to calculate sample size based on the statistical test, which can detect various levels of differences between the mean accident rates, expressed as a percentage of the overall average accident rate.

4.1 Introduction

Collecting accurate and complete road accident data is very important in developing a road safety strategy to reduce the road toll. We have seen from the previous chapter that time series road accident data obtained from various sources cannot provide accurate and complete road accident data. For that reason, sometimes accident risks are estimated from various road users, vehicle types and other characteristics based on transport exposure survey. Using an appropriate sample size, collecting road accident information for valid statistical tests is very important. In fact, estimating sample size to achieve statistical significance is a common problem. In this study, we are interested in testing the difference between the mean number of accidents per kilometer driven by high-power and low-power engine capacity of the riders. Hence, estimation of an appropriate sample size for the exposure survey is important to have a reasonable expectation of finding statistically significant differences between these means of two groups.

In general, the estimation of sample size is related to the following factors:

(a) the magnitude of the expected difference relative to the initial magnitude of the dependent variable;

38 ESTIMATION OF SAMPLE SIZE FOR ACCIDENT RISK

(b) the underlying variance of the dependent variable;

(c) The statistical test to be used;

(d) the confidence level considered acceptable for avoiding a Type I error; the probability of accepting that a given difference is statistically significant, when in fact it is not;

(e) the confidence level considered acceptable for avoiding a Type II error; the probability of failing to detect a significant difference when it really occurs; and

(f) The width of the confidence range of the estimate, i.e. the level of accuracy to estimate the magnitude of difference.

4.2 Derivation of the Sample Size

The derivation of the sample size here is based on three basic assumptions: (i) that relatively large samples are being considered, i.e. samples of 50 or more; (ii) that in comparing two sample means, standard normal test is applied; and (iii) that the most pressing consideration is the ability to detect that a change has taken place.

Therefore, our job is to determine the relationship between sample size, the amount of variation within the data, the level of change to be observed and the confidence level we wish to have in avoiding both Type I and Type II statistical errors.

4.3 A Simple Model

Under usual conditions, the following formula can be derived to test the significant differences between the population means:

$$\hat{\delta} = (Z_1 + Z_2)\left(\frac{\sigma_H^2}{n_H} + \frac{\sigma_L^2}{n_L}\right)^{1/2}$$

where $\hat{\delta} = \mu_H - \mu_L$ the minimum detectable difference in population means

μ_H = population mean accident rate/km for the high engine capacity riders

μ_L = population mean accident rate/km for the low engine capacity riders

ESTIMATION OF SAMPLE SIZE FOR ACCIDENT RISK

$\dfrac{\sigma_H^2}{n_H}$ = the variance of the estimated mean high engine capacity rate/km driven

$\dfrac{\sigma_L^2}{n_L}$ = the variance of the estimated mean low engine capacity rate/km driven

Z_1 = the critical value of the standard normal deviate associated with one or two-tailed test of significance at the c_1 level.

Z_2 = the critical value of the standard normal deviate Z associated with one-tailed test of significance at the c_2 level.

Now, if we assume: $\sigma_H^2 = \sigma_L^2 = \sigma^2$

and suppose: $n_H = 0.40\, n_L$

Then: $\hat{\delta} = (Z_1 + Z_2)\left(\dfrac{\sigma^2}{0.4\, n_L} + \dfrac{\sigma^2}{n_L}\right)^{1/2}$

$= (Z_1 + Z_2)\left(\dfrac{3.5\,\sigma^2}{n}\right)^{1/2} \qquad \therefore n_L = n$

Or: $\hat{\delta}^2 = (Z_1 + Z_2)^2 \left(\dfrac{3.5\,\sigma^2}{n}\right)$

$\therefore n = (Z_1 + Z_2)^2 \left(\dfrac{3.5\,\sigma^2}{\hat{\delta}^2}\right)$

It should be noted that the true σ^2 rather than estimated σ^2 is needed for the planning phase. Usually it is unknown and often available from past experience with the same or similar problem or can be obtained from a pilot survey.

4.4 Accident Rate Model

For the purpose of the present study, we use the two means to define accident rates:

$$Z_H = \frac{A_H}{R_H \overline{K_H}} \quad \text{and} \quad Z_L = \frac{A_L}{R_L \overline{K_L}}$$

where A = number of accidents involving motorcycles,
R = number of such motorcycles in the population,
$\overline{K}$ = average distance ridden on such motorcycles estimated from the proposed sample survey;

and the subscripts H and L stand for high engine capacity and low engine capacity respectively.

We made the following distribution assumptions:

$$\left. \begin{array}{l} A_i \approx \text{Poisson}\,(\lambda_i, \lambda_i) \\[6pt] \text{and} \quad \overline{K} \approx \text{NID}\,\left(\mu_i,\, \dfrac{\sigma_i^2}{N_i}\right) \end{array} \right\} \quad i = H, L$$

Further, if we assume that there is no covariance between A_H and $\overline{K_H}$, then the variance of Z_H can be expressed as:

$$\text{Var}\,(Z_H) = \text{Var}\left(\frac{A_H}{R_H \overline{K_H}}\right) = \frac{1}{R_H^2}\,\text{Var}\left(\frac{A_H}{\overline{K_H}}\right)$$

$$= \frac{1}{R_H^2}\left\{\frac{E(A_H)}{E(\overline{K_H})}\right\}^2 \left[\frac{\text{Var}(A_H)}{\{E(A_H)\}^2} + \frac{\text{Var}(\overline{K_H})}{\{E(\overline{K_H})\}^2}\right]$$

$$= \frac{1}{R_H^2}\left\{\frac{\lambda_H^2}{\mu_H^2}\right\}\left[\frac{\lambda_H}{\lambda_H^2} + \frac{\sigma_H^2/n_H}{\mu_H^2}\right]$$

$$= \frac{1}{R_H^2}\left\{\frac{\lambda_H^2}{\mu_H^2}\right\}\left[\frac{1}{\lambda_H} + \frac{\sigma_H^2}{n_H\,\mu_H^2}\right]$$

Similarly the variance of Z_L can be expressed as:

$$\text{Var}(Z_L) = \frac{1}{R_L^2}\left\{\frac{\lambda_L^2}{\mu_L^2}\right\}\left[\frac{1}{\lambda_L} + \frac{\sigma_L^2}{n_L\,\mu_L^2}\right]$$

$$\therefore \text{Var}(Z_H - Z_L) = \text{Var}(Z_H) + \text{Var}(Z_L)$$

$$= \frac{1}{R_H^2}\left\{\frac{\lambda_H^2}{\mu_H^2}\right\}\left[\frac{1}{\lambda_H} + \frac{\sigma_H^2}{n_H\,\mu_H^2}\right] + \frac{1}{R_L^2}\left\{\frac{\lambda_L^2}{\mu_L^2}\right\}\left[\frac{1}{\lambda_L} + \frac{\sigma_L^2}{n_L\,\mu_L^2}\right]$$

Our basic equation:

$$\hat{\delta} = (Z_H + Z_L)[\text{Var}(Z_H) + \text{Var}(Z_L)]^{1/2}$$

$$\therefore \hat{\delta}^2 = (Z_H + Z_L)^2\,[\text{Var}(Z_H) + \text{Var}(Z_L)]$$

$$= (Z_H + Z_L)^2\left[\frac{1}{R_H^2}\left\{\frac{\lambda_H^2}{\mu_H^2}\right\}\left[\frac{1}{\lambda_H} + \frac{\sigma_H^2}{n_H\,\mu_H^2}\right] + \frac{1}{R_L^2}\left\{\frac{\lambda_L^2}{\mu_L^2}\right\}\left[\frac{1}{\lambda_L} + \frac{\sigma_L^2}{n_L\,\mu_L^2}\right]\right] \quad (4.1)$$

4.5 Assumptions and Estimates

The assumptions and estimates are listed below.

1. $\sigma_H/\mu_H = \sigma_L/\mu_L = \dfrac{402055}{3177} = 1.2655$

2. $\mu_H = \mu_L = 3177$ km/year/rider

   From Wood and Bowen (1987)

3. $R_H = 2390\ rider.$

4. $R_L = 13544\ riders$

   These estimates are based on the assumption that 15% of the total motorcycle riders (provided by the RTA Head Office) use high engine capacity

ESTIMATION OF SAMPLE SIZE FOR ACCIDENT RISK

5. λ_H = 224 accidents / year
6. λ_L = 551 accidents / year $\Big\}$ In fact 3 years.

$$\frac{\hat{\lambda}_H}{R_H \mu_H} = \frac{224}{2390 \times 3177} = 29.5 \text{ accidents per million km}$$

$$\frac{\hat{\lambda}_L}{R_L \mu_L} = \frac{551}{13544 \times 3177} = 12.8 \text{ accidents per million km}$$

Average = 21.2 accidents per million km

7. Z_1 = 1.96, i.e., 5% two-tailed test

8. Z_2 = 0.84, i.e., 20% type 2 error probability (power 80%)

9. $n_H = n_L$ = n, i.e., equal sample sizes in each stratum

4.6 Formula with Assumptions and Estimates Having δ^2

Putting the above information in equation (4.1), we can get the following value for δ^2:

$$\delta^2 = 7.84 \left\{ 29.5^2 \left(\frac{1}{224} + \frac{1.2655^2}{n} \right) + 12.8^2 \left(\frac{1}{551} + \frac{1.2655^2}{n} \right) \right\} \times 10$$

$$= \left\{ 30.46 + \frac{10927}{n} + 2.33 + \frac{2057}{n} \right\} \times 10^{-12}$$

$$= \left\{ 32.79 + \frac{12984}{n} \right\} \times 10^{-12}$$

ESTIMATION OF SAMPLE SIZE FOR ACCIDENT RISK

4.7 Sample Size Required

The sample size, n, was calculated on the basis of the statistical test being able to detect various levels of difference between the mean accident rates, expressed as a percentage of the overall average accident rate.

4.7.1 20% Difference

$\delta = 0.2 \times 21.2 \times 10^{-6} = 4.24 \times 10^{-6}$

$\delta^2 = 17.98 < 32.79$ Not feasible

4.7.2 30% Difference

$\delta = 0.3 \times 21.2 \times 10^{-6} = 6.36 \times 10^{-6}$

$40.45 = 32.79 + \dfrac{12984}{n}$

$\therefore n = 1,695$ for $n_H = n_L$

4.7.3 35% Difference

$\delta = 0.35 \times 21.2 \times 10^{-6} = 7.42 \times 10^{-6}$

$55.06 = 32.79 + \dfrac{12984}{n}$

$\therefore n = 583$ for $n_H = n_L$

4.7.4 40% Difference

$\delta = 0.4 \times 21.2 \times 10^{-6} = 8.48 \times 10^{-6}$

$71.91 = 32.79 + \dfrac{12984}{n}$

$\therefore n = 332$ for $n_H = n_L$

These results show that a smaller sample size is required as the difference between the mean accident rates of two engine types expressed as a percentage of overall average accident rates is getting larger and larger.

4.8 Conclusions

This chapter provides statistical formulas for estimating sample size based on various level of differences between the mean accident rates of two types of motorcycle engines expressed as a percentage of overall average accidents. An empirical illustration is given based on the exposure survey. It shows that a reduced sample size is required if the difference between mean accident rates of two types of engines is large when expressed as a percentage of overall accidents. Further estimation of sample size for the comparison of two sample proportions is provided in Appendix 4A.

CHAPTER 5

DEVELOPING ROAD SAFETY COUNTERMEASURE INITIATIVES USING MONTHLY ROAD FATALITY DATA

Road accident deaths are a highly sensitive issue. For this reason, the government and society want to know very quickly the actual situation relating to what is happening on our roads. Monitoring fatality data can also let the government and society, know the current pattern of road fatalities and also let them know whether it is under control or not. If it exceeds the upper tolerable limit then they try to detect the causes and take precautionary measures to bring down the number of road accident deaths to within the control limits. In this chapter we have shown how to monitor monthly road accident deaths for a particular month, using road fatality data for the month of July 1990 and tried to find out whether road accident deaths are within the control limits or not. This technique can also be used to monitor other social and behavioral data.

5.1 Introduction

The government is very keen to know the number of road deaths per month, because it is a politically sensitive issue. The government wants to detect the causes of the number of monthly road fatalities if they go beyond the tolerable limits. More importantly, then it can take all necessary actions to bring down the number of monthly road fatality within tolerable limits. If fatalities exceed the upper tolerable limit, then the causes for such change will be investigated and remedial road safety countermeasures will be taken quickly to bring down the number within tolerable limits. On the other hand if the current trend of road fatalities falls below the lower tolerable limit then the causes can be identified and maintained so that low road fatalities continue in the future. In this chapter, we have shown how to monitor monthly road fatalities by road user types by

46 DEVELOPING ROAD SAFETY COUNTERMEASURE INITIATIVES

comparing the actual road fatality number with the forecasted number bounded by the estimated tolerable limits, using the short-term accident monitoring system. In addition to this, we have also compared the number of road fatalities for a particular month with the same month of the previous year, as well as last five years' average of that month's fatality number, to detect any changes in the current month's road fatalities. Total number of road fatalities as well as fatalities by road user type for the month of July 1990 is used to demonstrate how to monitor monthly road fatalities to detect any changes that might occur in recent months.

5.2   Methodologies

In order to monitor the current monthly road fatalities, two methods are used: (i) simple comparison with the previous year for the same month, as well as last five years' average for the same month; and (ii) trend analyses. We constructed the monthly (January to December) trend lines based on six years monthly road fatality data and then encompass this trend line by the upper and lower confidence limits. Current monthly road fatality data are then plotted in the same graph to see its position. If it falls within these limits, then it shows that the current road fatality numbers are tolerable. If it falls below the lower limit then the road safety people should be very pleased, but if it exceeds the upper limit then the government and other road safety bodies should take immediate action to bring down the number of road deaths within control.

5.3   Empirical Illustrations

It is clear from Table 5.1 that during the month of July 1990:

- 40 people were killed on Victorian roads. This is 12 below both the 1989 figure and the average for the last five years.

- Differences related mainly to the decrease in deaths of motorcyclists (0 compared to 6 last year), and pedestrians (7 compared to 10 last year).

5.3.1   For the Period January—July 1990

The number of deaths was 344, 70 fewer than the five-year average and 128 fewer than for 1989 (see Table 5.1 and Figure 5.1).

This is the lowest figure on record for this period since the series began in 1951. The figure for Australia for January—June was the lowest since 1960.

5.3.2 In Relation to the Five-year Averages

It is seen from Table 5.1 and Figures 5.1—5.6 that:

- There has been a 17% decrease in road fatalities in Victoria.

- The drop relates mainly to pedestrians (down 34 or 38%), driver (down 24 or 14%), passengers (down 9 or 9%), and motorcyclists (down 6 or 15%).

- Total fatalities in metropolitan and country areas decreased by 25% and 7% respectively.

- Motorcyclist fatalities have slightly reduced, while bicyclist fatalities have increased slightly.

- Fatalities from truck related accidents were 43, a decrease of 16 (see Figure 5.6).

Table 5.1: Persons Killed by Road User Type (Preliminary Figures for 1990)

Road User Type	1 - 31 July Victoria			1 Jan to 31 July Melbourne Metropolitan			1 Jan to 31 July Rest of State			1 Jan to 31 July Victoria		
	1990	1989	85-89 Av.	1990	1989	85-89 Av.	1990	1989	85-89 Av.	1990	1989	85-89 Av.
Pedestrians	7	10	14	45	72	73	11	23	17	56	95	90
Drivers	19	21	21	57	84	73	88	122	96	145	206	169
Passengers	10	10	11	35	53	46	56	53	54	91	106	100
Motorcyclists and pillion	0	6	4	17	24	21	16	19	18	33	43	39
Bicyclists	4	5	2	11	12	8	8	10	8	19	22	16
Total	40	52	52	165	245	221	179	227	193	344	472	414

Source: Road Traffic Accident Data File of the RTA of Victoria extracted from the Victorian Police Road Accident Report Form.

5.4 Conclusions

The reduction of road fatalities is a continuation of a significant downward trend since October 1989 as shown on the moving twelve-month total fatality figure presented in Appendix 5A (Figure 5A.1). During this period major road safety campaigns have related to increased random breath testing (see figures 5A.3 and 5A.4), and the introduction of speed cameras as a means of reducing

48 DEVELOPING ROAD SAFETY COUNTERMEASURE INITIATIVES

speeding, which can be seen from Figure 5A.2 of Appendix 5A. Figures 5A.2 to 5A.4 show that police activity as shown by speeding offences and random breath testing increased significantly in the last 15 months, although the number of speeding offences issued per month dropped after this.

Given the high correlation between accidents, speeding, alcohol consumption and young drivers, the success of the campaigns should be evident as reduced deaths amongst young drivers. This is shown on Table 5.2 that during January to July 1990, there were 49 deaths for drivers aged 17–20 and 21–25 compared to the five-year average of 60.

During January to July 1990, there was a significant drop in deaths of pedestrians, particularly those aged 60 years or older, 26 deaths compared to the five-year average of 40.

Figure 5.1: Total Road Fatalities, 1990 vs. Six-year Trend

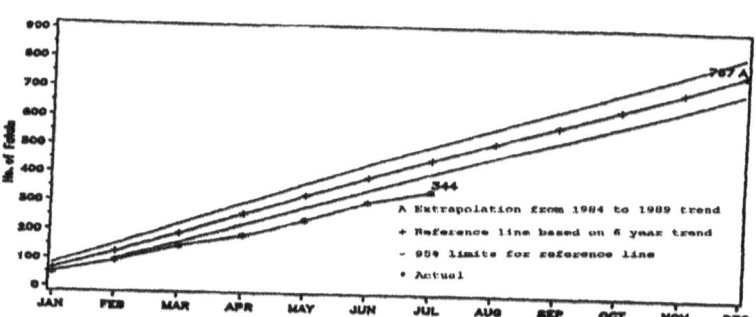

Source: Road Traffic Accident Data File of the RTA of Victoria extracted from the Victorian Police Road Accident Report Form.

Figure 5.2: Vehicle Occupant Fatalities, Cumulative 1990 vs. Six-year Trend

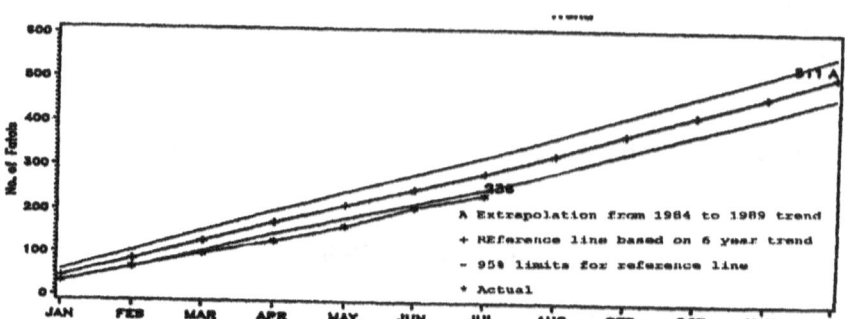

Source: Road Traffic Accident Data File of the RTA of Victoria extracted from the Victorian Police Road Accident Report Form.

Figure 5.3: Pedestrian Fatalities, Cumulative 1990 vs. Six-year Trend

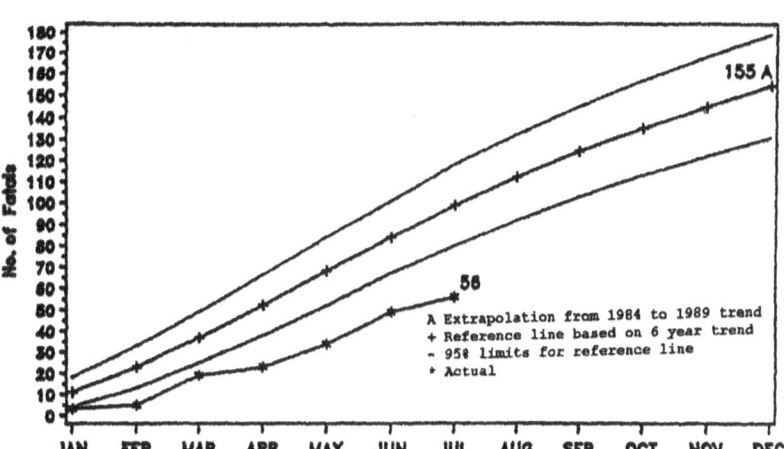

Source: Road Traffic Accident Data File of the RTA of Victoria extracted from the Victorian Police Road Accident Report Form.

Figure 5.4: Motorcyclist and Pillion Fatalities, Cumulative 1990 vs. Six-year Trend

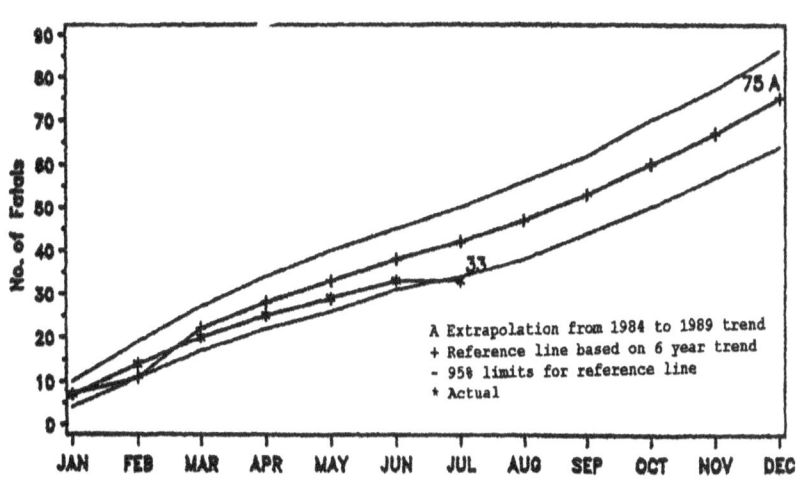

Source: Road Traffic Accident Data File of the RTA of Victoria extracted from the Victorian Police Road Accident Report Form.

Figure 5.5: Bicycle Fatalities, Cumulative 1990 vs. Six-year Trend

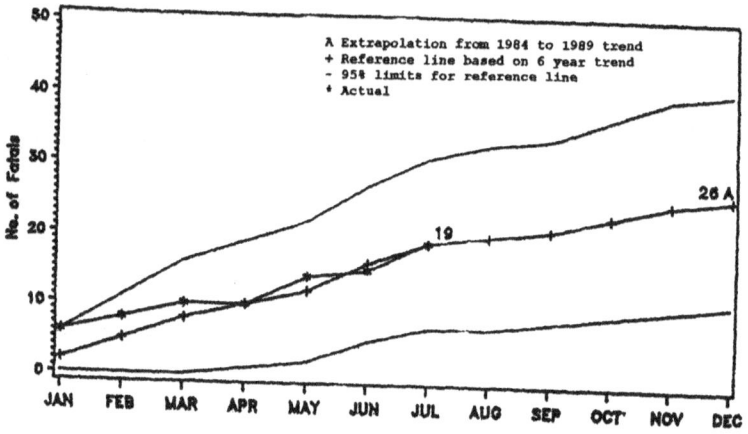

Source: Road Traffic Accident Data File of the RTA of Victoria extracted from the Victorian Police Road Accident Report Form.

Figure 5.6: Fatalities From Truck Accidents, Cumulative 1990 vs. Six-year Trend.

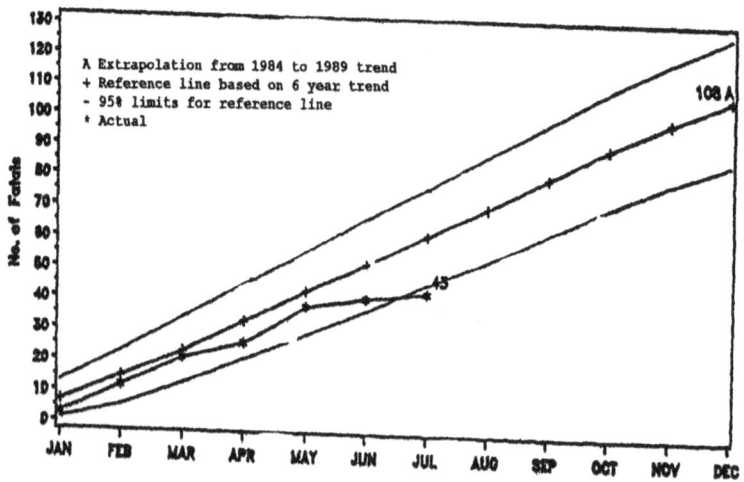

Source: Road Traffic Accident Data File of the RTA of Victoria extracted from the Victorian Police Road Accident Report Form.

Table 5.2: Number of Fatalities in Victoria by Age Group and Road User Type

Age \ Period	0-4	5-16	17-20	21-25	26-29	30-39	40-49	49-59	60+	Total
Drivers										
Jan–Jul Ave 85-89		0.4	24.8	35	18	30.8	20.6	16.4	23.6	169.6
Jan–Jul 1989			22	38	21	46	23	31	25	206
Jan–Jul 1990			26	23	16	22	16	15	27	145
Jul Ave 85-89			4.4	3.4	2	4.2	2.2	1.2	3.4	20.8
Jul 1989			3	3	2	3	4	2	4	21
Jul 1990*			4	1	1	3	2	4	4	19
Motorcycle riders										
Jan–Jul Ave 85-89		1.6	12.6	12.2	2.6	6.8	1.2	0.4	0.4	37.8
Jan–Jul 1989		2	12	10	3	9	3			39
Jan–Jul 1990		3	10	9	4	4	1			32
Jul Ave 85-89			1	1.8	0.4	0.8				4
Jul 1989			2	2	1	1				6
Jul 1990*										0
Pedestrians										
Jan–Jul Ave 85-89	1.6	11.4	6.2	4.2	4.8	5.6	6.8	9.4	39.6	89.6
Jan–Jul 1989		14	6	3	4	9	10	11	38	95
Jan–Jul 1990	3	6	6	2	1	3	3	6	26	56
Jul Ave 85-89	0.2	1.8	0.8	1	0.6	0.6	2	1.6	5.4	14
Jul 1989		2	1			1	2	1	3	10
Jul 1990*		1				1	1	1	3	7
Passengers and pillions										
Jan–Jul Ave 85-89	4.4	14	22.8	16.8	5.8	9.6	4.2	6.6	18.2	102.4
Jan–Jul 1989	5	13	16	25	6	10	3	9	23	110
Jan–Jul 1990	4	11	18	10	4	6	4	5	30	92
Jul Ave 85-89	0.2	1.6	3.8	2	0.2	0.8	0.4	1	1	11
Jul 1989		2	2	4		1		1		10
Jul 1990*		1	2	1	1	1		1	3	10
Pedal cyclists										
Jan–Jul Ave 85-89		7	16	1	0.6	1.6	1.2	1	1.8	15.8
Jan–Jul 1989		13	2		1	2	1	2	1	22
Jan–Jul 1990	1	7	2	3	1		2	2	1	19
Jul Ave 85-89		1	0.4			0.4		0.2	0.4	2.4
Jul 1989		3	1					1		5
Jul 1990*		1	1	1			1			4
Total										
Jan–Jul Ave 85-89	6	34.4	68	69.2	31.8	54.4	34	33.8	83.6	415.2
Jan–Jul 1989	5	42	58	76	35	76	40	53	87	472
Jan–Jul 1990	8	27	62	47	26	36	26	28	84	344
Jul Ave 85-89	0.4	4.4	10.4	8.2	3.2	6.8	4.6	4	10.2	52.2
Jul 1989	0	7	9	9	3	6	6	5	7	52
Jul 1990*	0	3	7	3	2	5	4	6	10	40

* Preliminary figures.
Source: Road Traffic Accident Data File of the RTA of Victoria extracted from the Victorian Police Road Accident Report Form.

CHAPTER 6

A SHORT-TERM ACCIDENT MONITORING SYSTEM: A CASE STUDY FOR VICTORIA

Short-term accident monitoring provides a timely and accurate picture of any changes in level rather than level per se of road safety. In this chapter, we review 'the various accident data sources with a view to developing a short-term accident monitoring system'. Tow-truck allocation data turns out to be the most suitable data for developing short-term road accident monitoring. It is demonstrated that like police fatality data used in previous chapter, tow-truck allocation data can also be used as a regular indicator of the extent of road trauma, for vehicles involved in accidents within the Melbourne Metropolitan Area. It is a large data set and can therefore provide a clear picture about the safety conditions on our roads. Techniques of time series analysis are applied to forecast monthly road accident numbers along with its 95% confidence limits. By reading this chapter, readers will be able to learn a technique, which will enable them to monitor the trend of road accidents to find out whether the current accident numbers are within the tolerable limits or not. This will help to understand the current road accident situation, if it goes beyond the tolerable limits.

6.1 Introduction

Road accidents are an indirect measure of road safety. Their frequency gives an index of 'un-safety' on the roads. Thus, traffic safety administrators and the government are interested in knowing quickly whether variations have occurred in the regular pattern of road accidents. The development of a system to do this was recommended for urgent attention in the 'Final Report on Road Safety in Victoria' prepared by the Social Development Committee (1984).

It is expected that a short-term monitoring system established from past data will show the regular patterns of road accidents. Accident data provided by a number of sources viz., police, hospital, ambulance services, Transport Accident Commission and tow-truck allocation scheme, etc., can be used for this purpose. The monitoring can also make use of other transport data, such as drivers licensed, vehicles registered, survey data on distances driven, fuel sales, etc. These data can be brought together to provide early warning of developing road accident problems requiring countermeasure interventions.

At present, road fatality data is used as an up-to-date assessment of the extent of road trauma on Victorian roads. This fatality data is very important, but gives only a small fraction of the total road trauma picture. Thus, there is an urgent need to establish a short-term monitoring system covering other aspects of road trauma.

This chapter gives the results of a broad review of accident data sources with a view to developing a short-term accident monitoring system to quickly determine quickly changes in road trauma trends in Victoria. Following this review a time series model was developed as a basis for a short-term accident monitoring system, using tow-truck allocation data.

It is demonstrated that like fatality data, tow-truck allocation data can be used as a regular indicator of the extent of road trauma, for vehicles involved in accidents within the Melbourne Metropolitan area.

The general objective of this chapter is to detect any change in road accidents from the established pattern based on the past data. This can then be taken as a basis for detailed research and development of countermeasure initiatives.

This chapter also investigates various data sources in terms of their suitability for inclusion within the short-term accident monitoring system and to develop a monitoring system with the use of a computer for suitable data sets. More specifically, the aim is to provide a timely and broad picture of the level and pattern of a large number of vehicles involved in casualty and/or property damage road accidents, using tow-truck allocation data.

6.2   A Brief Review on Some Monitoring Systems in Australia

The Road Traffic Authority of Victoria monitors the number of road fatalities daily as an indicator of the level of road trauma on Victorian roads. This monitoring system is regarded as a valuable management tool. However, Cameron and Russell (1981) indicated that road fatalities occur in insufficient numbers to get a true picture of the level of road trauma, using fatality data alone. They suggested the use of Serious Casualty Accident (SCA) data, which occurred in sufficient numbers to avoid misleading conclusions from chance fluctuations. A serious casualty accident is an accident in which at least one person is killed, or injured and admitted to hospital.

The Traffic Authority of New South Wales (1987) publishes a monthly bulletin of preliminary traffic accident data, using police, health, ambulance and Australian Bureau of Statistics data sources. This provides detailed road accident information of New South Wales and particular attention is given to the fatality data. They are also collecting accident data from the ambulance services intended for short-term monitoring purposes, using statistical techniques for revealing short-term changes. A report prepared by Douglas *et al.* (1986) contains recommendations only for their future plans.

Leggett (1985) has used quality-control techniques to monitor monthly accident data in both disaggregated and aggregated form for Transport Tasmania. A computer algorithm is developed for police accident data to provide regular control charts, using recent available data. In recent times, they also produce Traffic Safety Trend newsletter, which describes the cumulative totals of fatal accidents at different points of time.1

6.3 Criteria of a Data Set Suitable for Short-term Monitoring

A data series is considered suitable for short-term monitoring if the following criteria are satisfied.

- **Timeliness**

Recent accident data availability is an integral part of a short-term monitoring system. In this study, recent means information available within four weeks after the occurrence of an accident. Data sets are considered unsuitable when they are delayed more than four weeks.

- **Bias**

The expected values of the data series must reflect a true underlying trend in that aspect of road trauma for which the data is used. However, a small amount (probably 5% to 10%) of bias in a quickly available data set may be acceptable for short-term monitoring purposes. Ignoring a small amount of bias can be justified because the monitoring system is based on a number of short-term periods and hence the effects of variations between the periods are likely to average out for long-term data series.

- **Consistency**

The data series must possess the statistical property of consistency, which asserts that with increasing size of the sample, the probability that the estimated value lies close to the true value tends to unity. On the other hand, consistency neither implies completeness of information nor an absence of bias in the information. However, it does imply that the level of completeness and the degree of bias remain unchanged over time. If information is consistent, then changes in trend over time reflect changes in the level of road safety and are not an artifact of varying data collection procedures.

- **Content**

Content refers to the types of information that are readily available for short-term monitoring. Data should not necessarily be mutually exclusive and exhaustive. Data should be defined in specific terms, so that it can correctly describe the true picture of the road trauma for certain aspects of the road safety system. Aspects of data relevant here are road-user type, location, injury severity and injury type, age, sex, time of the day, crash type, etc. Some of these factors may prove either unsuitable or unavailable, and the data may not cover all levels of some factors in some data sets.

6.4 Data Sources

Data related to road accidents in Victoria can be collected for short-term monitoring purposes from the following sources:

(a) Police Traffic Accident Report Forms (Vic roads accident system)
(b) Transport Accident Commission (TAC)
(c) Hospital Morbidity File (HMF)
(d) Ambulance data
(e) Centralised Tow-Truck Allocation Scheme

These are now discussed below.

6.4.1 Police Traffic Accident Report Forms (VicRoads Accident System)

The Road Traffic Authority codes and stores information obtained from Police Accident Report Forms. Since January 1986, the accident Form type 510 is required to be completed for all road accidents reported to the police, regardless of severity.

The great advantage of the VicRoads accident system data is its comprehensive coverage of accident details. The data are reported by various factors such as: accident severity, road user movement (RUM) type, location, vehicle type, time of the day, etc., for the whole state.

Apart from fatality data, other accident information from the VicRoads system at present is available only after several months' delay and therefore is not suitable for short-term accident monitoring. A new data processing system introduced in 1987 however reduced delay in the provision to the VicRoads by police of unchecked data.

It is expected that fatality and serious injury accident data will be available within four weeks and possibly be suitable for short-term monitoring purposes. Once the system has stabilised, data suitability for inclusion within a monitoring system should be reassessed. For instance, serious casualty accident data from the system may be obtained quickly in a form, which can be used for short-term monitoring purposes. Meanwhile, historical data from this source can be used to check the consistency of data from other sources.

6.4.2 Transport Accident Commission (TAC)

The Motor Accident Board (MAB) previously provided no-fault compensation to road accident victims in the form of payment of hospital, medical and ambulance expenses as well as a certain amount for loss of earnings, even though the accident was not reported to the police in some cases. Substantial delays in receiving and entering claim data after the accident date (typically 6 weeks) are also a problem, which would have reduced the usefulness of this data for short-term monitoring purposes.

In January 1987 with .the introduction of the new Transport Accident Act, claims for compensation for a transport accident are liable for payment to the road victims within four weeks if the accident is reported to the Police.

At present, police traffic accident report forms are sent to the TAC daily. It is expected that both casualty and property damage accident data will be available quickly from TAC. Thus, property damage accident data can be taken from the TAC to supplement VicRoad's casualty accident data. The changing reporting criterion for accident recording suggests that, in the short term, this data series is unsuitable for the inclusion within a short-term accident monitoring system for time series analysis.

6.4.3 Hospital Morbidity File

The Hospital Morbidity File (HMF) administered by the Health Department of Victoria is a central registration authority to collect in-patient information for Victoria's public hospitals. The registration began in January 1979, but only a few public hospitals initially contributed to the scheme. By July 1983, however, all public hospitals, which admit road trauma victims, were contributing to the scheme.

The HMF contains detailed information about the victims, age, sex and date of hospital admission, hospital location, crash type, road user type, etc. However, there may be a problem of over counting, because of some accident victim's multiple admissions to a number of hospitals. Batch entry of data to the HMF from the hospitals occurs usually once or twice a month, although a few larger hospitals with in-house computing facilities took up to four months to enter data. Hence, the HMF data is also not suitable for short-term accident monitoring system for time series analysis.

6.4.4 Ambulance Services

The development of a similar scheme in the New South Wales (NSW) Ambulance Service data could likely be used for short-term monitoring. The advantage of such data is that it is obtained immediately after an accident, giving information about the victim's age, sex, road user type, accident type and location. But, the problem with ambulance data is that not every one uses an ambulance, even if they are admitted to hospitals after road accidents. Hence, this data is not complete and therefore is not suitable for short-term accident monitoring.

6.4.5 Centralised Tow Truck Allocation Scheme

The centralised tow-truck allocation scheme administered by the Royal Automobile Club of Victoria (RACV) operating solely within the Melbourne Metropolitan area, determines which tow-truck operator attends an accident. Operators are registered at the Control Centre with an address for each tow-truck licenee. Under this system, a tow-truck operator may attend an accident only when authorised to do so by the control centre.

Any metropolitan accident requiring a vehicle towed away is recorded by the center except perhaps where drivers organise their own tow. This data is regarded as reliable only after 1 April 1983, since before then a tow-truck operator was permitted to maintain his ranking in the job allocation queue if unable to locate the assigned vehicle. In practice this procedure may lead to an abuse of the system, because tow-truck operators might falsely claim that the vehicle could not be found.

The data collected within the 'Accident Towing Controlled Area' is smaller than the Melbourne Statistical Division (MSD). It excludes the following areas from the MSD:

- Flinders, Healesville, Pakenham, Hastings; and

- part of Cranbourne, Mornington, Berwick, Sherbrooke, Lilydale and Diamond Valley.

This data includes a large number of vehicles involved in casualty or property damage accidents, which may not be reported to the police. It is readily available soon after the end of each month, and thus can be used for short-term monitoring purposes.

There are some drawbacks in this data. First, at present this data is available in an aggregated form only. Disaggregation by accident severity, vehicle type, road user type, or location is not currently available.

Second, this data is indicative of accidents involving car and car derivatives (vehicles) only and does not adequately cover accidents involving unprotected road users (pedestrians, bicyclists and motorcyclists). As a result, a large number of serious injuries are missing from this series, which is of course a major concern for coverage of the data.

Third, this data is only collected within the 'Accident Towing Controlled Area'. Therefore it will not reflect the complete picture of accident patterns for larger regions such as the MSD or the whole of Victoria.

6.5 Methods of Analysis

The best means of detecting whether observed values differ from the expected can be judged by building an appropriate forecasting model. There are many forecasting models viz., classical, econometric and time series models, etc. Each model has merits and demerits; for example the regression and econometric models can give more accurate estimates of road accidents, using a number of independent predictive variables. However, data of such variables are difficult to obtain. Alternatively a time series model enables one to produce expected trends based on past accident data. Its chief drawback is that it assumes that a general trend established in previous years will continue into the future. It was decided to apply time series analysis for short-term accident monitoring, despite many problems associated with such data.

It is expected that this will produce reasonable forecasting values, which are generated from the past data, at least for short-term prediction periods. Observed values may then be compared with forecast values to examine whether the existing trends are significantly different from that of the expected trends.

In the sphere of time series analysis, the three methods: exponential smoothing, decomposition and Box-Jenkins are all appropriate for short-term prediction purposes. These methods will therefore be studied to find an appropriate model for a short-term accident-monitoring system, which will be discussed later in Section 6.7.

6.6 Short Term Monitoring System Using Tow-Truck Allocation Data

Judging from a number of criteria stated in Section 6.3 for a suitable data set for short-term accident monitoring, it is seen that apart from the VicRoads road fatality series, the tow-truck allocation data has proved to be most suitable for this purpose. A major attribute is its ready availability, although deficient in being restricted to accidents involving vehicles only in the Metropolitan area and not accessible in disaggregated form.

6.6.1 Comparison with the VicRoads Accident Data System

It is assumed that the VicRoads accident data system is the most reliable and comprehensive data set for casualty accidents in Victoria. If this assumption is taken as correct then there is sufficient basis to compare the trend of the tow-truck allocation data with various sets of VicRoads accident data. The tow-truck allocation data can be taken as a reliable subset of accident data if its trend consistently follows the same trends of various VicRoads accident data sets.

In order to verify the validity of the tow-truck allocation data, the monthly and twelve monthly moving totals of this data have been plotted together with three series of the VicRoads accident system data, viz., total reported accidents, total casualty accidents, and total vehicles involved in casualty accidents and towed away, for accidents occurring in the MSD only in each case. These are presented in figures 6.1 and 6.2.

It is clear from these graphs that tow-truck allocation data follows the same pattern as the VicRoads data and they all contain a strong seasonality. Furthermore, tow-truck allocations and the casualty accident data exhibit a slightly increasing trend. The total reported accidents (which contain a large number of property damage only accidents) began to drop in 1986, probably due to the influence of the new Form 510 introduced at the beginning of that year. This introduction may have caused a lesser number of property damage only accidents to be reported by the police in 1986 compared to 1985, as indicated by Table 6.1.

Table 6.1: Accidents Reported in the Melbourne Statistical Division

Severity	1985 Without Form 513*	1985 With Form 513*	1985 Total Form 512	1986 Form 510
Casualty	461	12094	12555	11937
Property damage only	12393	10053	22446	19100
Total	**12854**	**22147**	**35001**	**31037**

* Note that Form 513 is a subset of Form 512.

Source: Road Traffic Accident Data File of the RTA of Victoria extracted from the Victorian Police Road Accident Report Form.

Fewer property damage only accidents reported in 1986 may have been a direct result of the change in Report Form. Before 1986, police could only complete a 512 Report Form for property damage accidents. From 1986, there may have been a tendency for minor property damage accidents to go unreported in preference to completing the more detailed 510 Report Form.

Figure 6.1: Patterns of Monthly Road Accidents;
April 1983 to December 1986

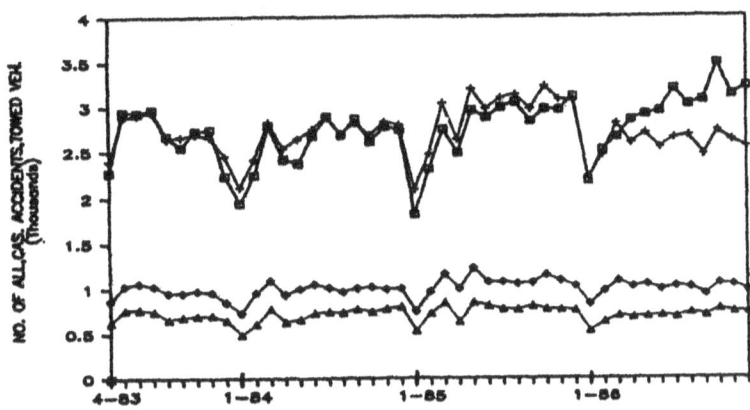

Source: □ Tow-truck allocation data from the RACV;
         + Total reported accidents from the RTA
         ◊ Total casualty accidents from the RTA
         Δ Total vehicles involved in casualty
            accidents and towed away from the RTA.

Figure 6.2: 12-month Moving Totals of Road Accidents

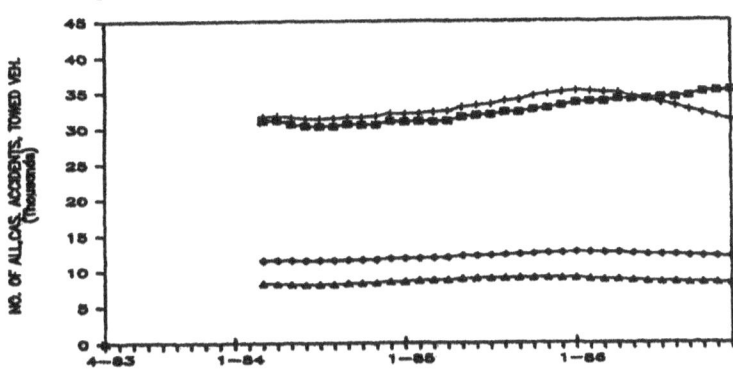

Source: □ Tow-truck allocation data from the RACV;
         + Total reported accidents from the RTA
         ◊ Total casualty accidents from the RTA
         Δ Total vehicles involved in casualty
            accidents and towed away from the RTA.

The reporting of casualty accidents should not be affected by changing the form because of its compulsory status, even though there was a 5% drop in the number of reported casualty accidents during 1986 compared to 1985. In general, the tow-truck allocation data varies consistently from month to month in the same way as the casualty accident data held by the VicRoads. Hence, tow-truck allocation data can be taken as a reliable data source for short-term accident monitoring.

6.7 Forecasting Tow-truck Allocation Data

We have considered the following models: (1) exponential smoothing (Winter's) method; (ii) decomposition method, and (iii) Box-Jenkins method as mentioned in Section 6.5 to model the tow-truck allocation data to produce the forecast values. A number of criteria are used to choose the best model among three alternatives, which are given below in Table 6.2.

Table 6.2: Comparison of Forecasting Models for Tow-truck Allocation Data[*]

Criteria	Winter's Method	Decomposition Method	Box Jenkins Method
Mean sum squares of errors (MSE)	67721	15030	78072
Use of computer software to calculate confidence intervals	Yes	No	Yes
Time to prepare forecast	Shortest	Medium	Longest
Interaction between users and method	Low	Medium	High

[*] The MSE figures are calculated for various models, using the tow-truck allocation data.

Source: Tow-truck allocation data are taken from the Royal Automobile Club of Victoria (RACV).

On the basis of the criteria set in Table 6.2, it clearly shows that Winter's model can be considered as the best forecasting model. Hence, Winter's method was chosen for forecasting purposes, which are used for our short-term accident monitoring system. It gives a reasonably good fit to the data. It is easy to understand, and various statistics including forecasted values and its confidence limits can be calculated quickly using available computer software. Further details of this method can be found in Appendix 6A.

Winter's model was applied to the available tow-truck allocation data for the period 1983 to 1986 to forecast values for each month of 1987. These forecasted values as well as the actual monthly number of tow-truck allocation from

January 1986 to October 1987 are presented in Table 6.3. This table shows that in the first ten months of 1987, 31,379 vehicles were towed away after crashes in the Melbourne Metropolitan area under the Centralised Tow-truck Allocation Scheme. In the corresponding period for 1986, 28,860 vehicles were towed away. Forecasted values for the first ten months of 1987 were 30,114, which lie between the actual figures of 1987 and 1986.

Forecast values based on Winter's model along with historical data are plotted in Figure 6.3. The historical data show a very gradual increase over time in the number of tow-away reports and this is reflected in the 1987 forecast values being slightly greater than the corresponding 1986 values. However, 1987 forecast values were lower than the actual numbers. This indicates that a greater number of vehicles were involved in accidents in 1987 than in 1986.

Figure 6.4 shows how 1987 monthly reports compare with forecast values. For six of the ten months, actual report numbers were greater than the expected numbers. Confidence limits at the 67% and 95% levels are also shown in this figure.

These limits provide a guide as to whether the amount by which actual figures differ from forecast values can reasonably be attributed to chance effects alone. There is about one chance in three that random effects are responsible for an observation falling outside the 67% limits and one chance in twenty that an observation falls outside the 95% limit. In 1987 only the May figure was outside the 67% limit, and no observation fell outside the 95% limit.

Figure 6.5 presents the cumulative number of tow-truck allocations to the end of October 1987 and compares this with the forecast values and 95% confidence limits. This figure shows that observed numbers exceeded forecast numbers but fell well within the 95% limits.

Figure 6.3: Short-term Accident Pattern Forecast of Tow-truck Allocations

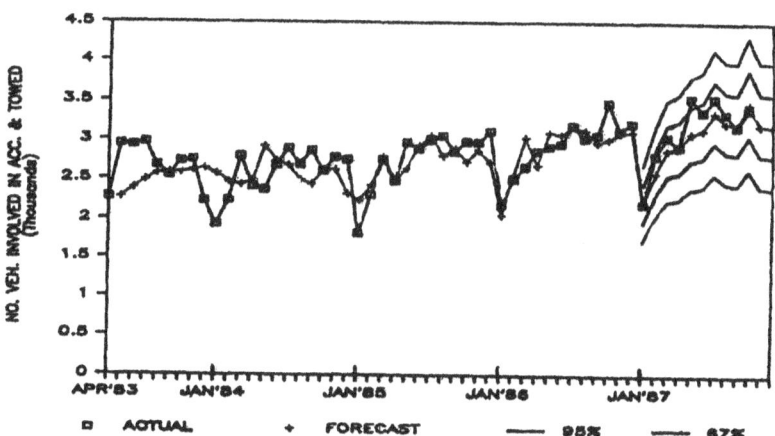

Source: Tow-truck allocation data are taken from the RACV.

Figure 6.4: Short-term Accident Pattern, 1987 Forecast of Tow-truck Allocations

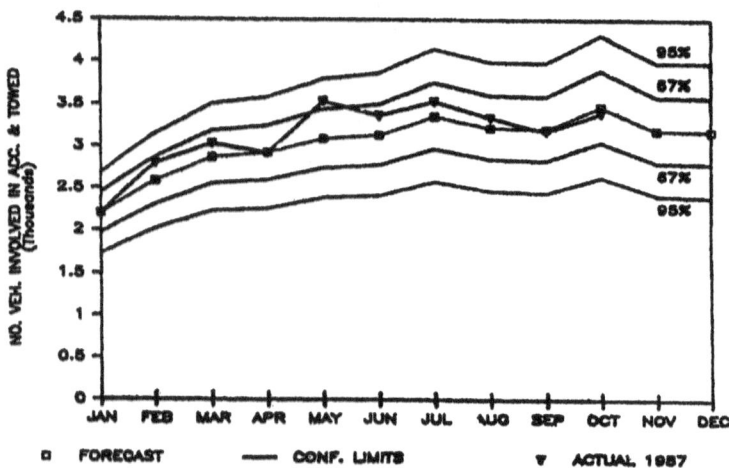

Source: Tow-truck allocation data are taken from the Royal Automobile Club of Victoria (RACV).

Figure 6.5: Cumulative Tow-truck Allocations

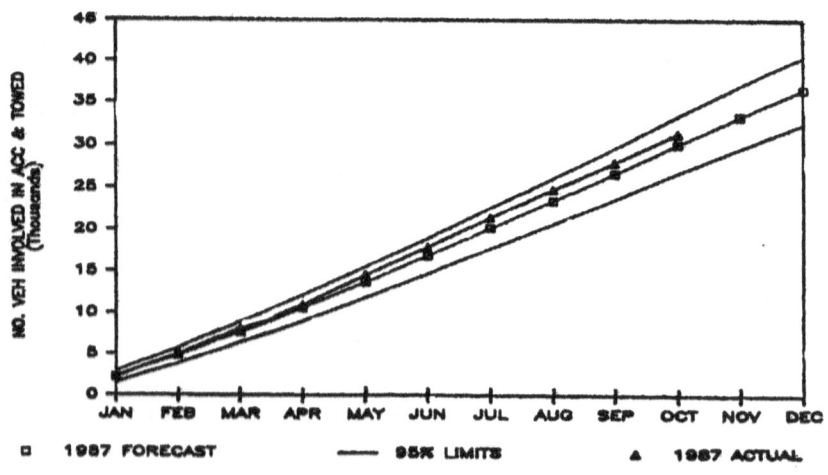

Source: Tow-truck allocation data are taken from the Royal Automobile

Club of Victoria (RACV).

Table 6.3: Monthly Report of Number of Vehicles Involved in Accidents and Towered Away Within Melbourne Metropolitan Areas*

Months of the years	1987 Actual*	1987 Forecast	1986 Actual
January	2202	2202	2178
February	2803	2590	2512
March	3040	2874	2666
April	2925	2927	2859
May	3542	3095	2918
June	3378	3141	2955
July	3541	3366	3196
August	3351	3230	3027
September	3189	3214	3069
October	3408	3475	3480
November	-	3204	3130
December	-	3191	3222
Total up to October	31379	30114	28860

* Area covered is the centralised tow-truck allocation scheme which covers an area slightly smaller than the Melbourne Statistical Division.

Source: RACV Tow-truck Allocation Data. In view of the tow-away criterion, crashes which involve pedestrians, cyclists or motor cyclists are less likely to be included in the statistics than are crashes involving other vehicle types only.

At this stage two technical points with regard to calculating the prediction based on the Winter's method should be mentioned, which are discussed below.

A method for calculating exact forecast confidence intervals for Winter's method was not available. The PROC FORECAST procedure of the SAS/ETS (1984) package was used for an approximation of confidence intervals.

A theoretical procedure for calculating the confidence limits for cumulative forecasts by the Winter's method is not currently available. However, the direct exponential smoothing method can be applied to calculate the prediction intervals for cumulative forecasts suggested by Montgomery and Johnson (1976).

At the end of 1987, if the pattern of the tow-truck allocation data remains unchanged, then the computerised Winter's model may well be used to forecast 1988 accidents, by adding the monthly 1987 data to the tow-truck allocation data series. However, a new model should be built to forecast 1988 accidents if a significant change is noted in the data series. Such investigations should be made at the end of each year and the model should be recalibrated or a new model be established.

6.8 Conclusions and Recommendations

Apart from the VicRoads fatality series, tow-truck allocation data is the only timely available series, which has been shown to be suitable for short-term monitoring purposes. In addition, this data have been shown to be consistent with police reported casualty accident data in terms of monthly variations.

The tow-truck allocation data provided a different view of the level of road trauma on Victorian roads to that provided by the consideration of road fatalities only. Both series will continue to be closely monitored to ensure that any significant deviations in levels of road trauma from the expected can be detected as early as possible. The VicRoads accident data may prove to be a very useful series for the short-term accident monitoring system in future, if the present delay can be reduced to four weeks. In addition, further investigation of the Hospital Morbidity File and ambulance services data may provide another promising source of information for the monitor.

Winter's method has been found to be a suitable method in forecasting tow-truck allocation data. It is recommended that:

(a) The tow-truck allocation data is used as a short-term accident monitoring tool for countermeasure initiatives in Victoria.

(b) The short-term accident monitoring system developed in this chapter could be applied to other data sources, such as the VicRoads accident data system, Hospital Morbidity File and ambulance services, etc.

(c) More theoretical research should be undertaken into development of a procedure for computing the exact confidence intervals for period and cumulative forecasts for Winter's method.

(d) A menu-driven program should be developed on a computer system to store, update and edit data, as well as interface with SPSSX (1986) or other packages. This can be used to produce monthly tables and graphs of presently available series (e.g. road fatalities and tow-truck allocations), for short-term accident monitoring in Victoria.

(e) This technique can also be used by a number of organisations to monitor any significant deviations of certain phenomenon, which can be detected as early as possible.

Notes

1 Federal Road Safety Commission (2005), AUSTROADS (2002) and most recently Haque (2006) also have developed a monthly road accident monitoring system to identify the current pattern of road accidents, and to introduce an appropriate road safety countermeasure initiative to bring down the number of future road casualties.

CHAPTER 7

EVALUATION OF SOME MAJOR STATEWIDE POLICE INITIATIVES

Road accident monitoring systems developed in previous chapters can be used to identify certain times of the day or events in a year or certain road user types and/or vehicle types, when historically road accidents are high. Road safety initiatives are then developed and implemented to reduce road toll. Extra measures are taken for these particular times/events to reduce road toll. Many organizations are working to achieve this objective. The police are the only one unified force who actively monitor the road safety situation on the road and target certain events to reduce road toll. In this chapter we evaluate some initiatives undertaken by the Victorian Police, which are aimed to reduce road toll in Victoria. It is thus expected that other states in Australia and other countries can follow such techniques of increasing extra police activities on the road in certain events to help to reduce road toll.1

7.1 Introduction

The Victorian Police (VP) has responsibility to control hazardous driving situations on Victorian roads through enforcement of road safety regulations with the aim of minimising the level of road trauma resulting from unsafe behaviour of the individuals in the community. In order to fulfill this objective, VP increases their effort in certain times of the year such as the Queen's Birthday and Easter holidays, when historically the road toll tended to be high, and at a time when an increased level of holiday traffic flow runs on the roads, which are designed to handle much lower levels of traffic. This is the time when many individuals drive their vehicles in an unsafe manner such as speeding, running red lights, etc. In addition to these, the VP also conducts other major statewide police initiatives, such as campaigns targeting commercial vehicles, Project '100', etc. to reduce traffic casualties on the roads. These four major police initiatives have been analysed to examine whether their objectives are met. Because of the nature of the events and the lack of directly comparable control (non-policed) times, these police initiatives have been evaluated by the traditional pre-post method.

7.2 Easter Holidays

Easter holidays travel starts on Thursday afternoon prior to Good Friday and ends on the following Tuesday (inclusive, i.e., 5 1/2 days), although school holidays are now extend to the following Monday for State schools, and may be longer for some private schools. The number of fatalities and serious casualties of equivalent to the Friday to Tuesday 5 1/2 days before, during and after Easter holidays are presented in Table 7.1.

Table 7.1: Persons Killed and Seriously Injured Due to Road Accident; for Before, During and After Easter Holidays, 1986–1990

Period	1986–990	
	Fatalities	Serious casualties
Before (EH)	10	149
During (EH)	12	149
After (EH)	10	139

Source: Road Traffic Accident Data File of the RTA of Victoria extracted from the Victorian Police Road Accident Report Form.

7.3 Queens Birthday

Every year Victorian Police increases their activity during the Queen's birthday weekend period, which lasts for 4 days. The number of fatalities and serious casualties for the equivalent Friday–Monday 4 days period just before, during and after Queen's birthday holidays are presented in Table 7.2.

Table 7.2: Persons Killed and Seriously Injured Due to Road Accidents, Friday to Monday Period Before, During and After Queen's Birthday Holidays, 1986–1990

Period	1986-1990	
	Fatalities	Serious casualties
Before (QBH)	5	89
During (QBH)	10	134
After (QBH)	9	103

Source: Road Traffic Accident Data File of the RTA of Victoria extracted from the Victorian Police Road Accident Report Form

7.4 Analysis of Easter Holiday and Queen's Birthday Road Toll

It is generally anticipated that any major police activity has a direct effect during the period of increased activity and that it would continue to impact on road behaviour for periods following the date of actual operations.

Tables 7.1 and 7.2 show that there is no significant difference in serious road casualties before, during and after Easter and the Queen's birthday holidays probably because of heavy police activities on Victorian roads, even though there was an expected increase in the level of high-risk holiday travel. Thus, it can be argued that police activity prevented an increase in road trauma, even though the magnitude of this effect cannot be measured, as there is no recent and/or equivalent holiday periods with no special police effect noted for comparison.

7.5 Campaigns Targeting Commercial Vehicles

Heavy commercial vehicles involved in accidents result in more serious injury levels than would be expected in equivalent accidents between cars or car derivatives. In order to control the level of such accidents involving commercial vehicles, the Victoria Police, VicRoads enforcement personnel and other police undertook major campaigns targeting commercial vehicles during the following periods.

In 1986	During 28/9–4/10	Called 'Operation Tri-State'
In 1987	During 21/6–26/6	Called 'Operation West Wheels'
In 1988	During 7/10–15/10	Called 'Operation Big Wheels'
In 1989	During 25/6–30/6	Called 'Operation Big Brother'
In 1990	During 11/2–13/2 *	Called 'Operation Big Brother'

* Shortened by transport strike.

The average number of fatalities and serious casualties of the equivalent time period before, during and after the campaigns of every year is presented in Table 7.3.

No significant change is observed, while fatalities are lower, it needs to be stated that heavy vehicles are involved in only about 12–20% of fatalities or about 2 to 3 out of the 10–15 shown above.

Table 7.3: Persons Killed and Seriously Injured of Equivalent Times; Before During and After Targeting Commercial Vehicles, 1986–1990

Period	1986–1990 (AV)	
	Fatalities	Serious casualties
Before (CVC)	15	163
During (CVC)	9	171
After (CVC)	11	164
Average	10	167

Source: Road Traffic Accident Data File of the RTA of Victoria extracted from the Victorian Police Road Accident Report Form

7.6 Project 100

Project 100 was conducted from 27/9/89 to 4/1/90 in Victoria as a result of the high road toll and aimed to reduce traffic casualties generally during the period, as well as during Christmas and New Year. Average number of fatalities and serious casualties during the same time period of the previous five years, and the total number for 89/90 are presented in Table 7.4.

This table clearly shows a decrease of 23 (12%) in fatalities and 437 (15%) in serious casualties during the period of Project 100. These reductions are significant and it clearly shows that police enforcement undertaking Project 100 was very efficient in reducing the road toll during Christmas and New Year eves, when many high risk drivers drive their vehicles on the roads. However, this decrease may be the result of a number of other road safety initiatives of publicity and public concern, including the Transport Accident Commission's (TAC) advertising and changes to penalties, etc. Hence it is not possible to measure the effects of Project 100 directly. It would however be possible to determine the effect of this campaign if Victoria Police supplies the details of road sections where Project 100 was targeted (5 per police region).

Table 7.4: Evaluation of Project 100

Year	Fatalities	Serious casualties
1989–90	171	2,484
Av. of 1985–89	194	2,921

Source: Road Traffic Accident Data File of the RTA of Victoria extracted from the Victorian Police Road Accident Report Form.

7.7 Conclusions

This study clearly shows that police initiatives targeting certain events are very successful in reducing road casualties. During the times of Easter holidays, Queen's birthdays, Christmas and New Year eves many risky drivers drive their cars on the roads, and are involved in SCAs, many of which can be saved by enforcing extra police on our roads. This could assist to reduce the road toll. - This is because, the presence of extra police on our roads create an important change of behaviour of high-risk drivers. It is thus expected that these risky drivers drive their vehicles very carefully to avoid accidents when they see a heavy police presence on the road. Therefore to reduce the number of SCAs, it is recommended that extra police should be deployed on the roads at certain times of the year when historically high a volume of traffic runs through the roads, many of whom are high risk drivers.

Notes

[1] Haque (1989), Ross (1998), Romão et al. (2003), Elliott and Broughton (2005) and Zaidel (2002) have strongly advocated increasing police activities on the road in certain events to reduce road casualties.

CHAPTER 8

METHODS OF EVALUATION OF IMPLEMENTED ROAD SAFETY LAWS

This chapter presents the most appropriate methods of evaluating implemented road safety legislations. There are many methods among which two: the pre-post and the intervention time series analysis are very popularly used to evaluate implemented road safety legislations. Preliminary evaluation of the Victorian Zero BAC legislation has been made to illustrate the empirical application of these methods. It was observed that both methods provided a statistically insignificant reduction of serious road casualties for the first six-month post-legislation period: July 1984 to December 1984. However, it is too early to make any conclusion about the effectiveness of the Victorian Zero BAC legislation, and power of the analysis is very poor.

8.1 Introduction

Zero Blood Alcohol Content (BAC) legislation was introduced in Victoria on May 22, 1984. Under this legislation no learner (L), first year probationary (P), disqualified or unlicensed driver or rider is allowed to drive or ride with any alcohol in his/her blood. Justification of this legislation is based on separating evidence that young drivers appear to be more adversely affected at lower BAC levels than standard licence holders [see Borkenstein et al. (1974); and Mayhew and Simpson (1983)]. The Victorian law also applies to unlicensed and disqualified drivers, because these groups have a much higher incidence of illegal BACs than standard licence holders [see South and Johnston (1984)]. Learner drivers were also included in the law for consistency reasons.

The accident effects of the legislation were examined only for car drivers involved in Serious Casualty Accidents (SCAs) at alcohol times, using the pre-post and intervention time series analysis.1 The effect was measured over the first six months post-legislation period (July 1984 to December 1984).

In order to measure the effect of the zero BAC legislation accurately, we have used two groups of drivers: a target group (learner, first-year probationary, disqualified and unlicensed), and a control group (standard license holders). To measure the effect of certain implemented road safety legislation, the traditional pre-post method compares the number of SCAs for target group drivers at post-legislation period with the same pre-legislation period. But, simple comparison of the SCAs of the target group of drivers between pre- and post-legislation period is subject to criticism on the grounds that other factors might have affected accident numbers within comparison periods. For that reason, another legislation free control group of drivers was used to see the relative change of the SCAs for target group drivers between the pre- and post-legislation period.

Moreover, the traditional pre-post method cannot incorporate the emerging pre-legislation trend, and hence cannot provide an accurate estimate of the effect of the legislation. This can be illustrated by an example. Let us suppose that there was a downward trend in the pre-legislation period, which is supposed to continue up to the post-legislation period. Now if one observes lower SCA numbers at the post-legislation period compared to the pre-legislation period, there is no way of knowing whether that reduction of SCA numbers is due to the implementation of the legislation or due to the trend effect. To take into account the effect of the pre-legislation trend, the intervention time series analyses are conducted to test the effect of the implemented road safety legislation. Earlier, Abraham (1987) and Vingilis *et al.* (1988) used the Box and Tiao (1975) intervention time series method to evaluate Ontario's road safety legislations. But, they only dealt with a single series of time series data. As a result, their estimates may be biased due to not incorporating the effects of other influences, which should be taken into account in assessing the effects of the legislation.

The Box and Tiao (1975) intervention time series method is also used in the present analysis on two separate groups (one target and one control) of drivers to estimate the effect of the zero BAC legislation for the target group drivers compared with control group drivers. In this way, we have avoided the effects of the other external factors from the post-legislation SCA numbers in order to estimate the actual effect of the legislation.

The major objective of this study is to evaluate the effect of the zero BAC legislation for target group drivers at 'alcohol' times (when alcohol related accidents are higher compared to other times), using the SCA data.

This chapter is organised as follows. Data used in the present study are described in Section 8.2. Section 8.3 is concerned with the evaluation methods. Analysis and results of the study are presented in Section 8.4, while some important discussions are made in the final section.

8.2 Data

At the time of the study, accident data from the Road Traffic Authority (RTA) accident file were available up to December 1984. This provided an opportunity to measure the effectiveness of the zero BAC legislation for the first six months after its implementation.

Accident data for drivers of car and car derivatives who were involved in serious casualty accidents were considered in this study. A serious casualty accident (SCA) is an accident in which at least one person is killed, or injured and admitted to hospital. Alcohol times were used to observe the number of serious road casualties. This is because Sloane and South (1985) and Haque *et al.* (1986) showed that the distribution of alcohol-related accidents is not uniform over the hours of the day and days of the week. In fact most of the alcohol related accidents happen during alcohol times (see Appendix 8A for more details about alcohol times).

Therefore, any reduction in the incidence of alcohol-related accidents, which might occur due to the implementation of the zero BAC legislation could be expected to be greater at these times. Thus, SCAs during the alcohol times were used in this study as surrogates for alcohol-involved accidents.

8.3 Evaluation Methods

8.3.1 Driver Groups

For the purpose of the analysis, learner, first year probationary, disqualified and unlicensed drivers were considered as the 'target' group drivers. The standard license holders were considered as the 'control' group drivers, although it was very difficult to find a suitable control group of drivers (who were free from the zero BAC legislation) for such complex analysis.

The following two separate series of drivers were analysed in the present analysis. These are:

- target group drivers at alcohol times; and
- standard licence holders at alcohol times.

Our primary focus is on the first group, because the effects of the zero BAC legislation were considered likely to be greater for the target group during the alcohol times. The second group was considered as a control group. The second group was included to measure and account for the effect of other influences which may have affected the first series in addition to the zero BAC legislation.

8.3.2 Statistical Methods

There are two basic types of statistical methods that can be used to evaluate road safety countermeasures. These are the 'pre-post' method and the 'intervention time series' method. The pre-post method attempts to evaluate the effect of road safety countermeasures by comparing the relative changes in the numbers of target and control group drivers involved in SCAs between the pre- and post-legislation periods. The intervention time-series method attempts to analyse the effect of road safety countermeasures by predicting the expected number of target group drivers involved in SCAs during the post-legislation period, using the available pre-legislation data.

Each of these methods has advantages and disadvantages. The advantage of the pre-post method is that it is easy to apply and understand. However, its principal disadvantage is that it cannot incorporate a pre-legislation trend, which might affect the measure of the actual benefit of the legislation. In contrast, the time series method has the advantage of controlling for long-term trends and is potentially more sensitive. In addition, a component representing the effect of an intervention can be added to examine whether there is any statistically significant effect due to the implementation of a countermeasure. Its main drawback is that it assumes that a general trend established in previous years would be continued into the future. These two evaluation methods are discussed below.

8.3.2.1 The Traditional Pre-post Method

The number of target and control group drivers involved in SCAs at alcohol times for pre and post legislation periods can be presented in a 2x2 contingency table. A measure of change in the target group drivers for alcohol times in the post legislation period relative to both control group drivers and pre-legislation period can then be calculated from SCA numbers presented in cells of the following contingency table.

Driver groups	Pre-legislation period	Post-legislation
Target group drivers	A	B
Control group drivers	C	D

The measure used to determine the size of the net change for target group drivers from pre- to post- legislation period at alcohol times relative to control group drivers is given by:

$$C_t = \frac{b}{a\left(d/c\right)} - 1 \qquad (8.1)$$

A negative result represents a reduction, while a positive number shows an increase in the post-legislation period. In order to examine whether such change is statistically significant, the traditional χ^2- test with 1 degree of freedom can be performed. Thus the simple pre-post comparison between 'target' and 'control' group drivers at alcohol times would give an indication of the effectiveness of the zero BAC legislation.

In order to avoid seasonal factors, SCAs in the pre-legislation period are compared with those in the post-legislation period for the same time period (i.e., same months of the years). In some cases, an average figure of SCAs for the pre-legislation years is used for comparison purposes when more than one year pre-legislation SCAs are compared with the one year post-legislation period for the same months of the years.

It should be noted that a one-tailed hypothesis testing procedure was used, because the test was designed to detect significant reductions from the pre- to the post-legislation period, rather than only significant changes between the pre- and post-legislation periods. Only 5% level of significance was used to conduct the test for all cases unless otherwise stated.

However, one of the major drawbacks of the traditional pre-post method is that it cannot take into account the effect of the pre-legislation trend, which is very important in measuring the effectiveness of implemented road safety legislation. On the other hand the intervention time series analysis can nicely incorporate the pre-legislation trend and can test the effect of implemented road safety legislation. Due to the pre-legislation downward trends identified by Haque *et al.* (1986) in the accident involvements of all car drivers, especially at night and especially for the target group, it was decided that the time series method is more likely to give valid conclusions in this study. However, for comparative purposes, both methods were used to assess the effects of the zero BAC law in the first six months of the post-legislation period July 1984 to December 1984.

8.3.2.2 Time Series Analysis

A three-step procedure is followed in performing time series analyses, which are described below.

(i) **Graphical Inspection**: First, the raw SCA data at alcohol times are plotted in Figure 8.1, which shows that the pre-legislation SCA data for both target and control group drivers followed a downward trend and continued for sometime after the implementation of the zero BAC legislation. Hence, it is highly likely that further time series analyses would provide a more accurate measure of the effectiveness of the zero BAC legislation.

(ii) **The Univariate Box-Jenkins Model**: Our visual inspection of the raw totals of SCA data show that the trend of the SCAs is quite compatible with the hypothesized effect. Hence, the autoregressive integrated moving averages (ARIMA) model developed by Box and Jenkins (1976) is used to forecast SCAs for the post-legislation period based on pre-legislation SCA data. These models are accomplished by the use of the auto-correlation and partial auto-correlation functions. By matching the known properties of models with the observed auto-correlation and partial auto-correlation functions, tentative models are identified, estimated and checked [see Box and Jenkins (1976) for more details]. If a number of models satisfy the portmanteau test on the residuals, MAICE criterion due to Akaike (1973) was used for final model selection. Using the estimated parameters of the chosen model, forecasts were made for the post-legislation period, which were then compared with the actual SCAs. If the actual values were consistent with the forecasted values, then they were considered to reflect the effects of long-term trends and seasonal factors, and the hypothesis was rejected without further analysis. However, if the actual SCAs differed from the forecasted values in a manner that was generally consistent with the hypothesized effect of the zero BAC legislation, then an intervention time series analysis was performed.

(iii)   **Intervention Time Series Analysis**: This is a further development of the ARIMA model, which enables one to measure the effect of an intervention. It differs in two respects from the ARIMA model in that: (i) it explicitly incorporates a mathematical representation of the intervention effect; and (ii) it uses both pre- and post-legislation data, whereas the ARIMA model uses only pre-legislation data.

The intervention model represents the consequential effect on the time series causes by the introduction of certain measures, e.g. change of policy. The intervention model enables one to find the expected form of trends and the size of the effects in the post-intervention period. Also, the statistical significance test of the intervention co-efficient could state whether any change in the post-legislation period is due to the implementation of certain policies.

The analysis of the effect of known intervention was first applied to traffic data by Cambell, Ross and Glass. Their methodology is discussed in Glass et al. (1975). Later, Box and Tiao (1975), Wiorkowski and Heckard (1977), and Bhattacharya et al. (1979) and many others etc., used the intervention time series techniques in analyzing road accident data. A few years later, Harvey and Durbin (1986) analysed the effects on casualty rates of a seatbelt law in Great Britain, using structural time series models. The historical development of the structural models is described in their paper, together with further references.

From the experiences with studies of Haque et al. (1986), and the Ontario study of Abraham (1987), we have decided to use the Box and Tiao (1975) intervention time series analysis based on Box-Jenkins (1976) ARIMA modelling. It is Box and Tiao who showed how the procedures for identifying time series models could be combined with regression analysis to measure the effects of intervention. Their method will be considered in the next sub-section. Before that, we would like to discuss the trends of the raw data of different series considered in this study.

Figure 8.1 presents the monthly number of target group drivers and standard licence holders involved in SCAs at alcohol times. These clearly show that there were decreasing trends in SCAs for both types of drivers at alcohol times until the middle of 1984. However, it is apparent from this figure that both target and control group drivers involved in SCAs at alcohol times increased from the middle of 1984. This might have happened due to many unknown reasons. At this stage of the analysis, it was not known for what group of drivers the rate of increase of SCAs was faster. In order to investigate this, the intervention coefficients for target and control group drivers have been tested for differences following the fitting of the intervention models.

Figure 8.1: Number of Serious Casualty Accidents for Target and Control Drivers at Alcohol Times in Victoria, 1977–1985

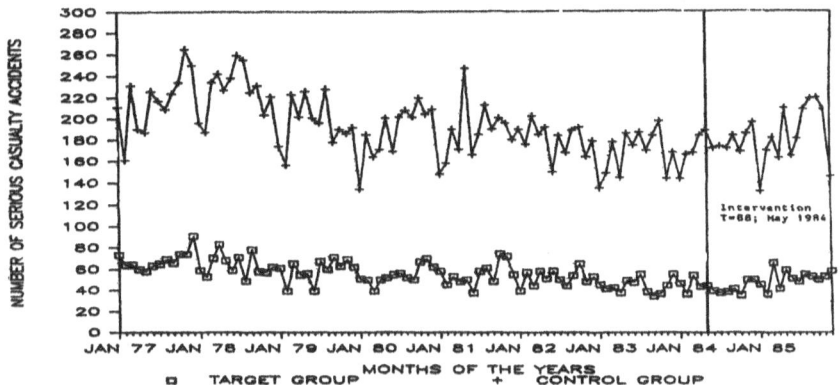

Source: Road Traffic Accident Data File of the RTA of Victoria extracted from the Victorian Police Road Accident Report Form.

8.3.2.2.1   Stochastic models for pre-intervention data

It is apparent from figure 8.1 that our series are non-stationary and autocorrelated. They are highly correlated at seasonal as well as at other lags. Following Box and Jenkins (1976, p. 305), we entertain a class of ARIMA model of the following form for the pre-legislation monthly data (January 1977–May 1984; 88 data points) for each of the two series separately:

$$\phi_p(B)\, \Phi_P(B^s)\, \Delta^d\, \Delta_s^D\, A_t \;=\; \theta_q(B)\, \Theta_Q(B^s)\, Z_t \qquad (8.1)$$

where B is the backshift operator such that $BA_t = A_{t-1}$, A_t is the output variable (number of SCAs) at time t:

$$\phi_p(B) = \left(1 - \phi_1 B - \phi_2 B^2 - \ldots - \phi_p B^p\right), \text{ and}$$

$$\theta_q(B) = \left(1 - \theta_1 B - \theta_2 B^2 - \ldots - \theta_q B^q\right)$$

are non-seasonal autoregressive and moving average polynomials in B of degrees p and q respectively.

$$\Phi_P(B^s) = \left(1 - \Phi_s B^s - \Phi_{2s} B^{2s} - \ldots - \Phi_{Ps} B^{Ps}\right) \text{ and}$$

$$\Theta_Q(B^s) = \left(1 - \Theta_s B^s - \Theta_{2s} B^{2s} - \ldots - \Theta_{Qs} B^{Qs}\right)$$

are seasonal autoregressive and moving average polynomials in B at seasonal length s of degrees P and Q respectively;

Δ^d is the non-seasonal differencing operator such that $\Delta^d = (1-B)^d$;

Δ_s^D is the seasonal differencing operator of length s such that $\Delta_s^D = (1-B^s)^D$;

d and D are the number of non-seasonal and seasonal differencing respectively; and Z_t stands for a set of uncorrelated random shocks with mean zero and variance σ_{zt}^2.

It is also assumed that the roots of $\phi_p(B)$ and $\Phi_P(B^s)$ lie outside, and those of $\theta_q(B)$ and $\Theta_Q(B^s)$ lie on or outside the unit circle.

The above equation (8.1) is referred to as an ARIMA (p, d, q) (P, D, Q)$_s$ process, where (p,d,q) indicates the non-seasonal orders and (P,D,Q)$_s$ denotes the seasonal orders of length s of the process.

8.3.2.2.2 Intervention models

The intervention time series model developed by Box and Tiao (1975) was used in the present analysis. There are four steps in the procedure.

(i) Fit an ARIMA model, which filters the series to a white noise process up to the period t, after which the intervention could be expected to affect the series (in this case May 1984).

(ii) Estimate the shape of the intervention on the series, meaning we have to find out whether the likely effect is a step or ramp function.

(iii) Evaluate the adequacy of the fitted model, using the Portmanteau test. Disputed models are finally selected by MAICE criterion developed by Akaike (1973).

(iv) Finally, perform a t-test to determine the significance of the intervention co-efficient.

Further, following Box and Tiao (1975), intervention models can be written as:

$$\Psi_t = \left[\frac{\omega(B)}{\partial(B)}\right] I_t^{(T)} \qquad (8.2)$$

Where: $\omega_{(B)} = \omega_0 - \omega_1 B - \ldots - \omega_s B^s$ and

$\partial_{(B)} = 1 - \partial_1 B - \ldots - \partial_r B^r$

are of degrees s and r respectively.

It is also assumed that the roots of $\omega_{(B)}$ and $\partial_{(B)}$ are outside, and on or outside the unit circle respectively. $I_t^{(T)}$ is an indicator variable and can be represented either by:

a step variable $\quad I_t^{(T)} = S_t^{(T)} = \begin{cases} 0, & t < T \\ 1, & t \geq T \end{cases} \qquad (8.3)$

or a pulse variable $\quad I_t^{(T)} = P_t^{(T)} = \begin{cases} 0, & t \neq T \\ 1, & t = T \end{cases} \qquad (8.4)$

Referring to our target group drivers, we expect an immediate step change in the input and, an output step change of unknown magnitude. This would result from the process:

$$\Psi_t = \omega S_t^{(T)} \tag{8.5}$$

In order to count the effects of other variables, we also wish to examine similar change in accident reduction for control group drivers. Later, a net effect of the legislation for target group drivers compared to the control group drivers will be evaluated on the basis of these changes.

The model (8.2) is flexible for various types of level change [see Box and Tiao (1975) for more details]. However, for present investigation the model (8.5) would be adequate, since our objective is to measure the road accidents due to the implementation of the zero BAC legislation. Hence our final intervention model can be expressed as:

$$A_t = \omega S_t^{(T)} + \frac{\theta_q(B)\,\Theta_Q(B^s)}{\phi_p(B)\,\Phi_P(B^s)\Delta^d \Delta_s^D} z_t \tag{8.6}$$

The model adequacy can be confirmed by the Ljung and Box (1978) Q statistics:

$$Q = n(n+2) \sum_{k=1}^{18} r_k^2 / (n-k)$$

Where: $r_k = \left[\sum_{k=1}^{n-k} z_t z_{t+k} \bigg/ \sum_{k=1}^{n} z_t^2 \right]$

8.4 Analysis and Results

8.4.1 ARIMA Model Fitting for Pre-intervention Data

Using the SAS (1982) computer software, the maximum likelihood (ML) estimation method is used to estimate a class of ARIMA models given in equation (8.1) for each of the two series separately. The ARIMA model selection procedure for each of the series was made on the basis of the sample autocorrelation, inverse autocorrelation [see Cleveland (1972); Chatfield (1980); Priestley (1981)]; partial autocorrelation; and Akaike's (1973) information criteria (AIC) and Schwarz's (1978) Bayesian criterion (SBC). A summary of the final ARIMA model selected for each of two series separately is given below.

Series	Number of models fitted	Best model selected	Estimation of best model
(1)	10	$(0, 1, 1)(1, 0, 0)_{12}$	$(1- B)(1- 0.17B^{12}) A_t = (1 - .82B) Z_t$; $\sigma_z^2 = 82.33$ [0.12] [0.06]
(2)	15	$(0,1,1)(1,1,0)_{12}$	$(1-B)(1-B^{12})(1+ 0.38B^{12})A_t=(1- .54B) Z_t$; $\sigma_z^2 = 422.33$ [0.09] [0.08]

Source: Road Traffic Accident Data File of the RTA of Victoria extracted from the Victorian Police Road Accident Report Form.

The ML estimates that the parameters of the final models for each of the two series have satisfied both the stationarity and invertibility conditions. The quantities in square brackets [ ] are standard errors. Diagnostic checks in terms of residuals and autocorrelations show that there is no inadequacy of the models.

It is now assumed that the pre-intervention model for each of the series continues to be adequate for the post-intervention period. This means that except for the effect of the intervention, the models described above are adequate for the post-intervention period.

8.4.2 Estimation and Checking of Intervention Models

An intervention model of the type given in equation (8.6) was applied to each best model, which was used for ARIMA forecasts, using all SCA data from January 1977 to December 1985. The parameters of those models were also estimated by the SAS computer software for each of the two series and are presented below.

The estimates of the parameters of the intervention models are not different from the pre-intervention data. Diagnostic checks in terms of residuals and their autocorrelations show that the models are quite satisfactory. This is confirmed by the Q statistic, which is significant when compared with the x^2 statistic with 4 degrees of freedom for each of the series.

Series	Estimation of the intervention model	σ_z^2	Q
(1)	$A_t = 0.65 \ S_t^{(T)} + \dfrac{(1-0.76B)\ [0.04]}{(1-B)(1-0.20B^{12})\ [0.081]} z_t$ [0.43]	72.95	11.81
(2)	$A_t = 1.01 \ S_t^{(T)} + \dfrac{(1-0.61B)\ [0.06]}{(1-B)(1-B^{12})(1+0.51B^{12})\ [0.09]} z_t$ [0.86]	411.16	11.98

* Numbers presented in brackets are standard errors.

Source: Road Traffic Accident Data File of the RTA of Victoria extracted from the Victorian Police Road Accident Report Form.

8.4.3 Results

8.4.3.1 Results from Time Series Models

The results of the ARIMA models and the actual number of drivers involved in SCAs for target and control groups in the alcohol times are given in Table 8.1. Forecast values based on intervention models are also presented in parentheses in this table. There were 251 target group drivers involved in SCAs during the alcohol times in the post-legislation period, compared with 267 forecasted by the ARIMA model, a difference of –6%. In contrast, the number of control group drivers involved in SCAs during the alcohol times was 3.1% greater than that forecast by the ARIMA model (Table 8.1); this difference was assumed to have been due to influences on the target group drivers other than the zero BAC legislation. It could be expected that a similar 3.1% difference for the target group would have occurred during the alcohol times in the absence of the legislation. Hence these results indicate that the net effect of the legislation was a –9.1% decrease in target group involvements during the alcohol times since this is the net difference (Table 8.1).

Table 8.1: Drivers Involved in Serious Casualty Accidents During July 1984 – December 1984 (Six Months Post-legislation)

Driver groups	ARIMA forecasts*	Actual numbers	Difference %
1. Target group	267.0 (144.7)	251	– 6.0
2. Standard license holders	1049.6 (1068.9)	1082	+ 3.1
3. Net difference for target group drivers relative to standard licence holders			– 9.1

* Intervention model forecasts are presented in parentheses.

Source: Road Traffic Accident Data File of the RTA of Victoria extracted from the Victorian Police Road Accident Report Form.

The statistical significance of this estimated effect was judged by appropriate differencing of the standardised intervention coefficients (dividing the intervention coefficients by the monthly average SCAs forecasted by the ARIMA model in the post-legislation period) for each of the two series, following the procedure above for calculating the adjusted net percentage difference. The adjusted net difference of the intervention coefficients is directly related to the adjusted net percentage difference, but has the advantage that a statistical test can be made to test whether it is real or due to chance variation.

An intervention coefficient (– 7.8) was observed for target group drivers when the step function was estimated for alcohol times. This coefficient was statistically insignificant since its t-value = – 0.68. On the other hand, a positive intervention coefficient (+2.4) was observed for control group drivers when a step function was estimated at alcohol times. This coefficient was also not statistically significant (t-value = +0.25). Furthermore, a test of the statistical significance of the adjusted net intervention coefficient based on the two intervention coefficients was carried out and was found to be insignificant (t-value = – 0.21).

These results are in conflict with those of Haque et al. (1986), who found a statistically significant positive effect of the legislation during the first six months of its implementation. However, they recognized the deficiency of the method, which had to be used at the time and were tentative in reaching a conclusion, recommending further work using time series methods. To resolve the conflict, and to provide results directly comparable with those found in this study, it was decided to apply the pre-post method also to evaluate the zero BAC legislation.

9.4.3.2 Results for the Pre-Post Method

Unlike Haque et al. (1986), only two six-month periods of pre-legislation (July to December of 1982 to 1983) average SCA data were used to compare with the six months post-legislation SCA data. This was done to minimize the effect of the pre-legislation trends and also to provide closer comparability to the time series results. The pre-post results are presented in the following Table 8.2.

Table 8.2: Effects of the Zero BAC Law in the First Six Months Post-legislation

Driver Groups	July–December (1982–83)	July–December (1984)	Change (%)
1. Target group	288.0	251	– 12.9
2. Control group	1063.5	1082	+ 1.8
3. **Net difference**: Target Group Drivers relative to control group drivers			– 14.7

Source: Road Traffic Accident Data File of the RTA of Victoria extracted from the Victorian Police Road Accident Report Form.

There were 251 target group drivers involved in SCAs during alcohol times of the week in the period July to December 1984, compared with an average of 288.0 for the same months in two previous years. This resulted in a reduction of 12.9% SCAs. On the other hand there was a 1.8% increase in SCA involvements for control group drivers at alcohol times between the same periods. Since 1.8% increase in SCAs would have been expected in the absence of the zero BAC legislation for target group drivers, the net effect of the legislation can be calculated as a 14.7% reduction in SCA involvements for target group drivers during the alcohol times. But, this net reduction was not statistically significant.

These results are consistent with those found in the time series analysis in that there was no statistically significant evidence of an effect of the zero BAC legislation during its first six months of the post-legislation period. However, the results indicate a magnitude of the effect of the legislation almost as large as that suggested by the results of Haque et al. (1986), so there is some consistency there. Nevertheless, the time series analysis results for the first six months post-legislation period should be regarded as more conclusive than the results earlier found by Haque et al. (1986).

Further evaluations of the zero BAC legislation were carried out for the first six months of its implementation based on alternative target and control group drivers, and were presented in Appendix 8B. Here, learner and first year probationary drivers were considered as the 'target group', while second and third year probationary drivers were considered as the 'control group'. This is a parallel study of the original work with alternative 'target' and 'control' group drivers involved in SCAs. The time series and pre-post results are presented in Tables 8B1 and 8B2 respectively in Appendix 8B. These results are quite consistent with those of the results already obtained from the main study based on the initial 'target, and 'control' group drivers.

8.4.4 Discussion

The results of this analysis show a statistically insignificant effect of the legislation during its first 6 months. The test performed was based on the adjusted difference of the intervention coefficients (Section 4.3.), which showed that there was a non-significant decrease (− 9.1%) for target group drivers during alcohol times, since the inception of the Zero BAC legislation.

We have analysed the power of the test, following the procedures discussed in Cohen (1977), to determine the minimum effect of the legislation, which could have been detected in the target group. It was found that the power of the test was poor (only 0.08). Low power may lead to ambiguous negative results, since failure to reject the null hypothesis cannot have much substantive meaning, even though to some degree the phenomenon does exist. This may be the situation in the present study because the a-prior probability of rejecting the null hypothesis appears to be due to low power.

There may be many reasons for the absence of an effect of the zero BAC legislation during its first 6 months post-legislation period. Among many others, the apparent absence of specific enforcement procedures and the on-going mass media publicity supporting enforcement of the legislation are important. These along with other reasons will be discussed in more details in Chapter 10.

The analysis showed that there was approximately a 9% to 15% SCA reduction for target group drivers at alcohol times as compared with the increase, which would have resulted in the absence of the zero BAC legislation in Victoria. This was not statistically significant, and the statistical power of the analysis was very poor.

Notes

1 Motorcycle riders were excluded from this study, because another law described in the next chapter was introduced on June 1983 for them, which might contaminate the effect of the Zero BAC law.

CHAPTER 9

EVALUATION OF IMPLEMENTED ROAD SAFETY COUNTERMEASURES USING INTERVENTION TIME SERIES ANALYSIS

Evaluating implemented road safety countermeasures is one of the major tasks for every traffic safety program (TSP). We have indicated in previous chapters that there are a number of methods, which can be used to evaluate the effectiveness of certain implemented road safety countermeasures. The intervention time series analysis is one of the most sophisticated techniques to evaluate the effectiveness of certain implemented road safety programs. In this chapter we have evaluated the effectiveness of two implemented road safety countermeasures, one dealing with the motorcycle rider training and licensing scheme and the other with evaluating the 1983 random breath testing campaign. By reading this chapter, readers will be able to learn how the intervention time series analysis can be used to evaluate various implemented road safety programs, using the Victorian road accident data. The SAS software program proved to be a very successful computer package to estimate and test the intervention coefficient of the time series model.

9.1 Introduction

The beneficial aspect of any road safety countermeasure depends on the active introduction and supervision of a suitable legislation, along with active cooperation of the driving population. In many cases, unsuitable methods are applied to show the benefits of such legislation rather than scientific analysis of relevant data. The intervention time series analysis is one of the most sophisticated methods to evaluate the effectiveness of an implemented road safety law. The SAS software program proved to be a very successful computer package to estimate the intervention time series model, which helped to test the intervention coefficient to see whether there was any significant effect due to the implementation of the countermeasure legislation.

In this chapter, we have evaluated two important implemented road safety countermeasures: (i) the evaluation of a motorcycle rider training and licensing scheme, and (ii) evaluating the 1983 random breath testing campaign with reference to Victorian road crash data, using the intervention time series analysis.

The main objective of the present chapter is to show how the techniques of the intervention time series method can be successfully used to evaluate the implemented road safety countermeasures, using the SAS computer software program.

This chapter is organised as follows. The techniques of time series analysis are discussed in Section 9.2. Evaluations of two implemented road safety countermeasures, using intervention time series analysis are presented in Section 9.3, while the final section provides some comments and limitations of the studies.

9.2 Time Series Analysis

The methods of time series as described by Box and Jenkins (1970) and modified by Box and Tiao (1975) were used to show the effect of certain implemented road safety countermeasures. Here the idea is to identify a pattern, based on the analysis of past data, and then make forecasts for the future. However, the validity of forecasts rests on the assumption that the pattern which was observed from the past data would continue into the future, which is more likely to be true in the short rather than long term. Road safety countermeasures act as an intervention to the established pattern. As a result, the effects of these countermeasures can be calculated as the difference between actual and forecasted values. Details of these techniques are described below.

9.2.1 The Autoregressive Integrated Moving Average (ARIMA) Models

Box and Jenkins (1970) developed the ARIMA model. The models are accomplished by the use of the auto-correlation and partial auto-correlation functions. By matching the known properties of models with the observed auto-correlation and partial auto-correlation functions, tentative models are identified, fitted and checked [for more details see Box and Jenkins (1970)]. If a number of models satisfy the portmanteau test on the residuals, the MAICE criterion due to Akaike (1973) was used for final model selection. Using the estimated parameters of the selected model, projections were made for the post-legislation period. The projected ARIMA and actual time series were then examined to see whether they were generally compatible with the hypothesized effect of the implemented road safety countermeasures. If the actual values were consistent with forecasted values, then they were considered to reflect the effects of long-term and seasonal trends and the hypothesis was rejected without further analysis. On the other hand, if the actual time series data departs from the forecasted values in a manner that was generally consonant with the hypothesized effect of the legislation, then an intervention technique is called for because the usual ARIMA models are unable to test the effect of such implemented road safety countermeasures.

9.2.1.1 Intervention Time Series Analysis

The technique of the intervention analysis is a development of the ARIMA model, which enables one to measure the consequential effect on the time series caused by the introduction of a certain policy or law (e.g. a road safety countermeasure). Also, the statistical significance test of the intervention co-efficient could state whether any change in the post-intervention period is due to the implementation of certain policy. Thus, intervention models differ in two respects from the ARIMA models, viz., (i) explicitly incorporating mathematical representation of the intervention form, and (ii) being based on both pre and post-legislation data rather than the only pre-legislation data used for ARIMA models.

Many authors viz., Glass *et al.* (1975), Box and Tiao (1975) and Wiorkowski and Beckard, (1977) etc., have applied intervention models to traffic data. Box and Tiao (1975) showed how the procedures for an identified time series model could be combined with regression analysis to determine the effects of intervention. The procedures developed by the latter authors were used in the present analyses.

There are four steps in the procedure. These are given below.

(i) Fit an ARIMA model, which filters the series to a white noise process up to the period t, after which the intervention could be expected to affect the series.

(ii) Estimate the shape of the intervention. That means, is the likely effect a step or a ramp?

(iii) Evaluate the adequacy of the fitted model using the Portmanteau test. Disputed models are finally selected by MAICE criterion developed by Akaike (1973).

(iv) Perform a t-test to determine the significance of the intervention co-efficient.

The general ARIMA model can be amended to incorporate a single intervention model, which can be expressed as follows:

$$X_t = \frac{\theta_1(B)\theta_2(B^s)U_t + \alpha}{\phi_1(B)\phi_2(B^s)(1-B)^d(1-B^s)^D} + \frac{(\omega_0 - \omega_1 B \ldots -\omega_s B^s)}{(1-\delta_1 \ldots -\delta_r B^r)} I_{t-b} \qquad (9.1)$$

where functions of operator B are expressed as:

$$\theta_1(B) = 1 - \theta_1 B - \theta_2 B^2 - \ldots \theta_q B^q$$

$$\theta_2(B^s) = 1 - \tilde{\theta}_1 B^s - \tilde{\theta}_2 B^{2s} - \ldots \tilde{\theta}_Q B^{sQ}$$

$$\phi_1(B) = 1 - \phi_1 B - \phi_2 B^2 - \ldots \phi_p B^p$$

$$\phi_2(B^s) = 1 - \tilde{\phi}_1 B^s - \tilde{\phi}_2 B^{2s} - \ldots \tilde{\phi}_P B^{sP}$$

Where:
P = the auto-regressive process
d = degree of non-seasonal diffencing
q = order of the moving average process
P = order of the seasonal auto regressive process
D = degree of seasonal differencing
Q = order of the seasonal moving average process
S = seasonal span
$\tilde{\phi}_1$ to $\tilde{\phi}_P$ = seasonal auto-regressive parameters
ϕ_1 to ϕ_p = Regular auto-regressive parameters
$\tilde{\theta}_1$ to $\tilde{\theta}_Q$ = seasonal moving average parameters
θ_1 to θ_q = regular moving average parameters
U_t = random (white noise) error component
α = constant
B = back-shift operator such that $B(Z_t)$ equals Z_{t-1}
ω_0 to ω_s = transfer function shift parameter
δ_1 to δ_r = transfer function memory parameters
b = delay parameter
I_t = step (or pulse function)

EVALUATION OF ROAD SAFETY COUNTERMEASURE

Intervention models represent the consequential effect on the time series caused by the introduction of certain measures, e.g. change of policy. An intervention model enables one to find the expected form of trends and the size of the effects in the post intervention period. Also, the statistical significance test of the intervention co-efficient could state whether any change in the post intervention period is due to the implementation of certain policy.

The behaviour of the multi-intervention model can generally be represented as the sum of the interventions and the pre-intervention (ARIMA) noise N_t, i.e:

$$Z_t = \sum_{j=1}^{k} I_{jt} + N_t \tag{9.2}$$

where:

$$N_t = \frac{\Theta_1(B)\Theta_2(B^s)a_t}{\Phi_1(B)\Phi_2(B^s)(1-B)^d(1-B^s)^D} \tag{9.3}$$

$$I_t = \frac{W_j(B)}{\delta_j(B)} \xi_{tj} ; \text{ and}$$

$\Phi_1(B)$, $\Phi_2(B^s)$, $\Theta_1(B)$, $\Theta_2(B^s)$, $W_j(B)$, and $\delta_j(B)$ are polynomials of degree p_1, p_2, q_1, q_2, r_j and s_j respectively.

B, a_t and $(1-B)^d(1-B^s)^D$ are operating on, which are all defined earlier.

ξ_{tj} is a step indicator; $S_t^{(T)} = \begin{cases} 0 & t < T \\ 1 & t \geq T \end{cases}$

or a pulse indicator $P_t^{(T)} = \begin{cases} 0 & t \neq T \\ 1 & t = T \end{cases}$

94   EVALUATION OF ROAD SAFETY COUNTERMEASURES

such that: $(1-B)S_t^{(T)} = P_t^{(T)}$

Thus the effect of an intervention I_t on the output variable Z_t can be viewed as the transfer between them.

9.2.1.2   Evaluation of Intervention Effect

The saving in casualty accident involvements (due to the introduction of the legislation) at a particular post-intervention time point (t_i) is the difference between the actual accident involvements (or alternatively the forecasted intervention values) and the projected ARIMA values i.e., ΔP_{t_i} as shown below. Thus, the total accident savings from the time of intervention t_0 and up to t_i, i.e. within the time interval (t_0, t_i) is given by

$$\sum_{j=t_0}^{t_i} \Delta P_j \qquad (9.4)$$

Figure 9.1:   Serious Casualty Accidents: Estimates Based on ARIMA and Intervention Models

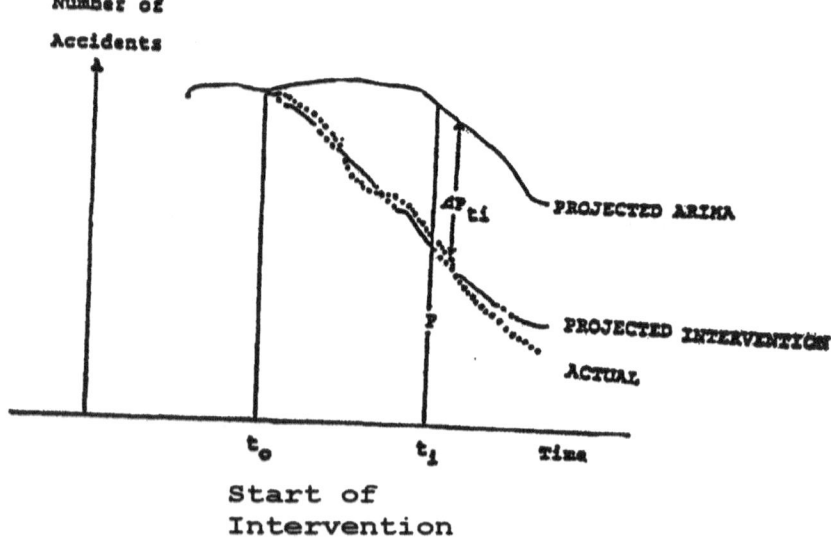

Therefore, total percentage savings of serious casualty accident involvements over the post-legislation period (t_0, t_i) is given by:

$$100 \left\{ \frac{\left(\sum_{j=t_0}^{t_i} \Delta P_j \right)}{\left(\sum_{j=t_0}^{t_i} P_j \right)} \right\} \% \qquad (9.5)$$

where p_j = the actual number of drivers involved in SCAs, j = $t_0, t_1, \ldots, t_i$.

The percentage change of target relative to control group drivers involved in SCAs in the post-legislation period can be estimated by:

$$[d/c(b/a)-1]\, 100\% \qquad (9.6)$$

where a and b are respectively the projected ARIMA and actual numbers of standard licence holders involved in SCAs, while c and d are the corresponding numbers for target group drivers.

9.2.1.3 Test of Intervention Co-efficient

The primary interest of the intervention model is to test the intervention co-efficient to examine whether there is any significant effect of the intervention. For our purpose, we should test the hypotheses that the number of individuals of a group (known as 'target group') likely to be affected by a certain countermeasure most likely would decrease road accidents. Therefore a one-tailed t-test can be used to find the significant decrease of the intervention co-efficient for this group. While a two-tailed t-test should be used to find any significant change for another group of individuals called the 'control group' who are free from the imposed intervention. The change of the adjusted effect of the legislation can be examined by testing whether the difference of the intervention coefficients differ from zero or not. This can also be done by the usual t-test. In all cases unless otherwise stated, the 5% level for statistical significance was used.

9.3 Evaluation of Two Implemented Road Safety Legislations Using Intervention Time Series Analysis

The Road Traffic Authority (RTA) is an authority of the Ministry of Transport in Victoria. One of the major tasks of the RTA is to evaluate the implemented road safety countermeasures in this state of Australia. Recently, one of the most sophisticated scientific techniques of time series methods has been used to evaluate some major road safety countermeasures, using SAS software program. In this chapter we have evaluated two important implemented road safety legislations, viz., (i) the evaluation of motorcycle rider training and licensing scheme and (ii) evaluating the 1983 random breath testing campaign, using the techniques of intervention time series analysis.

9.3.1 The Evaluation of Motorcycle Rider Training and License Scheme.1

An improved motorcycle rider training and licensing scheme was introduced in June 1983 with the aim of reducing the number of novice rider casualty accidents. The scheme included a new written test of motorcycle riding knowledge for learner permit applicants, as well as a basic riding skills test, which was initially applied in the Melbourne metropolitan area and later extended throughout Victoria. Four separate monthly series of persons involved in motorcycle casualty accidents for the period January 1977 to December 1984 were used in the main study. Only two series namely, (i) learner permit holders in the Melbourne Statistical Division (MSD) and (ii) standard licence holders in the MSD are presented here to demonstrate how the intervention time series analysis can be used to evaluate the motorcycle rider training and licensing scheme. The standard licence holder series is considered as a control series, so that any general downturn in accidents amongst all rider categories could be separated from that due to the new scheme.

First, many ARIMA models were fitted, tentative models were identified, fitted and checked, using January 1977 – June 1983 motorcycle casualty accident data for each of these series. These models were estimated using the SAS computer software. The best models selected for these two series are presented in Table 9.1.

The form of intervention for the learner permit holder series should theoretically be described by an infinite descending ramp [i.e. $W I_t (1 - B)$] as potential learner permit applicants are discouraged by the new procedures (an observed effect), leaving a decreasing number of permit holders, and as the better trained riders join the cohort of learner permit holders. Only current learner permit holders were given either one or both tests, would a step down in the level of casualty accidents would be expected. The SAS computer software program was also used to estimate the parameters of the best intervention models, using January 1977 to December 1984 rider casualty accident data.

The estimated parameters and the relevant statistics for the intervention models for these series are presented in Table 9.2.

The monthly accident forecasts based on the ARIMA and intervention models together with actual values for motorcycle learner riders and standard motorcycle riders in MSD are presented in figures 9.3 and 9.4 respectively. Figure 9.3 clearly shows that the number of SCAs for motorcycle learner riders has significantly reduced since the implementation of the motorcycle rider-training program in MSD. While Figure 9.4 shows that SCAs for standard motorcycle riders in MSD remains same at post-training period compared to the pre-training period. This clearly indicates that an improved motorcycle rider training and licensing scheme has reduced the number of novice rider casualty accidents.

Table 9.1: Best Models for Two Series Considered on the Basis of Akaike's Information Criterion and Portmanteau Test*

Series	Model	AIC	Fitted model	Residual variance	Significance of Q
(i)	(0,1,2)	316.78	$(1-B) X_t = (1-0.93B+0.24b^2) a_t$ [0.33] [0.33]	40.41	0.76
(ii)	(4,1,0)	340.05	$(1+.55B+.66B^2+.25B3$ (.33) (.35) (.36) $+.31B) (1-B) X_t = a_t$ [0.33]	50.97	0.47

*
   (1) In model (p, d, q), p represents the order of auto regression, d the data differentiating and q the order of moving average.
   (2) Product brackets mean that a seasonal model is being employed.
   (3) Bracketed [ ] terms denote standard error.
   (4) B is the back-shift operator i.e. $BX_t = X_{t-1}$.
   (5) X_t is the original series.
   (6) a_t is the white noise at time t taken from NID $(0, \sigma_a^2)$.

Source: Road Traffic Accident Data File of the RTA of Victoria extracted from the Victorian Police Road Accident Report Form.

The actual numbers of post-implementation learner permit riders, and standard licence holders involved in serious casualty accidents together with their estimates based on ARIMA and intervention models during July 1983 – December 1984 are presented in Table 9.3.

Table 9.3 shows that there was 26.8% significant reduction in casualty accidents involving learner permit holders in MSD during July 1983 – December 1984 following the introduction of the motorcycle training/licensing scheme. During the same period of time, a non-significant 5.3% increase in casualty accidents was observed for standard riders. Since, it could be expected that a similar 5.3% increase in accident involvements of learner permit holders would have occurred in the absence of the legislation, indicating that the net effect of the legislation was a 32.1% reduction in SCAs involvements for learner permit holders during July 1983 – December 1984. Further t-tests on intervention coefficients of these two series suggest that this reduction (32.1%) was statistically significant.2

Table 9.2: Estimated Parameters for Intervention Models

Series	Parameter estimates	Standard error	T-ratio	Model adequacy (Portmanteau test)	White noise variance
(i)	$\theta_1 = 1.11$	0.1	10.8		
	$\theta_2 = 0.31$	0.1	-3.00	0.447	34.09
	$W_1^2 = 1.52$	0.45	-3.35		
(ii)	$\theta_1 = -0.71$	0.1	-6.86		
	$\theta_2 = -0.76$	0.13	-6.05		
	$\theta_3 = -0.37$	0.12	-2.96	0.61	62.65
	$\theta_4 = -0.26$	0.11	-2.38		
	$W_1 = +1.01$	0.88	1.15		

Source: Road Traffic Accident Data File of the RTA of Victoria extracted from the Victorian Police Road Accident Report Form.

Table 9.3: Persons Involved in Motorcycle Casualty Accident Estimate of Intervention Effect: July 1983 – December 1984

Series	Actual	Forecasted* ARIMA	% change relative to ARIMA forecast	Significance of Intervention coefficient
(i)	338	461.9 (342.6)	-26.8	Significant
(ii)	702	666.9 (679.5)	$+5.3$	Non-significant
Net Change: Learner permit holders relative to standard licence holders			-32.1	Significant

*Forecasted intervention values are presented in parentheses ( ).

Source: Road Traffic Accident Data File of the RTA of Victoria extracted from the Victorian Police Road Accident Report Form.

9.3.2 Evaluating the 1983 Random Breath Testing Campaign. 3

A campaign of intensified random breath testing (RBT) was conducted during the period 24 October – 31 December 1983. Two RBT strategies were implemented separately for north and south of the Yarra River to compare the effectiveness of periods of high police visibility. This was supported by mass

EVALUATION OF ROAD SAFETY COUNTERMEASURE

media publicity during this period. In the area north of the Yarra (NY), RBT operations were conducted on Thursday to Saturday night (9.30 pm to 3.00 am) when the highest proportion of drinking driving was expected, whilst the other operations aimed to maximize the number of drivers aware of the present of RBT units by operating on Monday to Wednesday afternoon (4.30 pm to 8.00 pm) in the area south of the Yarra (SY).

Serious casualty accidents (SCAs) were used as the response variable, because they act as good surrogate for alcohol-involved accidents, particularly at nighttime. Two series are considered here to illustrate the analysis viz., (i) drivers involved in SCAs on Thursday to Sunday at night (8.00 pm to 4.00 am) in the NY and (ii) drivers involved in SCAs in the SY on Monday to Wednesday afternoon times (4.00am to 4.00pm). The first series is considered as the 'target group', while the second series is taken as the 'control group'.4

A number of ARIMA models were fitted, using four-weekly pre-RBT campaign SCAs data (commencing 26 December 1977). The best models were selected and projections were made on the basis of the estimated parameters for each of these two series.

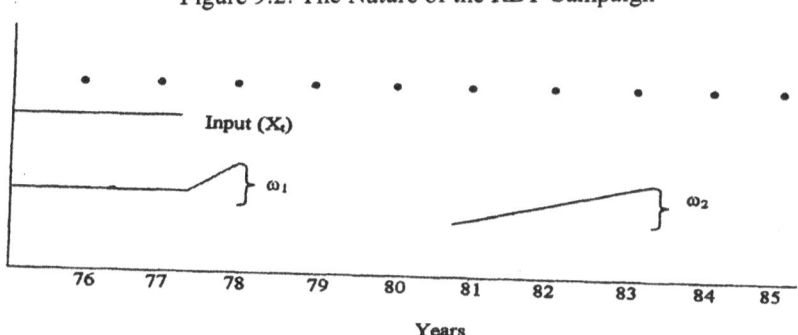

Figure 9.2: The Nature of the RBT Campaign

The nature of the RBT campaign is shown in Figure 9.2, which is incorporated to build the intervention model. This model comprised of two linear ramps to reflect the view that the effect of intensified RBT and TV advertising was cumulative, extending for at least four weeks beyond the termination of the RBT campaign.5 The indicator I_1 consequently measured the linear ramp over the RBT interval and one period beyond, with I_2 performing likewise for the succeeding five periods. The model can be expressed in mathematical form as,

$$Z_t = \frac{\Theta_1(B)\Theta_2(B^s)a_t}{(1-B)^d(1-B^s)^D \Phi_1(B)\Phi_2(B^s)} + \frac{W_1 I_1}{(1-B)^d(1-B^s)^D} + \frac{W_2 I_2}{(1-B)^d(1-B^s)^D} \quad (9.7)$$

The form of the indicator functions are given by:

$$I_1 = \begin{cases} 1 & t = \text{period } 12, 13, 1983; \text{ and period } 1, 1984 \\ 0 & \text{otherwise} \end{cases}$$

$$I_2 = \begin{cases} 1 & t \geq \text{Period } 2, 1984 \\ 0 & \text{otherwise} \end{cases}$$

The best models were identified, fitted and checked. In particular the magnitudes of W_1 and W_2 are evaluated and tested for statistical significance by t-tests to measure the size of the intervention. These are presented in the following Table 9.4.

Further, we have seen that the four weekly forecasts based on ARIMA and intervention models together with actual values on Thursday to Sunday nights at the north of the Yarra River. The actual numbers of drivers involved in SCAs on Thursday to Sunday night, and Monday to Wednesday day times, along with their estimates based on ARIMA and intervention models during the period 24 October – 31 December 1983, are presented in Table 9.5.

It is clear, from Table 9.5 that there was an 8.24% significant accident reduction on Thursday to Sunday nights in the north of the Yarra River during 24 October to 31 December 1983 due to the implementation of the intensive RBT campaign. However, there was a non-significant 10.61% increase in SCAs in the south of the Yarra River at day times. When these two figures are incorporated, it turns out that the net effect of the intensive RBT campaign was an 18.85% reduction in SCAs. Further t-tests on intervention co-efficient suggest that this net reduction was statistically significant.

9.4 Conclusions and Limitations

We have used the ARIMA and intervention models in evaluating two major implemented road safety countermeasures, using the SAS software. It appears that intervention time series analysis provides an estimate of the effectiveness of the road safety legislations. More importantly, the real benefit of the road safety countermeasures in Victoria can be evaluated by testing the intervention coefficient, which cannot be achieved by other methods.

The SAS computer program is very effective in producing forecasts based on the ARIMA and intervention models with step and linear ramp functions. However, it is still not clear how SAS can be used to estimate non-linear ramps and with multiple interventions. On the whole, the intervention time series model proved to be a very successful technique in evaluating and testing the effect of the implemented road safety countermeasures.

Table 9.4: Estimated Intervention Coefficients Fitted to the Serious Casualty Accident Data

Series	ARIMA model selected	RAMP effect period: 1977–79	RAMP effect after period: 1980–85	Residual variance	Significance of Q
(i)	$(4,1,0)(0,1,1)_{13}$	-7.06 (-2.10)	-3.38 (-1.40)	36.51	0.15
(ii)	$(0,1,1)_{13}$	3.01 (-0.79)	7.45 (-2.72)	50.33	0.55

* t-values are presented in parentheses.

Source: Road Traffic Accident Data File of the RTA of Victoria extracted from the Victorian Police Road Accident Report Form.

TABLE 9.5: Estimates of the Intervention Effects of Serious Casualty Accidents: 24 October – 31 December 1984

Series	Actual	Forecasted ARIMA*	% change relative to ARIMA forecast	Significance of intervention coefficient.
(i)	208	226.69 (213.04)	-8.24	Significant
(ii)	377	340.83 (375.90)	$+10.61$	Non-significant
	Net change: NY drivers at night relative to SY at day		-18.85	Significant

* Forecasted intervention values are presented in parentheses ( ).

Source: Road Traffic Accident Data File of the RTA of Victoria extracted from the Victorian Police Road Accident Report Form.

Figure 9.3: Motorcycle Riders in Casualty Accidents, Category: Learners, Regions: MSD, Post-intervention Period Only.

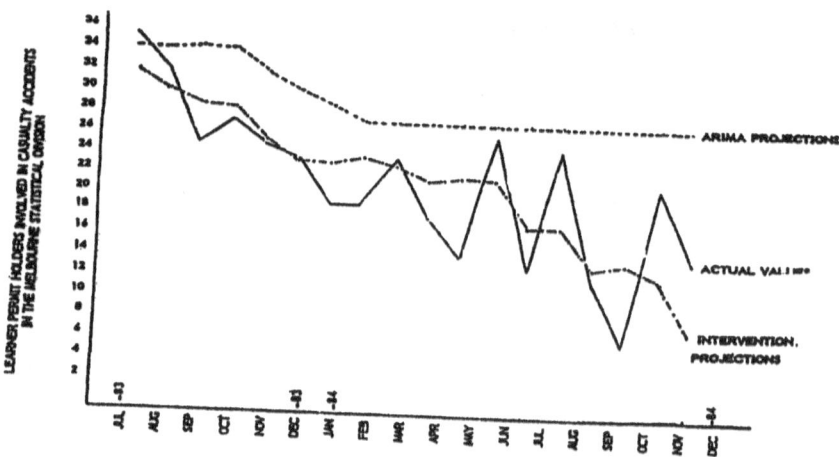

Source: Road Traffic Accident Data File of the RTA of Victoria extracted from the Victorian Police Road Accident Report Form.

Figure 9.4: Motorcycle Riders in Casualty Accidents, Category: Standard, Region: MSD, Post-intervention Period Only.

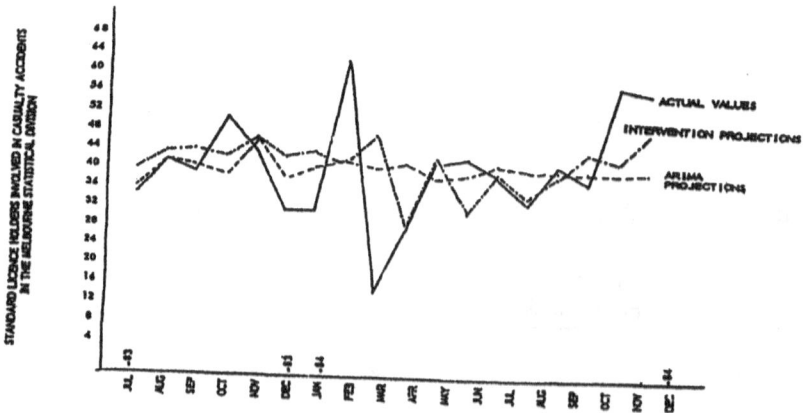

Source: Road Traffic Accident Data File of the RTA of Victoria extracted from the Victorian Police Road Accident Report Form.

Notes

1 See Daltry and Thomson (1986) for more details about Motorcycle Rider Training and Licensing Scheme in Victoria. There are many studies relating to motorcycle accidents, among which Hurt *et al.* (1981), Iamtrakul *et al.* (2003) and Fukuda (2006) are important. More importantly some authors such as Servadet *et al.* (2003), Supramaniam *et al.* (1984) and Sangowawa *et al.* (2006) have evaluated the effect of motorcycle helmet law and found that the use of a motorcycle helmet has significantly reduced the number of road casualties.

2 Traffic Safety Education programs are a most effective way of reducing road toll which can be found in Nagai *et al.* (2005), DFID (2004) and Fukuda *et al.* (2006).

3 See Daltery (1986) for more details about the 1983 Random Breath Testing Campaign. Saffer and Chaloupka (1989) have also evaluated the breath testing law and estimated its effects on highway fatality rates.

4 See Johnston (1980) and Cameron, Strang and Vulcan (1980) for more details about alcohol-related accidents in Victoria.

5 Such a direct residual influence has been reported by Cameron and Strang (1982).

CHAPTER 10

DETAILED ANALYSES OF THE VICTORIAN ZERO BAC LEGISLATION ON SERIOUS CASUALTY ACCIDENTS

By reading this chapter the readers will be able to learn how to evaluate an implemented public policy. In this chapter, we have evaluated the effect of the Victorian Zero Blood Alcohol Content (BAC) legislation over successive periods, following the availability of up-to-date and accurate data. In particular, readers will see how Victorian Zero BAC legislation was evaluated for the target (learner, first-year probationary, unlicensed and disqualified drivers) and control (standard drivers) group drivers at alcohol times and non-alcohol times, using the pre-post method and sophisticated intervention time series analysis. The aim of the legislation was to reduce the number of alcohol-related serious casualty accidents (SCAs) of the target group drivers. The analysis indicates an insignificant reduction of about 4% in the number involved in SCAs at alcohol times during the first 18-month post-legislation period. Hence, it was not possible to determine conclusively whether the result was due to chance variation or to the legislation, which did not achieve statistical significance because of poor analytical power.

10.1 Introduction

In Chapter 8, we analysed the Victorian Zero BAC legislation at alcohol times only for target group drivers: learner, first-year probationary, unlicensed and disqualified drivers to see whether the legislation had any effect in reducing the number of serious casualty accidents (SCAs) during the first six months post-legislation period. No significant effect of the legislation was found.

106   ANALYSES OF THE VICTORIAN ZERO BAC LEGISLATION

In this chapter, a detailed evaluation of the Victorian Zero BAC legislation will be under taken at alcohol and non-alcohol times for target and standard drivers. Motorcycle riders are excluded from this study, because in June 1983, new arrangements for the training and testing of motorcycle learner permit applicants were introduced. The proximity of this change to the introduction of the Zero BAC legislation prevented an evaluation of the effect of the latter on novice motorcyclists. Thus, this study evaluates the effect of the Zero BAC legislation for learner, first-year probationary, disqualified and unlicensed drivers only.

The purpose of the present study is to evaluate the effects of the Zero BAC legislation over successive post-legislation periods, for example: (i) first six months; (ii) second six months; (iii) first twelve months; and (iv) first eighteen months of the post-legislation period separately, following the availability of more up-to-date and accurate data. Further, a new definition of alcohol times (when the proportion of alcohol related SCAs is known to be higher than any other times) and non-alcohol times in hours of the day and days of the week have been incorporated to measure the effect of the legislation (see Appendix 8A for more details about alcohol and non-alcohol times).

This study is organised as follows. A brief review of the previous studies is provided in Section 10.2. Section 10.3 is concerned with the data used for the study. While, some methodological discussions are provided in Section 10.4. Analyses and results are presented in Section 10.5. Some important discussions about the study are provided in Section 10.6, while some concluding remarks and limitations of the study are presented in the final section.

10.2   Brief Review of Previous Studies

A surrogate for alcohol involvement was necessary, because no direct measure of BAC level for all drivers involved in SCAs was available. Cameron and Strang (1982) pointed out that SCAs were known to have a high probability of alcohol involvement, especially at night. Sloane and South (1985) showed that the distribution of alcohol-related accidents was not uniform over the hours of the day and days of the week. They observed that the proportion of accidents, which were related to alcohol, was higher on Thursday to Saturday nights than at other times. Haque *et al.* (1986) also observed a similar finding and reported this in their interim analysis of the effect of the zero BAC legislation.

Since then, South (1986) has indicated that there are alcohol times (certain hours of a week) during which the proportion of SCAs involving alcohol is higher than at other times (the complement of the alcohol times is taken as the so-called non-alcohol times). Any reduction in the incidence of alcohol-related accidents that might occur due to the implementation of the

Zero BAC legislation could be expected to be greater at alcohol times. Thus, SCAs during the alcohol times were used in this study as surrogates for alcohol-involved accidents.

Haque et al. (1986) investigated the effect of the Zero BAC legislation by comparing the number of drivers of target and control groups involved in SCAs during six months post-legislation (July to December 1984) with the average of the same months for the previous four years (July to December 1980–1983). They used two target group drivers: (i) first year probationary drivers only, and (ii) learners, first year probationary, unlicensed and disqualified drivers. They also used two control group drivers: (i) standard license holders, and (ii) this group together with second and third year probationary drivers. Simple contingency table tests were applied to measure the effectiveness of the Zero BAC legislation. It was observed that there was a significant reduction in the total number of target group drivers relative to the number of control group drivers. The overall reduction was 12%. There were also significant accident reductions of the order of 18% for learner, first year probationary, unlicensed and disqualified drivers compared to standard drivers at night (when alcohol involvement in SCAs is higher than at other times). More importantly, there was evidence that a significant higher accident reduction of 29% occurred on Thursday to Saturday nights for the first year probationary drivers (the main target group), when compared with the standard license holders (more conservative control group).

It was observed that there had been reductions in trend during the pre-legislation period in the number of drivers involved in SCAs for both target and control groups. There was a strong indication that the drop was greater for the target group than for the control group at alcohol times (see figures 10.1 and 10.2). Simple pre-post comparison cannot take fully into account any changes that are attributable to a long-term downward trend in the pre-legislation period and continued after the implementation of the legislation. Thus, Haque et al. (1986) suggested applying both the pre-post method and the time series analysis when additional post-legislation data became available. At a later date, Haque and Cameron (1987) made a comprehensive study and presented more detailed information about the effect of the Victorian Zero BAC legislation, using serious casualty accident data. They found insignificant small reduction of SCAs for target group drivers compared to control group drivers.

In order to achieve significant reduction of SCAs for target group drivers at alcohol times, Victorian road safety authorities made a large scale publicity and educational campaign.1 just before the introduction of the Zero BAC legislation (during May/June 1984) to ensure target group drivers were aware of the new law and the penalties associated with driving above 0.00/100ml. The costs of the campaign included A$124,000 paid advertising on television, radio and press; and A$74,000 for community service airtime. The new Victorian Traffic Handbook introduced in June 1985 contained a major section on the Zero BAC limits. Compulsory questions on these limits are included in the new written tests for learner permits (since July 1985) and probationary licences (since October 1985). The effects of the publicity and educational campaigns along with new testing procedures for learner permits and probationary licences are now discussed as follows.

10.2.1   Uses of "P" Plate

There was a possibility of not showing P plates by some first year probationary drivers (novice drivers) to avoid the detection of drink driving due to heavy penalties associated with the Zero BAC law. Such behaviour would have counteracted the intended deterrent effect of the legislation. A series of on-road interview surveys was undertaken in the Melbourne Metropolitan area between February 1984 and December 1984 to obtain estimates of P-plate use for first year probationary drivers before and after the introduction of the legislation. Bowen (1985) analysed these survey data, and found that there was no reduction in P-plate use rather than a short-term increase in use among 18-year-old drivers following the introduction of the Zero BAC legislation. The level of P-plate use by 18 to 25-year-olds ranged between approximately 40% and 60% over the five surveys. Eighteen-year olds were found to have higher levels of use than 19 to 25-year-olds.

10.2.2 Public Awareness

A market research survey was conducted in December 1984 to assess public awareness and acceptance of the legislation [see Monk and south (1985)]. An examination of the results reveals that 80% to 90% of all age groups of both sexes in metropolitan and country areas knew that the law applied to L and P plate drivers, and only 25%–40% mistakenly thought that the law also applies to second and third year probationary drivers. Approximately 60% of people interviewed knew that the law applies to unlicensed drivers as well. The survey of attitudes towards the law showed that more people approved than disapproved. People living in metropolitan areas were more likely to approve the law compared to the country people. No significant difference was observed within age or sex groups.

10.2.3 Exposure of Target Group Drivers

Accident reductions can be achieved through one of the two or both ways. First, an exposure reduction mechanism, i.e., the target group drivers may choose to drive less at alcohol times, because their opportunities to drink and drive have been restricted by the law. Second, a risk reduction mechanism, meaning target group drivers may choose to consume less alcohol without reducing their exposure. Drummond et al. (1986) analysed the 1984 and 1985 Melbourne on-road driver exposure surveys and found that the greatest reduction in the proportion of total travel undertaken by first year probationary drivers occurred at night over weekends, the time when the incidence of alcohol-related accidents is higher. More importantly he observed that novice drivers compared to experienced drivers are driving less at times when drinking and driving is traditionally most prevalent. It implies that the Zero BAC law may have deterred novice drivers from driving at times when otherwise they would have been both drinking and driving.

10.3 Data

At the time of this analysis was carried out, accident data from the RTA accident file were available up to December 1985. This gave an opportunity to measure the effectiveness of the Zero BAC legislation for the first eighteen months as opposed to the earlier study based on the first six months of its implementation. This resulted in the statistical tests being more powerful, enabling more realistic effects to be detected. More importantly, the extended (18 months post-legislation) data could be used to show the degree of effectiveness of the legislation for the target group in the first and second six months, first twelve months and first eighteen months of the post-legislation period separately.

It should be noted that specific definitions of day (4am–4pm) and night (4pm–4am) [when alcohol involvement in SCAs is higher] were used in the present study, a new definition of alcohol times, which consists of certain hours of the day and days of the week during which there is a high percentage of accidents known to involve a driver with BAC in excess of 0.05g/100ml, was used as a surrogate measure of alcohol-related accidents. The complement of the alcohol times is taken as the so called non-alcohol times [see Appendix 8A for more details about alcohol and non-alcohol times]. Thus, in this study the change of the SCA's for the target group at the alcohol times and non-alcohol times was measured instead of in the night and day periods previously defined. This is because Sloane and South (1985) have shown that the distribution of alcohol-related accidents is not uniform over the hours of the day and days of the week. They observed that the proportion of alcohol related-accident is higher on Thursday to Saturday nights than at any other times.

Another important difference from the previous study should be mentioned. There were certain omissions in the data used in the interim analysis due to conceptual problems. In the previous data set, no conditional licence holder drivers were included. As a result, 4.4% of drivers of the total target group (learner, P1, unlicensed and disqualified) and 2.7% of drivers of the total control group (standard licence holders) were excluded. More importantly an additional 23.4% of the total target group drivers were omitted from the previous accident data file due to the exclusion of unlicensed and disqualified drivers whose state of licence was coded by the police as either unknown or blank. These deficiencies of the previous data have been fully accounted for and complete data are used for the present study. The following table shows how many data were missing from previously used target and control groups. In essence, due to the omission of 91.0% of the unlicensed and disqualified drivers from the target group SCAs involvement, the results of the interim analysis apply to the effects of the Zero BAC legislation on learner and first year probationary drivers only. Accident data for all drivers of cars and car derivatives who were involved in SCAs were considered in the present study and are presented in Table 10.1. This criterion was chosen to provide a larger data set than fatal accidents. This results in the statistical test being more powerful, enabling smaller effects to be detected.

Table 10.1: Drivers of Cars and Car-derivatives Involved in Serious Casualty Accidents by License Type, 1980–1984

License type	Data used in previous study	Data used in present study	% of total present data missed in previous study
Learner	259	259	0
P1	3,158	3,159	0
Conditional P1	Not included	214	4.4
Unlicensed	71	974	18.5
Disqualified	42	281	4.9
Total Target	**3,530**	**4,887**	**27.8**
Standard	25,677	25,681	0
Conditional Standard	Not included	707	2.7
Total Control	**25,677**	**26,388**	**2.7**

Source: Road Traffic Accident Data File of the RTA of Victoria extracted from the Victorian Police Road Accident Report Form.

10.4 Methodology

10.4.1 Driver Groups and Times

For the purpose of the analysis, learner, first-year probationary, disqualified and unlicensed drivers were the target group. The standard license holders were the control group drivers, since they were not subject to the Zero BAC legislation. Further, the accident involvements of the target and control group drivers were disaggregated into alcohol and non-alcohol times of accident occurrence. The effects of the Zero BAC legislation were considered likely to be greatest for the target group during the alcohol times. Thus, the following combinations of drivers and times of their accident involvement were analyzed in the study:

1. target group drivers during alcohol times;
2. target group drivers during non-alcohol times;
3. control group drivers during alcohol times; and
4. control group drivers during non-alcohol times.

The first combination (target group drivers during alcohol times) was the primary focus of the study. The remaining combinations of drivers and times were included to measure and account for the effects of other influences that may have affected the first combination in addition to the Zero BAC legislation.

10.4.2 Statistical Methods

There are two basic types of statistical methods that can be used to evaluate road safety countermeasures. These are the pre-post method and the time-series method. The pre-post method attempts to evaluate the effect of road safety countermeasures by comparing the relative changes in the numbers of target and control group drivers involved in SCAs between the pre and post legislation periods. The time series method attempts to analyze the effect of road safety countermeasures by predicting the expected number of target group drivers involved in SCAs during the post-legislation period, using the available pre-legislation data. The relative merits of these two approaches are given in Haque and Cameron (1987).2

Because pre-legislation downward trends were identified by Haque *et al.* (1986) in the accident involvements of the target group and standard license holders, especially at night and especially for the target group, it was decided that time series analysis methods were more likely to give valid conclusions in this study. In addition, it was decided to use the pre-post method for comparative and illustrative purposes. When the results of the two methods are in conflict, however, the time series results should be preferred in this study.

10.4.3 Pre-Legislation Trend

Figures 10.1 and 10.2 present monthly number of target group drivers and standard licence holders involved in SCAs at alcohol and non-alcohol times. These show that there were decreasing trends in SCAs on Victorian roads during alcohol times, especially for the target group. It is generally believed that this achievement has been mainly due to the progressive introduction of drink-driving countermeasures since late 1978 consisting of:

- intensified random breath testing operations;
- increased penalties for drink-driving offences;
- intensive drink-driving publicity campaigns, and
- introduction of low-alcohol content beer.

RACV (1983) showed that there was a statistically significant reduction in the proportion of driver casualties with BAC level exceeding 0.05g/100ml during 1979–81 compared with 1977–78. They concluded that the package was effective in reducing drink driving by drivers of all age groups, but had a particularly strong effect on young drivers aged 18–25. Thus, this latter group appears to have received most benefits from the drink-driving countermeasures. Data presented by Harrison (1986) indicates that these trends in alcohol involvement in accidents continued up to 1984 (Figure 10.3).

The above trends are also presented when different license categories are examined, with novice drivers displaying the steepest downward trend in the proportion of serious casualties with BAC exceeding 0.05g/100ml (Figure 10.4). This is particularly true for first year probationary drivers, who account for the bulk of the accident involvements of the target group in this study.

The trends are reflected in figures 10.1 and 10.2, where 12-month moving totals for the target group and standard license holders involved in SCAs are plotted. The trends for both groups have been stable or increasing at non-alcohol times during the same period. These trends indicate that the changes in behaviour of the target group and standard licence holders involved in SCA's was similar before the introduction of the zero BAC legislation, not withstanding the fact that the proportion of their accident involvements occurring in the alcohol times was greater for the target group. This provides further support for the use of standard license holders as the control group.

Figure 10.1 indicates that 12-month moving total trends for target group drivers involved in SCAs at alcohol (and non-alcohol) times have stababilized or increased since early 1984, which is contrary to the hypothesis. On the other hand it is apparent from Figure 10.2 that the 12-month moving totals for control group drivers involved in SCAs both at alcohol and non-alcohol times have increased from early 1983. At this stage of the analysis, it was not known for what group of drivers the rate of increase of SCAs was faster. In order to investigate this, the intervention coefficients for target and control group drivers involved in SCAs (standardized for the monthly average forecasts in the post-legislation period) have been tested for differences following the fitting of the intervention models. Only standarised coefficients have been used for such comparisons.

10.5 Analysis and Results

In order to determine the effect of a certain intervention (Zero BAC legislation for our present study), a group of individuals known as the target group (in our case: learner, P1, unlicensed and disqualified drivers) likely to be affected by that measure should be compared with another set of individuals called the control group (here, standard license holders), who are entirely free from any type of simultaneously imposed intervention. Learner, P1, unlicensed and disqualified drivers; and standard license holder drivers; will be considered as target and control groups, respectively, throughout the present analysis.

One of the major objectives of the present study is to examine the effectiveness of the Zero BAC legislation in the first six months, second six months, first twelve months and first eighteen months separately. In order to do this, target group drivers involved in SCAs in the specified periods were compared with the standard license holders, which are presented separately as follows.

10.5.1 Pre-Post Comparisons 3

10.5.1.1   First Six Months

It is observed from Table 10.2 that there were 251 target group drivers involved in SCAs during the alcohol times of the week in the period July to December 1984, compared with an average of 325.25 in four previous years. This resulted in an accident reduction of order 22.8%. However, there was a 1.7% increase in SCAs for the target group in non-alcohol times between the same periods. Since it could be expected that a similar 1.7% increase in accident involvement of the target group would have occurred during the alcohol times in the absence of the legislation, these results indicate that the net effect of the legislation was a 24% reduction in SCA involvement for target group drivers during the alcohol times. This net reduction was statistically significant.

On the other side, a 7.7% net reduction in SCAs also occurred for the control group between the same periods when alcohol times were compared with non-alcohol times. In the absence of the legislation, this 7.7% reduction of SCA would have occurred for target group drivers as well. Thus, there is an overall 17.7% net net reduction in SCAs for the target group in the first six months post-legislation period when alcohol and non-alcohol time is compared relative to standard licence holders. The three way (2 x 2 x 2) contingency table test was carried out and it showed that this net net reduction in SCAs of order 17 7% was statistically significant (calculated $\chi^2 = 2.9$ compared with one-tailed theoretical $\chi^2_{0.05} = 2.7$).

Table 10.2 shows the number of involvement in SCAs for both target and control group drivers, together with changes in accident frequencies for both groups, in the first six months of the post-legislation period during the alcohol, and non-alcohol times of the week.

Table 10.2: Effects of the Zero BAC Law in the First Six Months Post-legislation

Driver Groups	July – December (1980/83 average)	July – December (1984)	Change (%)
Target Groups*			
Alcohol times	325.25	251.00	– 22.80
Non-alcohol times	188.75	192.00	+ 1.70
Net change: alcohol relative to non alcohol times		(a)	– 24.00
Standard license holders			
Alcohol times	1,134.50	1,082.00	– 4.60
Non-alcohol times	1,548.50	1,602.00	+ 3.40
Net change: alcohol relative to non alcohol times		(b)	– 7.70
Target group net change relative to standard license holders net Change			– 17.70

* Learner, first year probationary (P1), unlicensed and disqualified drivers.

Source: Road Traffic Accident Data File of the RTA of Victoria
extracted from the Victorian Police Road Accident Report Form.

10.5.1.2 Second Six Months

From Table 10.3, it shows that during the second six months of the legislation (January to June 1985), 279 target group drivers were involved in SCAs, compared with an average of 289 in the previous four years during the alcohol times of the week, a reduction of 3.4% only. Their accident involvements during the non-alcohol times increased by 11.4% between the same periods. This latter figure when incorporated with accident reduction in alcohol times produces a net reduction of 13.3% in SCAs for target group drivers during the alcohol times relative to the non-alcohol times. This net reduction was not statistically significant.

In contrast, the net change in the accident involvement of standard licence holders during the alcohol times relative to the non-alcohol times was a 10.2% reduction. Therefore, only a 3.4% net reduction in SCAs occurred in the second six months of the post-legislation period for target group drivers relative to control group when the alcohol times are compared with non-alcohol times. This was not statistically significant. Both target and control group drivers involved in SCAs, together with their changes in accident frequencies in the second six months of the post-legislation period during the alcohol and non-alcohol times of the week, are presented in Table 10.3.

Table 10.3: Effects of the Zero BAC Law in the Second Six Months Post-legislation

Driver Groups	July – December (1980/83 average)	January – June (1985)	Change (%)
Target Groups*			
Alcohol times	289.00	279.00	– 3.3
Non-alcohol times	192.75	215.00	11.4
Net change: alcohol relative to non-alcohol times		(a)	– 13.3
Standard license holders			
Alcohol times	1,042.00	979.00	– 6.00
Non-alcohol times	1,519.25	1,589.00	+ 4.60
Net change: alcohol relative to non-alcohol times		(b)	– 10.20
Target group net change relative to standard license holders net change			– 3.40

* Learner, first year probationary (P1), unlicensed and disqualified drivers.

Source: Road Traffic Accident Data File of the RTA of Victoria extracted from the Victorian Police Road Accident Report Form.

10.5.1.3 First Twelve Months

When the effects of the Zero BAC legislation for the first and second six months are combined, a clear picture emerges and shows an over and above improvement in safety for all drivers. In the first 12 months of the legislation (July 1984 to June 1985), there were 530 and 407 target group drivers involved in SCAs during alcohol and non-alcohol times compared with the averages of 614.25 and 381.50 in the months of four previous years (January 1980 to December 1984) respectively. Thus, the accident involvement of the target group drivers were reduced by 13.6% during the alcohol times of the week, and increased by 6.8% during non-alcohol times. A combination of these results represent a net reduction of 19.1% during alcohol times. This reduction was statistically significant.

In contrast, the net reduction in SCAs for standard licence holders during the alcohol times relative to the non-alcohol times was only 9.0%, perhaps representing the effects of the drink-driving countermeasures aimed at all drivers over the period 1982 to 1985. Therefore, there was an 11.1% net reduction in SCAs for the target group in the first twelve months post-legislation period when alcohol time is compared to non-alcohol time relative to control groups. The overall apparent accident reduction was not statistically significant (calculated $\chi^2 = 2.2$ compared with one-tailed theoretical $\chi^2_{20.05,1} = 2.7$). These results are shown in Table 10.4.

10.5.1.4 First Eighteen Months

The effects of the Zero BAC legislation were also examined by comparing the post-legislation period with a comparable 18-month pre-legislation period (July 1982 to December 1983). However, it should be noted that this method of analysis does not take into account the pre-legislation trends and hence the results should only be used for comparative purposes with the more definitive time series analysis results.

Table 10.5 shows that there were 866 target group drivers involved in SCAs during alcohol times in the post-legislation period compared to 837 in the pre-legislation period, an increase of about 3.6%. However, there was an 11.0% increase in SCA involvements for the target group in the non-alcohol times between the same two periods. As it could be expected that a similar 11.9% increase in the target group's SCAs would have occurred during the alcohol times in the absence of the legislation, these results indicate that the net effect of the legislation was a 7.4% reduction in SCA involvements for target group drivers during the alcohol times. This net reduction was not statistically significant.

A 1.5% net reduction in SCAs also occurred for the standard license holders between the same periods when alcohol times were compared with non-alcohol times. Thus, compared to standard license holders, target group drivers had an overall 6.0% net reduction in SCAs during alcohol times in the first 18-month post-legislation period. A one-tailed 2 x 2 x 2 contingency table test shows that this reduction was not statistically significant (Bishop, Fienberg and Holland, 1978).

The results in Table 10.5 are in good agreement with those in Table 10.6 where the time series results are summarized. The largest difference is that the forecast post-legislation SCA involvement of the target group in the alcohol times is only 803.3 (Table 10.6) compared with 837 during the 18-month pre-legislation period (Table 10.5); this illustrates that the pre-legislation trend which the pre-post method is unable to take into account.

Nevertheless, the critical net changes in the two tables are in the same direction and approximately the same magnitude. Thus, the results in Table 10.5 provide confirmation of the more conclusive results in Table 10.6.

Table 10.4: Effects of the Zero BAC Law in the
First Twelve Months Post-legislation

Driver Groups	July – December (1980/83 average)	July – December (1984) & January – June (1985)	Change (%)
Target groups*			
Alcohol times	614.25	530.00	– 13.56
Non-alcohol times	381.50	407.00	+ 6.84
Net change: alcohol relative to non-alcohol times		(a)	– 19.09
Standard license holders			
Alcohol times	2,176.50	2,061.00	– 5.31
Non-alcohol times	3,067.75	3,191.00	+ 4.01
Net change: alcohol relative to non-alcohol times		(b)	– 8.96
Target group net change relative to standard license holders net change			– 11.13

* Learner, first year probationary (P1), unlicensed and disqualified drivers.

Source: Road Traffic Accident Data File of the RTA of Victoria extracted from the Victorian Police Road Accident Report Form

10.5.2 Time Series Analysis

The usual Box-Jenkins (1976) ARIMA models were fitted to the pre-legislation data (i.e., January 1977 to May 1984) for all four driver/time combinations or series. Projections were then made on the basis of the best available model for each separate series.

Next, intervention techniques due to Box and Tiao (1975), were applied to those best models that were used for ARIMA forecasts, using all SCA data from January 1977 to December 1985. The intervention approach involved: (a) formulating a model of the expected effect of the intervention (i.e., the Zero BAC legislation); (b) incorporating this in the ARIMA model previously found for each series; and (c) fitting the combined (intervention) model to the pre- and post-legislation data simultaneously. The presence of an intervention effect is tested statistically by a test of whether the intervention coefficient in the model is significantly different from zero.

Table 10.5: Effects of the Zero BAC Law in the First Eighteen Months Post-legislation

Group	Before (July 1982-Dec. 1983)	After (July 1984-Dec. 1985)	% Change
Target group			
Alcohol times	837	866	+ 3.6
Non-alcohol times	586	655	+ 11.9
Net change: alcohol relative to non-alcohol times		(a)	– 7.4
Standard license Holders			
Alcohol times	3,095	3288	+ 6.3
Non-alcohol times	4,593	4958	+ 7.9
Net change: alcohol relative to non-alcohol times		(b)	– 1.5
Target group net change adjusted for standard licence holders net change			– 6.0

a Alcohol times relative to non-alcohol times for target group drivers.
b Alcohol times relative to non-alcohol times for standard license holders.

Source: Road Traffic Accident Data File of the RTA of Victoria extracted from the Victorian Police Road Accident Report Form.

This approach was adopted for each of the four series of data, even though there was no hypothesized intervention effect for the three control series, series 2, 3 and 4. For these three series, any measured intervention effect is a measure of the effect of other influences that should be taken into account in assessing the effect of the Zero BAC legislation on Series 1, target group drivers during alcohol times.

Correction for the effect of other influences was made by subtracting the estimated intervention coefficient of the control series from that of Series 1. Before this was done, dividing the intervention coefficients by the monthly average SCA involvements forecast by the ARIMA model in the post-legislation period standardized the intervention effects. The effect of the Zero BAC legislation can then be tested by the statistical significance of the corrected intervention coefficient for Series 1.4

10.5.2.1 Pre-legislation Trends

Figure 10.1 indicates that the 12-month moving total trends for target group drivers involved in SCAs at alcohol (and non-alcohol) times have stabilized or increased since early 1984, which is contrary to the hypothesis. On the other hand, it is apparent from Figure 10.2 that the 12-month moving totals for control group drivers involved in SCAs both at alcohol and non-alcohol times have increased from early 1983. At this stage of the analysis, it was not known for what group of drivers the rate of increase of SCAs was faster. In order to investigate this, the intervention coefficients for target and control group drivers involved in SCAs (standardized for the monthly average forecasts in the post-legislation period) have been tested for differences following the fitting of the intervention models. Only standardized coefficients have been used for such comparisons.

10.5.2.2 Results of the Time Series Analysis

The results of the ARIMA and intervention models together with the actual numbers of target and control group drivers involved in SCAs during alcohol and non-alcohol times are given in Table 10.6.

There were 866 target group drivers involved in SCAs during the alcohol times in the post-legislation period, compared with 803.3 forecasts by the ARIMA model, a difference of 7.8 %. In contrast, the number of target group drivers involved in SCAs during the non-alcohol times was 11.3% greater than that forecast by the ARIMA model; this difference was assumed to have been due to influences on the target group drivers other than the Zero BAC legislation. It could be expected that a similar 11.3% difference for the target group would have occurred during the alcohol times in the absence of the legislation. Hence, these results indicate that the net effect of the legislation was a 3.1% reduction in the target group's involvement in SCAs during the alcohol times (the net difference shown in Table 10.6).

The standard license holders' SCA involvement during the alcohol times is another indicator of the effect of other influences. In this case, their post-legislation SCA involvements were 7.4% greater than forecast by the ARIMA model (Table 10.6). This was similar to the difference for the target group during the alcohol times. However, during the non-alcohol times the standard license holders were involved in only 6.6% more SCAs than forecast. Thus, the pattern of differences for the standard license holders is different from that of the target group. The net difference for standard license holders is a 0.7% increase.

Figure 10.1: Time Series Analysis; 12 Month Moving Totals of Serious Casualty Accidents for Target Group Drivers

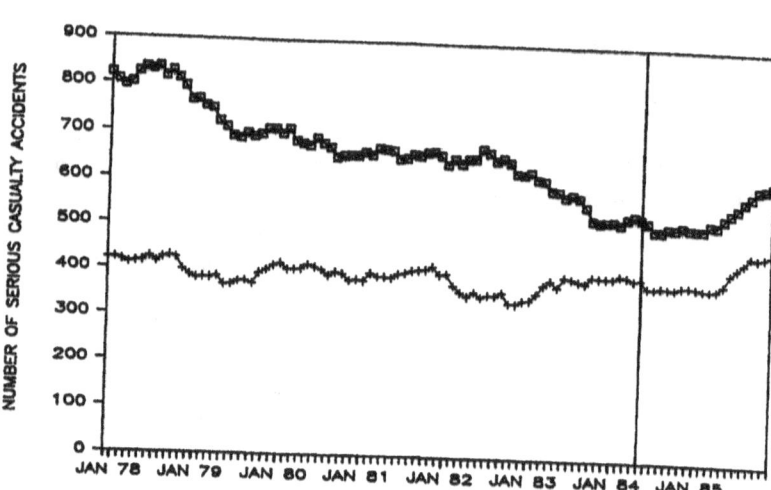

Source: Road Traffic Accident Data File of the RTA of Victoria extracted from the Victorian Police Road Accident Report Form.

To fully take into account the effects of influences on the target group drivers other than the Zero BAC legislation, the net difference for the target group needs to be adjusted for the net difference for the standard license holders (although the latter is small in this instance). The adjusted net difference for the target group was a 3.8% reduction (Table 10.6). This is the best estimate of the effect of the Zero BAC legislation on the SCA involvements of target group drivers during the alcohol times in the post-legislation period.

The statistical significance of this estimated effect was judged by appropriate differencing of the standardized intervention coefficients for each of the four series, following the procedure above for calculating the adjusted net percentage difference. The adjusted net difference of the intervention coefficients is directly related to the adjusted net percentage difference, but has the advantage that a statistical test can be made to test whether it is real or due to chance variation.

A positive intervention coefficient (+1.7%) was observed for target group drivers when the step function was estimated for alcohol times. This coefficient was not statistically significant $(t = 1.43)$. On the other hand, a positive intervention coefficient (+9.2%) was observed for target group drivers when a step function was estimated at non-alcohol times. This coefficient was also not statistically significant $(t = 1.23)$. Further, the difference between these two standardized intervention coefficients was not statistically significant (t = − 0.99).

Figure 10.2: Time Series Analysis; 12-month Moving Totals of Serious Casualty Accidents for Control Group (Standard License) Drivers

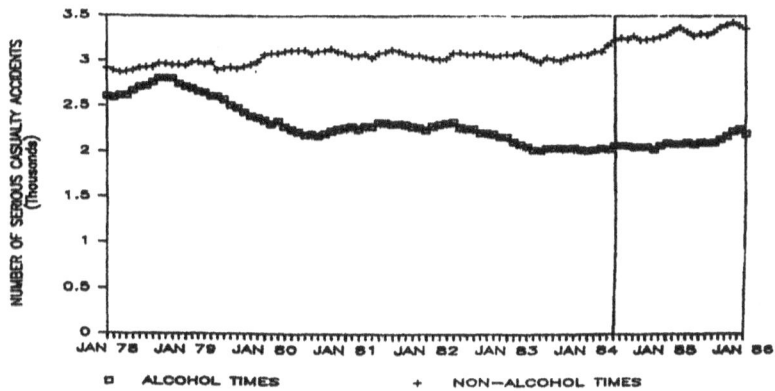

Source: Road Traffic Accident Data File of the RTA of Victoria extracted from the Victorian Police Road Accident Report Form.

Figure 10.3: Drivers Killed or Hospitalised in Victoria by Age for Whom Their Blood Alcohol is Known

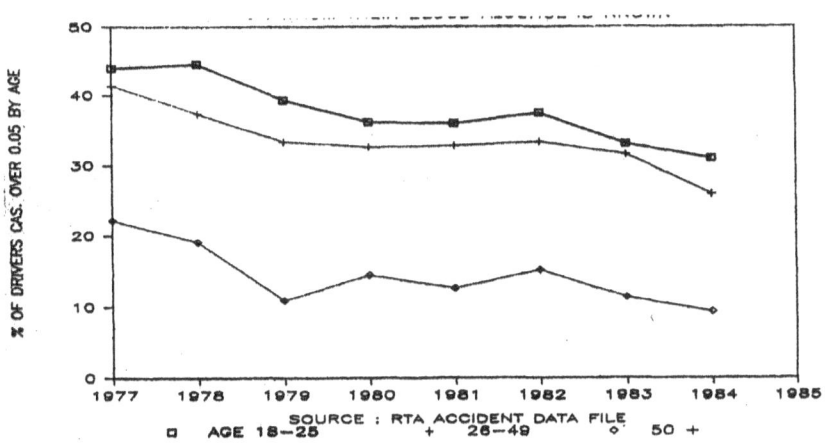

Source: Road Traffic Accident Data File of the RTA of Victoria extracted from the Victorian Police Road Accident Report Form.

ANALYSES OF THE VICTORIAN ZERO BAC LEGISLATION

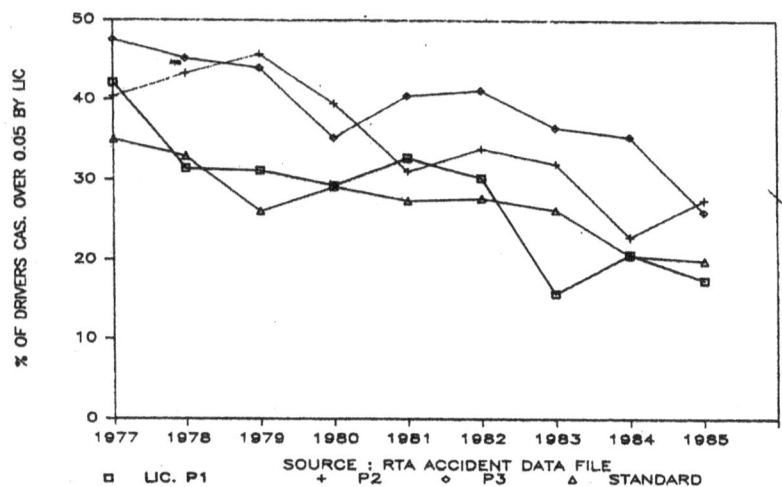

Figure 10.4: Drivers Killed or Hospitalized in Victoria by License Type for Whom Their Blood Alcohol is Known

Source: Road Traffic Accident Data File of the RTA of Victoria extracted from the Victorian Police Road Accident Report Form.

For standard license holders during alcohol times, the intervention coefficient was positive (+0.6%), although not statistically significant (t = 1.14). However, the intervention coefficient was + 8.2% (t = 3.65) for standard license holders at non-alcohol times. This implies that the increase in standard license holders' SCAs at non-alcohol times was significantly above that expected from the ARIMA model forecasts.

When the adjusted net difference of the four estimated intervention coefficients was calculated, it was not statistically significant (t = − 0.004). Thus, the estimated effect of the Zero BAC legislation (i.e., 3.8% reduction in target group driver involvements during the alcohol times) must be concluded as due to chance variation.

Further analyses of the Zero BAC legislation based on alternative target and control group drivers for the first eighteen and six month post-legislation periods are reported in Tables 10A.1 to Table 10A.4 of Appendix 10A. These results are consistent with those found for the initial analyses.

10.6 Discussion

10.6.1 Power of the Statistical Tests

The results of the analyses show the absence of a statistically significant effect of the legislation during its first 18 months. The most definitive test performed was that based on the adjusted net difference of the intervention coefficients, which showed that the adjusted net percentage reduction (3.8%) in the target group drivers' SCAs during the alcohol times was not statistically significant.

Table 10.6: Drivers Involved in Serious Casualty Accidents During July 1984 to December 1985 (18 Months Post-legislation)

Group	ARIMA Forecasts[a]	Actual numbers	% Difference
Target Group			
Alcohol times	803.3	866	+ 7.8
	(751.6)		
Non-alcohol times	588.5	655	+ 11.3
	(642.5)		
Net difference[b]			– 3.1
Standard License Holders			
Alcohol times	3061.7	3288	+ 7.4
	(3078.9)		
Non-alcohol times	4650.7	4958	+ 6.6
	(4977.4)		
Net difference[b]			+ 0.7
Target group net difference adjusted for standard licence holders net difference			– 3.8

a Intervention model forecasts in parentheses ;
b Alcohol times relative to non-alcohol times.

Source: Road Traffic Accident Data File of the RTA of Victoria extracted from theVictorian Police Road Accident Report Form.

However, if it is assumed that the actual effect was, in fact, the measured effect of a 3.8% reduction, the power of this test is only 0.21. The power of a statistical test of a null hypothesis is the probability that it will lead to the rejection of the null hypothesis when it is false, i.e., the probability that it will result in the conclusion that the phenomenon exists. This is a vital piece of information about a statistical test. For example, low power may lead to ambiguous negative results, since failure to reject the null hypothesis cannot have much substantive meaning, even though to some degree the phenomenon exists. This may be the situation in the present study, because the a priori probability of rejecting the null hypothesis appears low.

Power analysis has been carried out to determine the minimum effect of the legislation, which could have been detected in the target group. The results of the power analysis are presented in the following Table 10.7.

Table 10.7: Power Analysis for the Test for an Effect of the Zero BAC Legislation

Effect size of the legislation*	One-tailed level of significance	Sample size = n	Power
– 3.8%	0.05	18	0.21
– 5%	0.05	18	0.29
– 10%	0.05	18	0.70
– 20%	0.05	18	0.99

* Change in target group SCA involvements during alcohol times

Source: Road Traffic Accident Data File of the RTA of Victoria extracted from the Victorian Police Road Accident Report Form.

The results show that the power of the test is not sufficient for the 18-month post-legislation data unless a 20% SCA reduction can be expected, which is possible but unlikely. Given that 25% to 50% of SCAs during the alcohol times involved a driver with a BAC exceeding 0.05/100ml (see Appendix 8A), a reduction of 20% in SCA involvements of target group drivers due to the legislation is possible, but unlikely. Past experience suggests that drink-driving countermeasures are likely to achieve no more than a 10% to 20% reduction in the accidents they are aimed at, those involving alcohol. Thus the Zero BAC legislation could be expected to achieve no more than 2.5% to 10% reduction in the target group's SCA involvement during the alcohol times.

Further power analysis revealed that if the actual effect of the legislation was a 10 % reduction, then this effect would be detected with adequate power only if 40 months post-legislation data were used. The analysis to date suggests that an effect of this magnitude is possible. However, premature analysis would have a high probability of inconclusive results because a 10% reduction is the maximum effect that appears possible, and smaller effects would require a longer post-legislation period before conclusive results could be reached.

10.6.2 Possible Factors Diluting the Effect of the Zero BAC Legislation

Notwithstanding the lack of power of the statistical tests, the results of the analyses indicate the absence of a substantial effect of the legislation during its first 18 months. This absence may be explained by at least four factors:

1. The apparent absence of specific enforcement procedures supporting the legislation. It is understood that if a first-year driver is detected at a random breath test station with a positive BAC below 0.05g/100ml, and is not displaying a P-plate or carrying a licence, then the driver may claim to have had more than one year's experience without fear of follow-up procedures to establish whether this is the case. The low level of P-plate use (40%-60%) by first-year probationary drivers [see Bowen (1985)] also weakens the specific effect of other drink-driving enforcement procedures on this primary target group of the legislation.

2. The absence of mass media publicity supporting enforcement of the legislation, in particular, publicity aimed specifically at deterring the target group. No publicity campaign was made since the introduction of the legislation, even though a large scale publicity and educational campaign was carried out prior to the introduction of the Zero BAC legislation as mentioned in Section 1.5.

3. The existence of decreasing trends in SCAs during alcohol times in the pre-legislation period, especially for the target group of the legislation, apparently due to a package of drinking-driving countermeasures introduced progressively since 1976 [see South, Swan and Vulcan (1983); RACV (1983)] which has meant that any additional countermeasure such as the Zero BAC legislation could only be expected to have a relatively small incremental effect at the margin.

4. Some insensitivity in the method of using alcohol times as a proxy for alcohol involvement in serious casualty accidents, and non-alcohol times as a proxy for the absence of alcohol involvement (neither category is pure and this dilutes the measured effect).

No other factor is apparent to explain the absence of a substantial effect. Random breath testing activity continued at a similar or greater level during the period up to December 1985. This measure was not specifically aimed at the target group drivers, but, coupled with mass media publicity aimed at drinking and driving in general, was currently the principal mechanism by which the target group was expected to be deterred from committing the Zero BAC offense.

Variations in the number of prosecutions under the Zero BAC legislation and attendance at the RTA education program were considered as factors explaining the absence of a substantial effect. However the number of drivers prosecuted under the legislation was much too small to have any noticeable deterrent effect. The number attending the course was even smaller, and any educative value of their attendance would not have been apparent among target group drivers in general.

10.6.3 Post-legislation Trends

Throughout the preceding analysis, there was a general pattern of increased SCA involvement during the post-legislation period (compared with ARIMA forecasts or with SCA involvement in the pre-legislation period) for all categories of drivers and especially for the target group drivers during the non-alcohol times (see tables 10.5 and 10.6 and figures 10.1 and 10.2). Although the analysis method was able to take this pattern into account while assessing the effect of the Zero BAC legislation, the post-legislation trends still demand some explanation.

The patterns of increased SCA involvements may be explained by the following factors:

1. Up to June 1984, there appeared to have been generally downward trends in new issues of car learner permits and car probationary licenses per month (see figures 10.5 and 10.6. Since then, the probationary license issue rate increased by 5.7% in July to December 1984 (relative to 1983–1984), by 11.2% in January to June 1985, and by 18.7% in July to December 1985. These increases in new licensing rate took some time to affect the number of current first-year probationary licenses, but by July to December 1985 this number was 9.5% greater than the 1983–1984 average. Thus, these increases probably explain a substantial proportion of the target group's SCA involvements during the post-legislation period, especially in the non-alcohol times.

2. Introduction of Sunday bar trading may also have had an effect on the number of SCAs involving all categories of drivers. Sunday bar trading was first introduced in July 1983 for 4 hours in 2 periods on Sundays. In November 1984, this was relaxed and extended to 8 hours. In the interim analysis of the Zero BAC legislation, Haque *et al.* (1986) found that there was an increasing trend of SCAs involving standard license holders on Sundays from late 1983. Experience from other states shows that Sunday bar trading has increased the number of SCAs (Lind 1982; Smith 1980). These findings suggest that the introduction of Sunday bar trading and its later relaxation may have caused an increasing number of driver involvements in SCAs from late 1983.

Figure 10.5: Car Learner Permits Issues Per Month

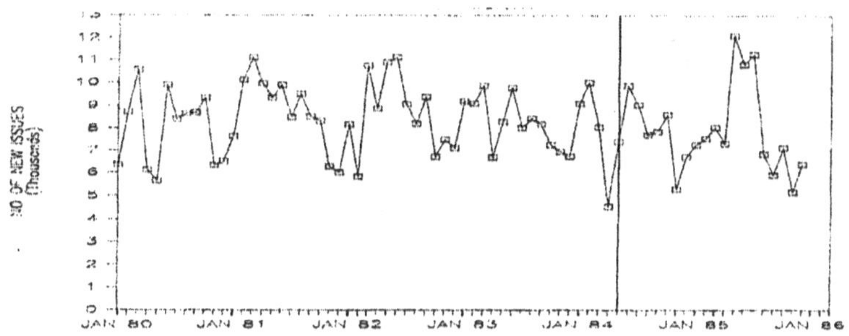

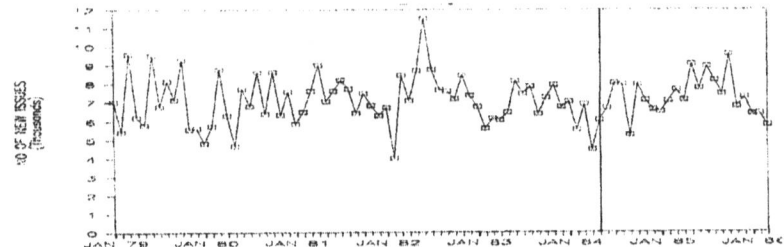

Source: Vehicle Learner Permit Data File of RTA of Victoria.

Figure 10.6: Car Probationary Licences Issues Per Month

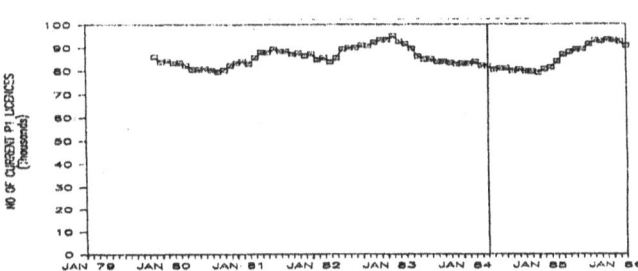

Source: Vehicle Licence Data File from the RTA of Victoria.

Figure 10.7: First Year Car P Licences Current 12 Months, Cumulative Total of New Issues

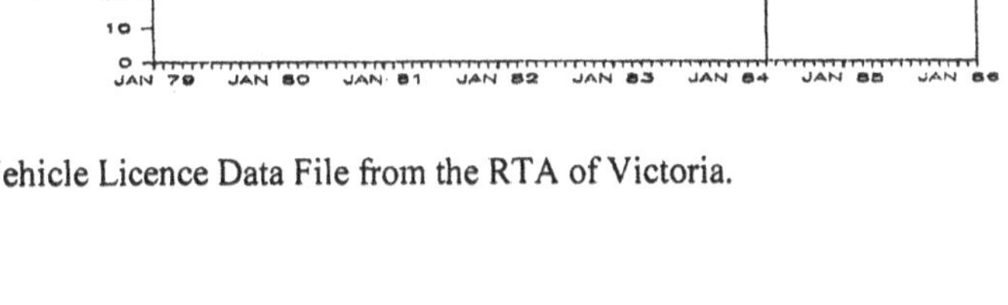

Source: Vehicle Licence Data File from the RTA of Victoria.

128   ANALYSES OF THE VICTORIAN ZERO BAC LEGISLATION

Figure 10.8: Number of Preliminary Breath Tests in Victoria

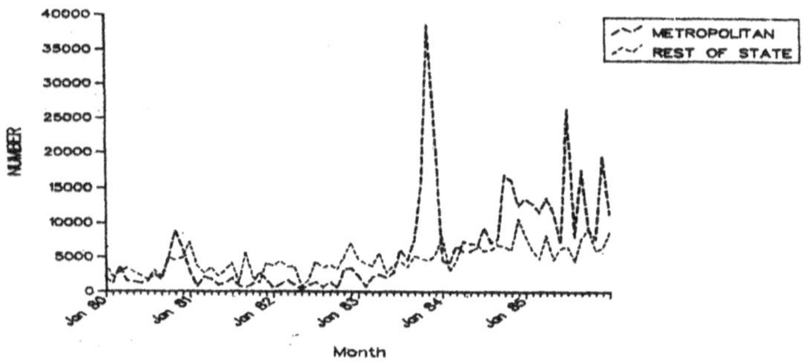

Source: Victorian Police RBT Data File.

10.6.4 Comments

The measured effect of the Zero BAC legislation during the 18-month post-legislation period was estimated by the pre-post and time series method, indicating approximately 4% reduction in SCA involvements of the target group drivers during the alcohol times of the week. While, it was not possible to say either method of analysis, whether the measured effect was other than due to chance variation, its magnitude seems small given the high level of public awareness of the law in December 1984 (Monk and South 1985) and the reduction in weekend night driving by first-year probationary drivers between 1984 and 1985 (Drummond *et al.* 1986). An effect of up to a 10% reduction may have reasonably been expected. Further, the measured effect during the six months of July to December 1984 does not appear to have been any larger (a 3.5% reduction estimated by time series analysis), though this estimate is subject to a greater degree of statistical error (however, the much large reduction found in the preliminary analysis of the six-month period appears to have been due to the methods of analysis that had to be used at that point).

A small effect may not be unexpected when it is noted that P-plate use rates remained essentially unchanged at a low 40-60% up to December 1984 (Bowen 1985), suggesting little or no behavioural change in compliance with relevant laws by many first-year drivers. In addition, the absence of specific enforcement procedures supporting the legislation and mass media publicity aimed specifically at deterring the target group, did not capitalized on the increase in random breath testing activity (Figure 10.8) to produce a general deterrent effect on the target group.

The level of random breath testing was increased still further during 1986. Given the results of this study, it may be appropriate to capitalize on

ANALYSES OF THE VICTORIAN ZERO BAC LEGISLATION   129

this activity by introducing specific enforcement procedures at random breath test stations and mass media publicity supporting enforcement of the Zero BAC legislation, aimed at increasing compliance with the legislation by:

- the original target group of learner, first year probationary, disqualified and unlicensed drivers (applicable since May 1984); and

- probationary drivers moving into their second year of licensing, for whom the Zero BAC limit has been extended to their second year (applicable since 1 March 1987).

10.7 Conclusions and Limitations

The analysis showed that there was no significant accident reduction (only 4%) due to the implementation of the Zero BAC legislation in Victoria, probably due to the absence of specific enforcement procedures and a mass media publicity campaign. Hence, in order to achieve a significant accident reduction, it is essential to implement the various specific procedures and mass media publicity supporting enforcement of the legislation.

While, this was not statistically significant, the statistical power of the analysis was very poor which meant that there was a high probability of falsely concluding that the legislation had no effect. Thus, although the measured effect size was consistent with expected values, it was not possible to determine conclusively whether:

- the result was due to chance variation;

- the result demonstrated a small effect due to the legislation, which did not achieve statistical significance because of the poor analytical power;

- a reduction of up to 10% in the number of target group drivers involved in alcohol related serious casualty accidents may reasonably be expected for an accident countermeasure of the Zero BAC legislation type if adequately publicized and supported by highly visible, specific enforcement. An effect of the 10% reduction could only be detected with adequate statistical power from 40 months post-legislation data.

The absence of a substantial effect of the legislation during its first 18 months may have been due to;

- the absence of specific enforcement procedures supporting the legislation (the low level of P-plate use by first-year probationary drivers made it very difficult for police to identify potential offenders);

- the absence of on-going mass media publicity supporting enforcement of the legislation (random breath testing continued at a similar or greater level during the period, but there was no supporting publicity aimed specifically at deterring the target group of the legislation); and

- the pre-existing decreasing trends in alcohol related accidents involving the target group drivers, which meant that the legislation could only be expected to have a relatively small incremental effect.

Notes

1 All drivers convicted of infringements of the law are required to undergo an educational program approved by the RTA. It is intended that this early intervention program should interrupt the drink-driving pattern of novice drivers especially before it becomes established behaviour.

2 Griffin and Flower (1997) have discussed six different procedures for evaluating highway safety projects. More importantly, Todd Litman (2004) evaluated mobility management traffic safety impacts, while AUSTROADS evaluated various actions emanating from road safety audits. Further safety data analysis and evaluation techniques can be found in Transport Research Circular (2006).

3 Hauer and Persand (1983), Hauer (1997) and Lum and Wong (2003) have extensively discussed the merits and demerits of pre-post comparison for the evaluation of road safety programms.

4 Odero *et al.* (2003) and Ghaffar *et al.* (2002, 2004) used the intervention method to analyse road accident data. While Chin and Huang (2006) used the safety Evaluation Procedure on Traffic treatments using the Empirical Bayesian Approach.

5 Williams (1994) has highlighted the contribution of education and publicity to reducing alcohol-impaired driving.

CHAPTER 11

EVALUATION OF THE DEMERIT POINTS SYSTEM IN DETERRING TRAFFIC OFFENSES

A statistical model for the evaluation of the effectiveness of the Demerit Points System (DPS) in reducing traffic offenses is presented. The model for the waiting times between detected traffic offenses is based on an exponential distribution. Since traffic offences are relatively rare events, the length of the study period was such that censoring was unavoidable. Under these circumstances maximum likelihood (ML) estimates of the waiting time between offenses are determined and the corresponding hypotheses are tested. The empirical results showed that the DPS was responsible for most of the deterrent effect reflected in the increased mean time until the third offense subsequent to the first and second offense detected was less than three years apart.

11.1 Introduction

The Demerit Points System (DPS) was introduced in Victoria (a state in Australia) in 1970 in order to identify drivers with high offense rates and to take remedial action against those who repeatedly violate traffic laws. The DPS is nominally still in operation, but now excludes speeding and red light offenses due to the introduction of the owner-onus provisions of the photographic detection devices legislations.

The general objective of the present study is to examine whether the DPS had a significant effect in reducing subsequent traffic offenses using offense records of 63,449 standard license-holder drivers during a period prior to the introduction of the owner-onus provision. More specifically, this study is designed:

- to estimate the expected time interval between first and second offenses;
- to estimate the expected time interval between second and third offenses; and
- to test the differences of the expected mean time intervals between first and second and between second and third offenses, adjusted for different levels of driving experience at the start of each interval.

A statistical model for waiting times between detected traffic offenses was established based on the exponential distribution. Detected traffic offenses are relatively rare events, and the length of study period is such that censoring of some waiting time occurs. Under these circumstances an (unconditional) estimate of the mean waiting time of an offense can be obtained from a conditional exponential distribution, using maximum likelihood (ML) estimation methods.

11.2 Background and Implementation of the DPS System

11.2.1 Background

The Demerit Points System (DPS) was introduced in Victoria in 1970 to achieve the following objectives:

(i) to identify drivers with high conviction rates that cause or contribute to the increasing number of accidents;

(ii) to take remedial action against those who repeatedly violate the traffic regulations by suspension of licenses and/or by requiring participation in a Driver Improvement Program (DIP); and

(iii) to determine the relationship between the drivers with frequent accidents and those with persistent moving traffic offenses.

11.2.2 Implementation of the DPS System

Punitive provisions were only applied in 1982. In that year numerical values called demerit points were placed on the drivers' records for various traffic offenses.[1]

In March 1982, the Driver Improvement Program (DIP) was implemented to reinforce the existing DPS's ability to meet its objective to reduce accidents. To permit an evaluation, all eligible drivers who incurred two entries (not necessarily totalling six points) in the demerit register within a three-year period were randomly selected to enter the DIP program. The DIP drivers received a personalized low-threat letter mentioning the penalties likely to follow further offenses.

Those incurring a third demerit entry in the next 15 months received an invitation to attend a group educational meeting (GEM) aimed at improving their attitudes toward driving.2 Those who continued to accumulate points increased their risk of having to pay the surcharges and having their licenses suspended.3 The rest of the drivers continued within the punitive-only program, known as the Motor Registration Branch (MRB) program. The MRB drivers continued to receive police-initiated warning letters if six points were accumulated within three consecutive years.

The DPS became less effective when it began to exclude speeding and red light offenses, owing to the introduction of the owner-onus legislation. This is because the latter offenses can be detected through cameras, and in those cases it is not possible to identify offending drivers.

It is estimated that these offenses would account for about 75% of pointable offenses detected. Thus the chance of reaching the two-offense entry at which further action was taken is now small. The substantial reduction in the probability of drivers reaching these levels resulted in the DPS becoming essentially inoperative.4

This evaluation of the deterrent effect of demerit points is thus confined to the period before the owner-onus provision was introduced.

This chapter is organized as follows. Background and implementation of the DPS system are described in Section 11.2. Data used in the present study are described in Section 11.3. Section 11.4 is concerned with the evaluation method used. Analysis and results of the study are presented in Section 11.5, followed by a discussion in Section 11.6, with some concluding remarks in the final section.

11.3 Data

The drivers studied were all standard license holders who committed a second demerit-point offense (within three years of the first offense), subsequent to the commencement of the Driver Improvement Program (DIP) in March 1982 and up to the end of February 1985. All eligible drivers were randomly allocated at the time of their second offense on a 74:26 split either to the DIP or to the MRB Program. The latter received no treatment except for the MRB warning letter if six points were accumulated within three consecutive years.

A total of 46,982 DIP drivers received an initial warning letter, and 11,691 of these committed a third offense. A total of 16,467 drivers had been randomly allocated to the MRB group and, of these, 4,302 committed a third offense. It should be noted that although the rates of third offense are close, they are statistically different, with those for the drivers in the MRB group higher than those for the DIP drivers. This suggests that the threats involved in the DIP scheme had an effect.

11.4 Methods

11.4.1 Statistical Model

The Poisson distribution has been found to be applicable to problems in which the random variable represents the number of occurrences of a rare event in a given time or space interval. The events are rare in the sense that there are only a few events occurring in the interval, and the interval can be conceived of as consisting of a large number of small subinterval units. For such a Poisson process, it can be shown (Parzen 1962:135) that the random variable representing the time or distance between successive occurrences of the events possesses an exponential distribution. That is, the exponential distribution can model the length of time between two successive Poisson events that occur independently and at a constant rate. In other words, the probability of present or future events does not depend on such events happening in the past. Thus the probability of a unit failing during a specified time interval depends only on the length of that interval and not on how long the unit has been in operation.

The exponential distribution is extensively used as a time-to-failure model in reliability problems and as a model for random time lengths in waiting time problems. Benjamin and Cornell (1970) mentioned that observed data is often suggestive of an exponential distribution even when the assumptions of a Poisson process may not seem wholly appropriate. They also pointed out that 'the exponential distribution ... is often adopted simply as a convenient representation of a phenomenon when no more than the shape of the observed data or the analytical tractability of the exponential function seems to suggest it'. Epstein (1958, 1960) has extensively discussed the tests for the validity of the assumption of the exponential distribution and its role in life testing. Maguire, Pearson and Wynn (1952) showed that time intervals between industrial accidents in Great Britain followed an exponential distribution. Other studies of accidents also showed that the distribution of time intervals was approximately exponential.[5]

Following the foregoing discussion, there is enough reason to believe that the time intervals between successive traffic offenses that are independent of an individual being detected multiple times can be considered to be a first approximation to the exponential distribution.

The analysis of time intervals between traffic offenses may provide an earlier indication about the shape of the distribution of the data. A histogram of the second and third time intervals between offenses is presented in Figure 11.1. This figure shows that it is approximately exponentially distributed.

The exponential distribution would be a good fit if the risk of the offence were constant. In order to show this, we have fitted the exponential distribution for the time intervals between offenses of the type:

EVALUATION OF THE DEMERIT POINTS SYSTEM

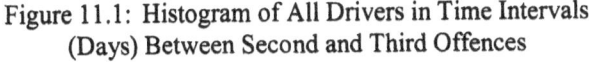

$$f(t, \theta) = \left(\frac{1}{\theta}\right) e^{(-t/\theta)}; \quad t > 0, \ \theta > 0; \quad (11.1)$$

where θ is the mean time between detected traffic offenses. We then performed a goodness of fit test for this model.

Figure 11.1: Histogram of All Drivers in Time Intervals (Days) Between Second and Third Offences

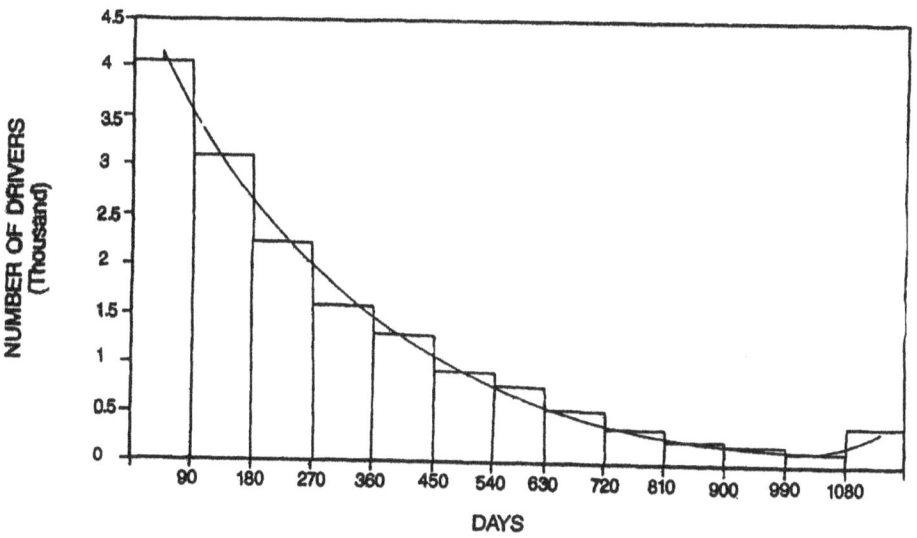

Source: DIP and MRB Data Files of the RTA of Victoria.

Table 11.1 presents the actual and expected number of drivers in various time intervals between second and third offenses. This table shows that there is good agreement between the observed and expected frequencies. The standard χ^2-test indicates that the time intervals between detected traffic offenses fit the exponential distribution.[6]

Moreover, the mean time predicted for the occurrence of a subsequent detected offense is, in many cases, considerably greater than the time available to study the effectiveness of the DPS program. The majority of drivers in the study would pass the entire period without a third offense and would not be followed past the end of the study. Since detected traffic offenses are relatively rare events, the length of the study period is such that censoring of some waiting time occurs. A detailed discussion of the censoring mechanism used can be found in Kalbfleisch and Prentice (1980). Under these circumstances, an (unconditional) estimate of the mean waiting time of an offense can still be obtained using the conditional exponential distribution (see Appendix 11A.1 for more details about these techniques).

11.4.2 Testing the Specific Hypothesis

If the accumulation of points has a deterrent effect, then the time between the second and third traffic offenses should be greater than that to be expected from the first to the second offenses. For this reason, a comparison was made between the interoffense intervals from the second to the third offense with that expected from the interval between the first to the second offense.

Table 11.1 Distribution of Time Intervals Between Second and Third Detected Traffic Offenses

Time (days) between second and third offences	Number of drivers who committed traffic offenses	
	Actual	Expected
0-90	4,027	4,145.09
90-180	3,102	3,070.76
180—270	2,248	2,274.88
270 – 360	1,654	1,685.27
360 – 450	1,304	1,248.47
450 – 540	908	924.89
540-630	721	685.18
630- 720	532	507.59
720-810	401	376.04
810- 900	297	278.58
900 – 990	202	206.37
990-1080	152	152.88
1080 – over	445	437.00
χ^2	13.52	(11 d f)
P		0.26

Notes:

1. The driver is older and more experienced during the later interval and could be expected to be more skilled in avoiding traffic offenses or detection.
2. The driver is deterred from committing a third offense by the knowledge that a system exists (the DPS) to punish repeated traffic offenders, with penalties (license surcharge and license suspension) in addition to the penalties applied to the individual traffic offenses.

Source: DIP and MRB Data Files of the RTA of Victoria.

The interval between the second and third offense could be expected to be greater than that between the first and second offense for one or more of the following reasons.

The specific objective of the study was to test for the presence of the form of deterrence described in Note 2 of Table 11.1. The effects of greater age and increased experience of drivers were recognized as likely to be significant and would be able to be taken into account in the analysis. A comparison was made between groups of drivers categorized by years of driving experience at the start of the interoffense intervals. It was necessary to compare the groups of drivers matched by their experiences, as it was clear from the data that the interoffense intervals increased with the driving experience. Since drivers in the later interoffense interval were (on average, about three years) more experienced, this could in itself result in the mean interval between the second and third offenses being greater than that between the first and second offenses. However, we have controlled the driving experience to evaluate the effect of the interoffense time interval for subsequent involvements to the detected traffic offenses for this analysis.

After estimating the mean interoffense intervals, the hypothesis can be tested through a standard test of difference of means. More details of this hypothesis-testing procedure are presented in the Appendix 11A.2.

11.5 Analysis and Results

11.5.1 Time Interval between First and Second Offences for DIP and MRB Drivers

Table 11.2 shows the number of standard license-holder drivers considered in this study, with their driving experience at different levels in years. Here, the driving experience is calculated by subtracting the date of license issue from the date of first offense.

Conditional and unconditional mean time intervals (in days) between first and second offenses are also presented in this table. The conditional mean time interval is calculated by averaging the values calculated by subtracting the date of first offense from the date of second offense. The unconditional mean time interval between first and second offenses for all DIP and MRB drivers is calculated by recognizing that the observed intervals are based on the conditional exponential distribution. The condition is that drivers must have had a second traffic offense entry within three years of the first offense. The theoretical formula for estimating the unconditional mean time interval between first and second offenses is derived in equation (11A.3) in Appendix 11A1.

Table 11.2 shows that, in all, 63,449 persons who had more than three years' driving experience were considered for this study. More than 60% of these drivers had more than 10 years' driving experience, while only 14% of them had less than five years' driving experience. It is apparent from this table that the unconditional mean time intervals between first and second offenses are generally higher than the conditional mean time intervals at different levels of driving experiences.

The pooled unconditional mean expected time intervals between first and second offenses for all drivers at various experience levels were calculated by the weighted average method and are presented in Table 11.4. It was observed that an overall unconditional mean expected time interval between first and second offenses for all drivers was 1,186 days, with an estimated standard error of 18.04.

11.5.2 Time Interval Between Second and Third Offences for DIP AND MRB Drivers

Table 11.3 presents the procedure for calculating the estimated average (unconditional) time intervals between second and third offenses for the DIP and MRB drivers. Here the driving experience was calculated by subtracting the date of license issue from the date of second offense.

Table 11.2: Drivers Experience and Estimated Mean Time Intervals (in Days) Between First and Second Offenses for DIP and MRB Drivers

Experience in years (at first offence)	Number of drivers	Estimated mean time interval between first and second offences (in days)	
		Conditional mean	Unconditional mean
3.0 - < 4.0	3,345 (1,156)	464 (462)	1,185 (1,165)
4.0 - < 5.0	3.298 (1,115)	436 (445)	872 (944)
5.0 - < 6.0	2,881 (1,025)	451 (450)	1,018 (1,009)
6.0 - < 7.0	2553 (943)	443 (456)	935 (1,044)
7.0 - < 8.0	2370 (878)	461 (447)	1,128 (974)
8.0 - < 9.0	2190 (773)	457 (445)	1,084 (954)
9.0 - < 10.0	2081 (752)	457 (456)	1,088 (1,082)
10.0 - < 11.0	1946 (728)	471 (453)	1,275 (1,038)
≥ 11.0	26,318 (9,097)	471 (470)	1,294 (1,283)
Overall	46,982 (16,467)	464 (462)	1,192 (2,169)

Note: The MRB figures are presented in parentheses.

Source: DIP and MRB Data Files of the RTA of Victoria.

The average actual time intervals between second and third offense of those drivers who committed a third offense, and the average time exposure of the drivers who did not commit any offense after the second and before the end of the study period, are also presented in this table.

It is noted that about one-fourth of both the DIP and MRB drivers committed a third offense. Of these, more than 60% had over 10 years driving experience. However, only 23% of the DIP and 24% of the MRB drivers who had more than 10 years driving experience committed a third offense, compared to 37% of those who had less than five years driving experience. This suggests that drivers in both groups who committed a third offense behave very similarly with respect to committing traffic offenses.

A conditional exponential distribution was used to estimate the unconditional mean time intervals between second and third offenses for the DIP and MRB drivers. The unconditional estimates are presented in the last column of Table 11.3. The weighted average estimated time interval between the second and the third offenses was 1,954 days with 18.07 standard error for the DIP drivers; the corresponding figure for the MRB drivers was 1,855 days with a standard error of 28.28.

It is interesting to note that the estimated unconditional mean time interval between second and third offenses for the DIP drivers is significantly higher than that for the MRB drivers (z value = 2.95). This reflects the effect of the DIP program, which is consistent with the findings of Drummond and Torpey (1985), who compared the survival time distributions to the third offense for these two groups to evaluate the warning letter component of the DIP Program.

The pooled unconditional time intervals between second and third offenses at different experience levels for all drivers were estimated by the weighted average method and are presented in Table 11.4. It was found that an overall unconditional mean time interval between second and third offenses for all drivers was 1,928 days with a standard error of 15.54.

11.5.3 Comparison of Estimated Unconditional Mean Interoffence Time Intervals Between First and Second, and between Second and Third offence

Comparison of the estimated unconditional mean interoffense time intervals between first and second and between second and third offenses for all drivers at different experience levels can be seen in Figure 11.2. This figure clearly demonstrates that the interoffense time interval gradually increases with the increase of driving experience for either type of offense interval. A similar picture emerges for both DIP and MRB drivers.

Comparison shows that the unconditional weighted average time interval between second and third offenses of 1,928 days is significantly longer than the unconditional weighted average time interval between first and second offenses of 1,186 days (Z = 31.16; see Appendix 11A.1 for details of the test) for all drivers.

However, it is also clear from the data that the interoffense intervals increased with driving experience. Since drivers in the later interoffense interval were (on average, about three years) more experienced, this could in itself result in the mean interval between the second and third offenses being greater than that between the first and second offenses.

Thus it was necessary to compare groups of drivers matched by experience at the start of the interoffense interval, if the estimated mean interval between the first and second offenses were to be used as an estimate of the expected mean interval between the second and third offenses (expected under the assumption of no deterrent effect due to the DPS). These intervals, for first to second and second to third offenses, were then compared, tested and presented in Table 11.4.

Table 11.4 shows that in every case, except for drivers with three to four years experience, there was a statistically significant difference between the interoffense time interval for the first to second and the second to third offenses.

Table 11.3: Estimates of the Average Time Intervals (in Days) Between Second and Third Offenses of the DIP and MRB Drivers

Experience in years (at second offence)	Number of drivers, who committed third offence	Average time interval between second and third offences for drivers who committed third offence	Number of drivers, who are free from third offence	Average time interval between second offence and end of study period, who are free from third offence	Estimated unconditional mean time interval between second and third Offence (in days)
3.0 - <4.0	323 (111)	301 (292)	383 (127)	768 (748)	1212 (1148)
4.0 - <5.0	708 (242)	289 (294)	1358 (473)	589 (612)	1418 (1490)
5.0 - <6.0	877 (327)	288 (301)	2205 (734)	533 (515)	1628 (1457)
6.0 - <7.0	805 (306)	285 (271)	2107 (720)	535 (525)	1685 (1506)
7.0 - <8.0	714 (250)	275 (300)	1918 (699)	516 (522)	1661 (1760)
8.0 - <9.0	666 (259)	304 (285)	1793 (659)	534 (517)	1742 (1600)
9.0 - <10.0	556 (217)	288 (328)	1632 (564)	539 (533)	1870 (1713)
10.0 - <11.0	519 (199)	319 (316)	1553 (568)	545 (533)	1950 (1837)
≥ 11	6523 (2391)	302 (313)	22343 (7621)	532 (536)	2124 (2021)
Overall	11,691 (4302)	298 (306)	35,291 (12165)	537 (537)	1954 (1855)

Note: The MRB figures are presented in parentheses

Source: DIP and MRB Data Files of the RTA of Victoria.

One noticeable feature of these data is the high average time interval between the first and second offense for those drivers who have three to four years driving experience. This could be explained by decreased driving exposure during this time. Unfortunately, there is no exposure data for this specific set of drivers. However, the 1986 Melbourne (the capital of Victoria) Metropolitan Exposure Survey showed that on average a driver with three to five years experience derived 7,693 km per year on all major arterial roads in the Melbourne Statistical Division during non-holiday periods compared to 8,521 km for a comparable driver with five to eight years experience.

Table 11.4: Test for the Unconditional Mean Time Intervals Between First and Second, and Second and Third Offenses at Various Driving Experience Levels for All Drivers

Driving experience in years[a] (at start of Interoffence interval)	Unconditional means between first & second offence (in days)	Unconditional means between second & third offence (in days)	Difference between unconditional means of the first & second, and second & third offence (in days)	Standard error	Z value	Significance or non-significance
3.0 -<4.0	1180	1196	16	88.27	0.18	NS
4.0 -<5.0	890	1437	547	60.87	8.99	S
5.0 -<6.0	1016	1583	567	70.52	8.04	S
6.0 -<7.0	964	1635	671	70.98	9.45	S
7.0 -<8.0	1086	1687	601	86.37	6.96	S
8.0 -<9.0	1050	1701	651	86.37	7.54	S
9.0 -<10.0	1086	1825	739	97.33	7.59	S
10.0 -<11.0	1210	1919	709	116.12	6.1	S
≥11	1291	2097	806	36.14	22.3	S
Overall	1186	1928	742	23.81	31.16	S

a. Driving experience is calculated by taking the interval between license issue and the first offense for the first and second offenses and the second offense for the second and third offenses, that is the driving experience at the start of interoffence interval. S = significant at 1% level and NS= non-significant

Source: DIP and MRB Data Files of the RTA of Victoria.

Figure 11.2: Unconditional Average Time Interval Between Offences and Experiences for All Drivers

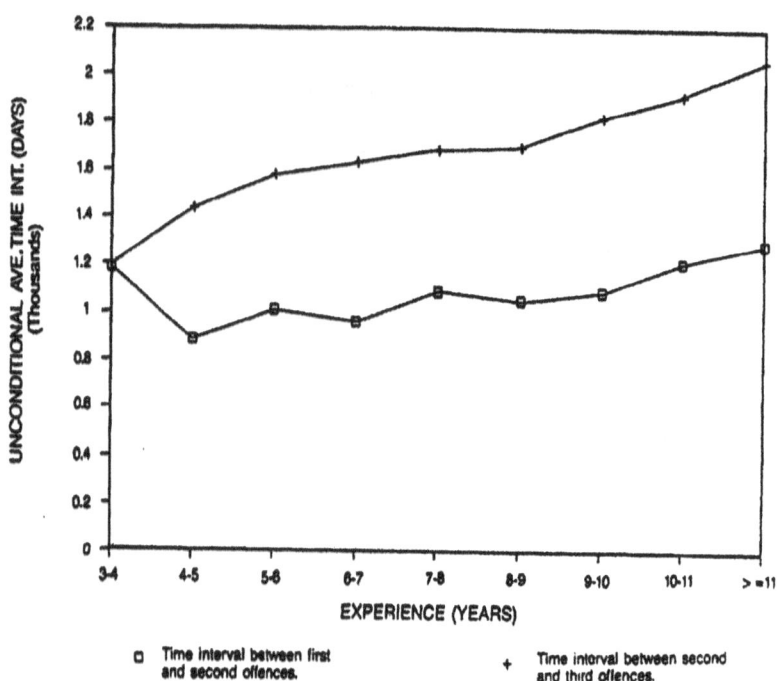

Source: DIP and MRB Data Files of the RTA of Victoria.

11.6   Discussion

It was argued in Section 11.5.1 that the effectiveness of point accumulation as a deterrent would be reflected in the difference between the time periods of first and second traffic offenses and between second and third traffic offenses (after correcting for differences in driving experience when making the comparison). The data analyzed here indicated that, with the exception of one level of driving experience, there was a significantly longer time interval between the second and third offenses than between the first and second offenses.

Moreover, it can be shown that the DIP has a deterrent effect that can be strengthened by comparing the offense rates up to the third offense across drivers' experience. As seen in Table 11.3, these are statistically greater for the MRB drivers than for these in the DIP scheme.

This finding is consistent with the view that the DPS provides a deterrent against traffic offenses. The results of this analysis demonstrate that there has been a significant effect in reducing traffic offenses subsequent to the second offense by increasing the mean time to the third offense. An objective of the DPS is to produce such an effect by deterrence.

The effect of the driver being older and more experienced has been eliminated by the analysis. The analysis method used was the only method available to assess the deterrent effect of the DPS.

The present analysis did not attempt to establish the relationship between the traffic offenses and accidents. However, other studies such as Corbett *et al.* (1997) and Diamantopoulou *et al.* (1997) showed that there existed a relationship between traffic convictions and accidents. While, Campbell (1958), Coppin, Lew and Peck (1965), Peck and Kuan (1982) and Chipman (1982) showed that for a large number of drivers, the accident rate increased steadily with conviction rate. Additionally, Chipman and Morgan (1975) and Chen *et al.* (1995) also indicated that demerit points were more strongly associated with future risk of collision than age, sex or class of license.

However, these authors were cautious about predicting future accident numbers from past driving records because of the low value of the correlation coefficient, even though it was statistically significant.

Empirical analyses from other fields also indicate that the coefficient of determination (R^2) is usually low for individual data. However, a high value of the R^2 can be achieved by using the grouped data for the same phenomenon, leaving the properties of the regression estimates largely intact. For example, in an Engel curve analysis, Cramer (1973:153) has shown that the R^2 increases systematically and quite considerably as the number of groups decreased, with little or no effect on the elasticity estimates for various household consumption items.

Thus there is enough reason to expect a significant effect in reducing future road accidents due to the DPS, although a low coefficient of determination (R^2) value is observed from individual data.

It should be noted here that the present analysis is a univariate technique, and it takes into account the driver's experience only, ignoring the effect of other variables. For this reason, Cox's (1972) regression method and MacKenzie's (1986) proportional hazard model should be used for further analysis, as they may provide a stronger statistical underpinning for the evaluation. Both Cox's regression method and Maclenzie's proportional hazard models are multivariate techniques that provide a prediction model to explain the length of offense-free intervals between various groups and circumstances, such as the driver's previous offense record, previous accident history, age, sex, marital status and so on.

11.7 Conclusions

Records of 63,449 standard license-holder drivers who committed a second offense (within three years of the first offense), between March 1982 and the end of February 1985 were used to evaluate the effectiveness of the DPS. The estimate of the unconditional mean time interval between the first and second offenses was 1,186 days. The estimated mean interoffense time interval between second and third offenses for these drivers was 1,928 days, which was significantly longer than the interoffense time interval between first and second offenses. More specifically, the estimated mean time intervals between first and second and between second and third offences were compared for groups of drivers matched by their experience at the start of the interoffense interval, and it was found that the latter interoffense time intervals were significantly longer than were the first and second offense time intervals at various levels of driving experience greater than four years. It is concluded that the DPS was responsible for most of the deterrent effect reflected in the increased mean time until the third offense subsequent to a first and second offense detected less than three years apart.

Notes

1 See Haque (1987) for more details about various measures that were taken against repeated traffic offenders.

2 Utzelman and Jacobshagen (1996) provided the validation of the German system of diagnosis and rehabilitation of traffic offenders.

3 See the Home Office (2000) Communication Directorate for the Road Traffic Penalties for UK drivers.

4 Road Safety Committee (2004) of Victoria made an inquiry into the Demerit Points Scheme of 1994 and prepared a report for Parliament of Victoria.

5 Chin and Quddus (2003) and Poch and Mannering (1996) used the Negative Binomial model to examine traffic accident occurrence at signalized intersections, while Salifu (2004) used accident prediction models for unsignalised urban junctions in Ghana . Gelman *et al.* (2003) analysed road accident data using Bayesian data analysis techniques, while Iamtrakul *et al.* (2006) analysed road accident data using the Pralbearty Survival Method.

6 Examination of time intervals between first and second offenses shows that the exponential distribution fits well to these data.

CHAPTER 12

UNEMPLOYMENT AND ROAD FATALITIES

It is demonstrated in this chapter that the effect of unemployment on road fatalities is very strong, after controlling for the amount of fuel sales (proxy for motor vehicle travel) and some important road safety countermeasure initiatives. The model developed in this chapter also helps to evaluate the effectiveness of some implemented road safety initiatives such as compulsory seatbelt wearing in motor vehicles, a package of drink driving reduction measures, the 1989/90 road safety initiatives, and the travel reduction due to the 1974 and 1980 oil price increases in reducing road fatalities. The influence of each of these factors on the total road fatalities has been measured by an econometric method and it shows that unemployment has negative association with road fatalities for the Victorian (a state in Australia) data. It also provides evidence of the effectiveness of some major road safety initiatives in Victoria.

12.1 Introduction

For sometime road safety experts such as Partyka (1984), Joksch (1984), Wagenaar (1984), Evans and Graham (1988) and Legget (1990) have noted that there exists a relationship between business activity and road fatalities.

An increase in automotive fuel 'consumption' (a proxy for motor vehicle travel) is expected to lead to more fatalities, because increased vehicle travel increases the likelihood of accidents, and hence fatalities. If the number of people unemployed is taken as an indicator of economic performance then it is expected that the higher unemployment number may lead to a lower number of road fatalities and vice-versa for the following reasons. In periods of recession, when unemployment increases, various forms of more risky travel are likely to be reduced to a greater degree than all travel. For example, young drivers whose accident rate per kilometre travel is generally higher than that of other drivers are more severely affected by unemployment than other groups and hence have less disposable income and it is expected that they would travel less.1 Further, commercial heavy vehicle travel tends to be more severely affected by a recession than commuter travel, and whilst the accident rate per kilometre of travel of this group of vehicles is low, the severity of accidents due to vehicle mass is high and contributes significantly to fatalities and severe injuries.2

People may choose to drink at home more than at bars at the time of recession and hence one can expect relatively less drink driving on roads. On the other hand, during economic prosperity, recreational, social and vocational travel increases and as this form of travel is more risky than utility and commuter travel, road trauma is anticipated to rise. These arguments suggest that there exists a procyclical relationship between the numbers of road fatalities and unemployment. Factors that may have an opposite effect on road fatalities may include psychological depression, stress from economic hardship or increased risk taking with a perception that there is nothing to lose. However, the number of road fatalities affected by these factors is likely to be low as those fatalities known to be suicides are not accounted as contributing to the road toll. Further overseas studies such as Tsuang, Boor and Fleming (1985) and Kesinen and Pasanen (1990) have shown that the number of fatalities that may have been suicides is small.

The net effect of unemployment on road fatalities has never been examined in Australia. Also, the theoretical predictions are conflicting. Hence the theory of the effect of unemployment on road fatalities is plausible. In this chapter, we analyse and document the net effect of unemployment on road fatalities using Victorian data.

Motor vehicle fuel sales and some major road safety variables such as compulsory seatbelt wearing in motor vehicles, various drink driving reduction measures, the 1989/90 road safety initiatives, travel reduction due to the 1974 and 1980 oil price increases, and the trend effect, are also examined.

Linear functions are used to analyse the data as a first approximation to a class of regular curve. The ordinary least squares (OLS) method is used to estimate the parameters of the regression equation after transformation of time-series data due to autocorrelation. These estimated parameters are then used to evaluate the effect of different independent variables. Victorian long-term (yearly: 1966 – 1990) and short-term (monthly: January 1985 to December 1990) data of road fatalities, unemployment numbers, fuel sales and some road safety variables are used for the analyses. 3

The main objective of the study is to identify the effect of unemployment on road fatalities using econometric methods, which can disentangle the effects of various road safety countermeasures, growth of travel and other external travel related factors. More specifically, it aims:

> to estimate the reduction in the number of fatalities per year due to compulsory seatbelt legislation;

UNEMPLOYMENT AND ROAD FATALITIES 147

- to estimate the yearly reduction in the number of fatalities due to the introduction of a number of drink driving reduction measures;

- to estimate the effectiveness of recent road safety initiatives; and

- to estimate the trend effect (which can be viewed as the effectiveness of progressive road safety initiatives and other effects other than seat-belt and drink driving measures).

The outline of this chapter is as follows. Data used in the present analysis are discussed in Section 12.2. Section 12.3 is concerned with the methodology used for the analyses. Numerical illustrations are given in Section 12.4. Some valuable discussions are made in Section 12.5, while some limitations and future options are provided in Section 12.6. Some concluding remarks are made in the final section.

12.2 Data

Two sets of road fatality data were taken from the VicRoads (Roads Corporation of Victoria) accident data file. These are long-term yearly data (1966 – 1990, and short-time monthly data January 1985 – December 1990).

Unemployment numbers for Victoria are taken from 'The Labour Force, Australia: Historical Summary 1966 to 1984', and the Australian Bureau of Statistics (ABS) monthly time series data on labour force from 1985 to 1990. Historical data are available for the month of August, as being representative of the unemployment situation for the whole year and are used for this study.4

Motor vehicle exposure data as represented by travel are not available for every year in Victoria. However, yearly motor vehicle fuel sales data are available, which have been taken as the proxy for motor vehicle exposure in this study, although it is recognised that motor vehicle fuel sales do not accurately represent vehicle travel. This is because the regular surveys of motor vehicle usages in Australia, which are conducted by the ABS every three years since 1976 show that the kilometres driven per litre has increased during the study period due to more fuel efficient cars. However, the introduction of a time trend in the model is assumed to take care of such an effect and it is thus expected that motor vehicle fuel sales data would give a good representation for motor vehicle travel. Yearly petroleum product sales in megalitres for motor vehicle usage for the state marketing area of Victoria were taken from the Bureau of Resource Economics (1987) publication for the years 1966 to 1984. The Australian Bureau of Agricultural Economics also provided later monthly figures. The State marketing area of Victoria includes the whole of the State, less the Murrayville district, but includes the Riverina district of New South Wales.

It is quite reasonable to assume that the fuel sales in the Victorian State marketing area represent the total petroleum products consumed by Victorian motorists. This is because the rolling stocks of motor vehicle petroleum products held at service stations do not vary significantly from month to month. Total motor vehicle fuel sale is obtained by adding the components of automotive gasoline (leaded, unleaded), liquefied petroleum gas (LPG) for motor vehicle usages only and automotive diesel oil.

Road safety variables and other significant exogenous events are used in the model as "interventions" via the use of appropriate dummy variables. Finally, a trend variable is allocated values that vary with time in years/months from the beginning of the series.

12.3   The Model

It was our desire to develop a comprehensive model that related various socio-economic and road safety intervention variables to the number of most motor vehicle accidents, deaths and injuries. However, data in the road safety field are not consistent, and in many cases not available due to non-reporting and under-reporting. This restricts the ability to estimate any comprehensive model, but leaves a challenge to determine whether and how changes of unemployment numbers affect the number of road fatalities. In this regard, one of the main challenges is to disentangle the effect of unemployment on road fatalities from the effects of various road safety initiatives and other related trends. Fortunately, econometric techniques can determine the effect of each independent variable separately, under *ceteris-paribus* condition (that is if other things remain constant).

In order to find the effect of unemployment, fuel sales for motor vehicle usage, road safety initiatives, other exogenous events and secular trends on road fatalities, the following model of the general form can be expressed as:

$$D_t = f(U_t, F_t, P_{it}, T, E_t) \qquad (12.1)$$

where D_t = number of fatalities in period t

U_t = number of unemployed in period t,

F_t = amount of fuel sales for motor vehicles usage in period t,

P_{it} = $\begin{cases} \text{Proportion of the effectiveness of} \\ \text{ith road safety initiative and} \\ \text{other extraneous events at period t .5} \\ \text{0 otherwise,} \end{cases}$

T = secular trend and can take the values 1,2,3, from the beginning to the end of the series,

E_t = variation due to chance and unidentified factors which may be seen as error term for the period t.

12.3.1 Specification of the Functional Form

Specification of the functional form is an important issue in econometrics. This is because the interpretation of the estimated parameters of the regression coefficient of different factors, which can explain road toll mainly, depends on the functional form used. Usually, the inspection of the scatter diagram of the various socio-economic and road safety data does not give a clear picture of the appropriate functional form. Researchers often determine the functional form of the relationship on an *ad-hoc basis*. In general it should be simple and satisfy the following properties:

- the possibility of a threshold effect, i.e. there *is* a low level of road toll, below which unemployment, travel or road safety activities or trend have little or no effect;

- existence of saturation level, i.e. there is a high level of road trauma above which high level of motor vehicle or unemployment or road safety activities have little effect;

- the criterion is that the sum of changes of road fatalities factors must add up to total changes in fatalities; and

- the best representation of the data on statistical grounds.

There is no unique functional form that can satisfy all these properties simultaneously. Therefore options are given to the investigators to choose the functional form to analyse the road fatality data. A linear function is often taken as a first approximation to a class of regular curve. Partyka (1984) used the linear function to model the fatality trend using the United States of America (USA) employment and population data, for the period 1960 to 1982, Loeb (1987) used the linear function to model the determinants of automobile fatalities with special consideration to policy variables, using the USA cross sectional data for the year 1979. Most recently, Evans and Graham (1988) used the logarithmic function to analyse the USA national time-series data for the post-war period and pooled state data for the past decade in order to examine the effect of unemployment on road fatalities for various road user groups, without introducing any road safety variables. They inferred that the performance of the economy exerts a powerful influence on traffic safety. In the present analyses, we have selected the linear function on the grounds of goodness of fit. It can satisfy the property of threshold, but cannot attain the saturation level, which is quite appropriate in the road safety area.

12.4 Numerical Illustrations

12.4.1 Long-term Road Fatality Analysis

A linear model was fitted by the ordinary least squares method to the 25 years (1966 – 1990) of the yearly number of road fatalities, using the number of persons unemployed divided by 1000, fuel sales in mega-liters, four dummy variables (the seat-belt legislation introduced in December 1970, various drink-driving measures introduced during the period 1978 – 1990, the 1974 and 1980 oil price rise, one for the recent road safety initiative); and one trend variable as an explanatory variable.

The SAS computer software package was used to estimate the various statistics and parameters of the model. Every care has been taken to avoid problems, which are associated with regression procedures in SAS as pointed out by Ugar and Edem (1990). The Durbin-Watson DW-statistic showed no problem of autocorrelation. The model was also tested for heteroscedasticity according to the procedure given in Glejser (1969) and again no evidence of this problem was found. Multicollinearity was highly pronounced among the various independent variables for the original observations. In order to avoid this problem, we removed trend effects from U, F, SB and DD, and then a separate regression was run with these trend free data for these variables along with other variables, which removed most of the collinearities among various independent variables (see Table 13A.1 of Appendix 13A). The final long-term estimated model for road fatalities for Victoria is given below. The absolute value of the t statistic of different estimated parameters of the model is given in parentheses.

$D_t = 1033.42 - 1.01\ U_t + 0.26 F_t - 154.94\ (SB)_t - 123.04\ (DD)_t - 108.26\ (OP)_t - 37.0\ (RRSI)_t - 15.6\ T;$
$\quad\ \ (68.95)\ \ (2.22)\ \ (4.48)\ \ \ \ (1.96)\ \ \ \ \ \ \ \ \ (2.18)\ \ \ \ \ \ \ \ \ (3.77)\ \ \ \ \ \ \ (0.89)\ \ \ \ \ \ \ \ \ (15.07)$

$F_{7,17} = 50.35$, DW - statistic = 2.06 and $R^2 = 0.95$

The summary statistics indicate that the model explains total road fatalities very well. The F-statistic shows that there exists a very high significant association between the number of road fatalities and various independent variables (viz. U, F, SB, DD, OP, RRSI and T) considered in the model. The estimates explain 95% of the variation in the yearly total road fatalities. Plots of residual against time showed that no important factor was unaccounted for in the model.

It should be noted that these estimated coefficients are very similar to those estimates when regressions were run to fit the model to all data points up to 1988 and up to 1989 respectively as shown in Table 12.1 below.

Table 12.1: Estimated Regression Coefficients for Various
Road Safety and Socio-economic Variables

Variables	1966–1988	1966–1989	1966–1990
Unemployment effect	– 0.907	– 1.011	– 1.011
Fuel sales	0.250	0.256	0.256
Seatbelt (at 100% wearing)	– 145.130*	– 155.00	– 155.00
Drink driving	– 121.159	– 123.00	– 123.00
Oil embargos/Price rises	– 108.542	– 108.265	– 108.265
Trend effect	– 16.00	– 16.00	– 16.00
Recent road safety initiatives	-	-	– 37.00**

* Significance at 10% level.

** Non-significance.

Source: Fatality, seatbelt wearing and drink driving data are taken from the RTA Accident Data File; unemployment data from the ABS Labour Force Survey; and fuel sales data are taken from the Australian petroleum sales data.

Thus, these estimates can be considered fairly robust. The t-statistic of the different estimated parameters of the model shows that each of them except RRSI is significantly different from zero and has the expected sign. The meaning of each of the estimated parameters attached to its variables is explained below:

- $-1.01 U_t$ means there would be an expected decrease of 1.01 fatalities per 1000 increase of unemployment number;

- $0.26 F_t$ means there would be an expected increase of 0.26 fatalities per 1 megalitre increase of fuel sales;

- $-154.94\ (SB)_t$ means the effect of seatbelt legislation would have been to reduce deaths by 155 per year for a wearing rate 100%;

- $-123.04\ (DD)_t$ means that because of the introduction of various drink-driving measures up to 1990, there would have been 123 fewer deaths in 1990 and a specified proportion of this number in each year since 1978;

- $-108.26\ (OP)_t$ means the effect of the 1974 oil shortage combined with the reduced rural speed limit and the 1980 oil price rise are estimated as 108 fatality reduction in those years;

- $-37.0\ (RRSI)_t$ means the immediate effect of the recent road safety initiatives would have a non-significant (probably because of lack of power of the test due to this factor being presented at one point only) reduction of 37 fatalities in 1990; and

- $-15.67\ T$ means there would have been 16 less fatalities per year due to trend effect (i.e., the progressive road safety initiatives and other effects over the years other than seatbelt and drink-driving measures).

On the whole, there is a good agreement between the actual (776 and 548) and fitted (763 and 548) fatalities (see Figure 12.1) for 1989 and 1990; the worst and best year for Victorian road toll in the 1980s. If the effect of the RRSI was not taken into account then the model predicts 585 fatalities for 1990 based on all data points except the last point. Similarly, 752 and 581 fatalities were predicted for 1989 and 1990 respectively, when all data points up to 1988 were used. This implies that the fatality increase/decrease in 1989/90 is consistent with the historical relationship between traffic fatalities and various road safety measures undertaken over the unemployment figures.

12.4.2 Short-term Road Fatality Analysis

The recent variation in the number of road fatalities is better understood by incorporating the current road safety initiatives and changes on the social and economic fronts. In order to see the effect of recent changes in various road safety and socio-economic factors on road fatalities, we have restricted the period of analysis from 1985 to 1990 for the following reasons:

- all monthly fatalities, fuel sales and unemployment numbers are available from the various official records;

- no major adjustment is needed to account for the seatbelt, drink-driving measures and also for the 1974 and 1980 oil price increases;

- recent changes in motor vehicle travel (less business travel, less social activity and less drink driving) due to rise of unemployment are reflected in the model; and

- recent road safety initiatives, which were implemented and or announced during 1989/90, can also be evaluated.

Here, we have used the monthly (January 1985 – December 1990) data of road fatalities, unemployment numbers ('000), fuel sales (megalitres) and one dummy variable for a package of recently implemented/announced road safety initiatives taking the value 1 for October 1989, 6 and later months and 0 elsewhere, and a trend variable, to estimate the parameters of the model.

In order to avoid seasonality, which is common in road fatalities due to a number of identified influences (viz, traffic volumes for a certain month, weather, hours of darkness, etc.) and unidentified or un-measurable ones, we have used 11 dummy variables (one each for February to December) to estimate the parameters of the linear model.

The same OLS method is used to estimate the parameters of the model. The data were appropriately transformed according to Durbin's (1960) two-stage procedure to overcome the autocorrelation problems and the parameters of the model were re-estimated. The model was also tested for heteroscedasticity according to the procedure given in Glejser (1969) and no such problem was observed. In order to avoid multicollinearity from the original observations, we have removed the trend effects from U and F and a fresh regression was run with these trend free variables together with other variables. The final estimated model is presented below.7

$$D_t = 65.80 - 0.15\ U_t + 0.05\ F_t - 15.80\ (RRSI)_t + 0.15\ T,$$
$$(14.12)\ (2.36)\quad (1.04)\quad (5.38)\quad\quad (2.66)$$

$$F_{15,5} = 6.52,\ DW\text{-statistic} = 2.0\ \text{and}\ R^2 = 0.64$$

The absolute values of the t-statistic of different estimated parameters are presented in parentheses and show that all parameters are significantly different from zero except for fuel sales. However, all have the expected sign. The estimated parameters can be interpreted exactly in the same way as the long-term model. It should be noted that estimated parameters of the 11-monthly dummy variables are not presented here in order to save space. Significant negative coefficients are observed for the months of July, August and November in recent years, while other monthly dummies fail to gain significance.

The F-statistic shows that there exists a significant association between dependent (D_t) and independent variables (U_t, F_t, $(RRSI)_t$, T and 11-monthly dummy variables to account for seasonal variation). The R^2 value is comparatively lower than the long-term historical model based on yearly (addition of 12 monthly grouped) data. This is probably because of using individual monthly data. There is evidence (see Cramer 1973:153) that R^2 is usually low for individual data, but high for grouped data for the same phenomenon, leaving the properties of the regression estimates largely intact.

The short-term model shows that there has been a significant reduction of about 190 in numbers of fatalities due to the recent road safety initiatives. These should continue for future years if these initiatives are successfully maintained with community support. The model also indicates that overall there is a significant increase in road fatalities due to the trend effect in the months of recent years, which is contrary to the long-term model that shows a significant decrease.

It is interesting to note from the long-term model that there was an insignificant fatality reduction of about 37 per year due to recent road safety initiatives, which is quite low compared to a high significant reduction of about 190 fatalities based on the short-term model. This might have happened probably because of lack of power of the test for the long-term model due to the presence of recent road safety initiatives at the end of the series, i.e., for 1990 only. While, the short-term model has incorporated the presence of recent road safety variables for 15 months from October 1989 to December 1990, which would be expected to measure the effect of road fatalities more accurately than the long-term model for recent months. Actual and fitted fatalities based on the short-term model can be found in Figure 12.2.

12.5   Discussions

The number of Victorian road fatalities reached its peak in 1970 when 1,061 road fatalities occurred in a state of 3.4 million people. There were 31 road fatalities for every 100,000 population in that year, a high death rate in relation to other motorised countries in the world. Up to that time it was explained that the number of road fatalities would increase with the increasing usage of motor vehicles. At that time the Victorian community pressure demanded increased safety on roads. Subsequently, there was increased public expenditure to improve Victorian roads and a number of road safety measures such as seatbelt wearing, a package of drink-driving and vehicle improvement programs, etc. were introduced and implemented in order to bring down the yearly road toll.

The response was immediate with a significant reduction in road fatalities. In 1971, there were 923 road deaths, a reduction of 138 fatalities compared to 1970. This downward trend continued steadily until 1984 with few exceptions (low road fatality numbers of 657 were observed in 1980). Then the road fatality numbers increased and reached a peak in 1989 when road fatalities of 776 were the highest in the 1980s. Politicians, road safety experts and enforcement authorities implemented and announced a series of road safety measures to avoid the annual road carnage on an *ad-hoc* basis.8 Victoria's road toll was favourable in 1990, when 548 people died, the lowest recorded in about 35 years. There were 228 fewer fatalities than in 1989 and 157 fewer compared to the average of previous five years. The death rate per 100,000 people was 12.7, which was lower than Australian national average of 13.9.

This study has attempted to underpin the causes of variation of road fatalities. It offsets the earlier concepts of variation of the road toll due to the variation of vehicle exposures alone and establishes a new relation that the variation of road fatalities depends on vehicle travel, road safety activity and economic activity as represented by the level of unemployment. In this study, vehicle fuel sales (which may be a surrogate for economic activity, as well as a proxy for exposure), some major road safety initiatives, unemployment numbers and trend effects were treated as independent variables in order to explain the variation in road fatalities. It is observed that a significant reduction of road fatalities is possible with the introduction and proper implementation of appropriate road safety legislation (such as the seatbelt law). More importantly, it shows that there exists a negative association between unemployment and road fatalities. This finding corroborates the findings of Partyka (1984) and Evans and Graham (1988) for U.S.A. studies.

Finally, a review of the correlation matrix of the original variables shows that there exists a high correlation among various independent variables. These problems reflect the fact that fatalities, unemployment, fuel sales and road safety activities have each been increasing over time. This tendency can reduce the precision of the estimate of the parameters. In order to avoid this problem, we first remove the trend effects from unemployment, fuel sales, seatbelt wearing rates and drink-driving variables and then run a fresh regression with the relevant variables, which eliminated most of the collinearities among independent variables (see tables 12A.2(a) and 12A.2(b) of Appendix 12A). This is a new contribution in the road safety field, which has never been achieved previously.9

12. 6 Problems and Future Options

There are several limitations in using the unemployment numbers and fuel sales data. The August unemployment numbers were used for the long-term fatality analysis as a representative of the whole year's unemployment, which may not be true in reality, although it is not significantly different from the yearly average of some later years. Total fuel sales data may not be a good indicator for total vehicle exposure data, because the distance travelled using a liter of fuel varies with fuel type (the 1988 ABS survey of motor vehicle usage shows that the average kilometres driven per liter of petroleum, LPG and distillate are 8.26, 5.38 and 3.5 respectively). Similarly, kilometres driven per liter has increased during the study period, due to more fuel efficient cars and hence fuel sales data may not accurately represent vehicle travel, although a time trend is assumed to take care for such an effect for the present analyses.

In the present analyses, we have used only linear functions to show the effect of road fatalities due to an increase in unemployment numbers or an increase of one megalitre of fuel usage, etc. The choice of the best functional form based on some selected criterion, viz., distance function criterion, non-nested hypothesis testing procedure or some parametric test among various alternatives, was not made. As a result, the current estimates may not be as accurate as that of other functions, although results may not be significantly different to those found by using other than the linear function. Further analysis along this line would be interesting and is left for further study.

We did not estimate the elasticity of road fatalities of different independent variables. Elasticity estimates are important to forecast the future road safety demand of both operational and construction standpoints. Elasticity measures the responsiveness of road fatalities due to change in unemployment, fuel sales and/or road safety activities. It also helps to measure the relative importance of road fatalities for different road user groups. Thus, elasticities indicate which groups are most likely to gain or lose due to change in policies.

It cannot tell us anything about the price responsiveness of demand, which is very important at the times of inflation and oil crises. The effect of distribution of national income and wealth on road fatalities can also be interesting for further development in the road safety area.

The present analysis also did not consider some economic, demographic, geographical and environmental factors, which might affect our estimated parameters of the model. Inclusion of these variables in the model will give more precise estimates of road fatalities and is left for further study.

The present analysis also did not consider road fatalities within specific road users groups, viz, pedestrians, motorcyclists, bicyclists and drivers of certain age groups. The risk of death on roads is highly variable between different groups of road users. A bicyclist (unprotected road user) and a driver (protected road user) are subject to different level of risk on the road. Further, most drivers carry a very insignificant probability of death on the roads, while a few have a much larger risk of death such as young drink drivers. The model may be improved by treating these groups separately. Thus, a more detailed (group by group) analysis covering a number of years data, and allowing for the variation of different socio-economic, geographical and environmental effects would be interesting and is left for further study. 10

12.7 Conclusions

This study uses the linear regression to estimate models, which explain total vehicle deaths, using long-term (yearly) and short-term (monthly) time series data. This is a more rigorous and extensive model than that of Partyka (1984) and Evans and Graham (1988) and supports the findings of those studies that 'as unemployment increases road fatality decreases and vice-versa'. The study also successfully evaluates a number of road safety initiatives and it is concluded that: a significant reduction of 155 road fatalities would be achieved if there would be a seatbelt wearing rate of 100%; 123 fewer deaths would have resulted due to the full implementation of the drink-driving measures in 1990 and a specified proportions of this number since 1978; a significant reduction of 108 fatalities would have been occurred due to the oil price increase in 1974 and in 1980; and there would have been a reduction of 16 fatalities per year due to trend effect; based on the short-term model, it is found that a significant reduction of about 16 fatalities per month is due to recent road safety initiative and/or further reinforcement of the previously imposed road safety legislations, although a non-significant much lower number of road fatality is observed from the long-term model.

Thus, the model developed here allows us to measure the effects of various relevant factors on road toll, which can assist policy makers in determining the effectiveness of various road safety countermeasures and other contributing factors.

The model is also able to forecast the road toll for future years based on predicted changes in the economy and social and other factors assuming road safety activities remain constant. Hence it can help policy makers to make decisions about how to use limited funds in order to achieve a maximum benefit to the community, by targeting more risky road user groups and/or factors, which can contribute to future road toll.

The model we have used is very simple, easily understood by non-technical people and can be estimated through readily available computer packages such as SPSS, SAS, GLIM, etc. Generalisation of our model is quite straightforward and many independent variables can be incorporated to explain road fatalities without difficulty.

This study demonstrates that road fatality does not only depend on numbers of motor vehicle or travel, but also depends on the performance of the economy, various road safety activities and other socio-demographic and environmental factors including extraneous effects such as oil crises. This is the most comprehensive study of its kind yet attempted in the road safety field.

It is clear from this analysis that the performance of the economy exerts a powerful influence on traffic casualties. It is recommended that this technique be applied to other states/countries and specific groups of road users to further examine the effect of economic activity as reflected by unemployment on road fatalities. It is also recommended that more general and sophisticated models be developed to test the hypotheses of appropriate model selection, economic and road safety determinants on traffic fatalities.

Figure 12.1: Fit of the Victorian Long-term Road Fatality Model, 1960–90

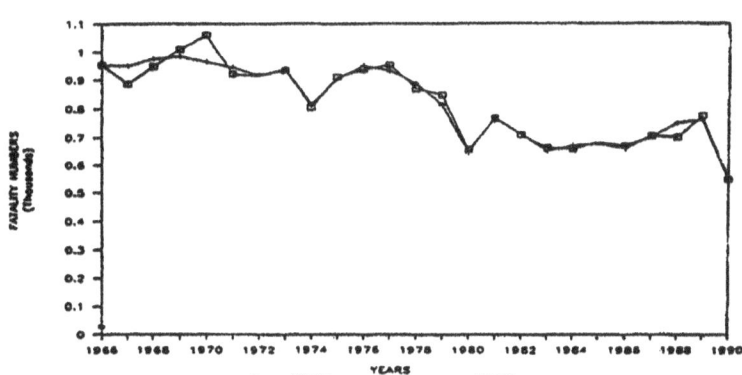

Source: Road Traffic Accident Data File of the RTA of Victoria extracted from the Victorian Police Road Accident Report Form.

Figure 12.2: Fit of the Victorian Short-term Road Fatality Model, with the Seasonally Adjusted Monthly Data, 1985–1990

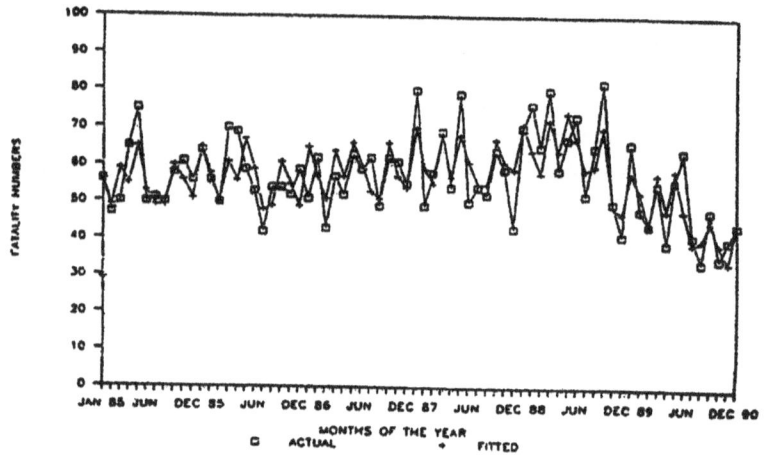

Source: Road Traffic Accident Data File of the RTA of Victoria extracted from the Victorian Police Road Accident Report Form

Notes

1 The unemployment rates (in percentage) for 20–24 age group and total population were 13.3 and 9.0 in 1983 (recession year) compared to 9.4 and 6.6 in 1982 (non-recession year) respectively. Similarly, the corresponding figures for these two groups were 9.5 and 6.1 in 1990 (recession year) compared to 6.4 and 5.0 in 1989 (non-recession year) respectively.

2 The Cul-way data system, which records the movements of trucks shows that only 969 trucks came to Melbourne (capital of Victoria and also the 2nd largest city in Australia) from Sydney (capital of New South Wales and the largest city in Australian) in 1990 (recession year) compared to 1323, 1128 and 1132 in 1987, 1988 and 1989 respectively. Fatalities per 100,000 registered trucks are also significantly lower in 1983 and 1990 (recession years) compared to other years. See Appendix 12A for fatalities involving trucks.

3 The impact of socio-economic variables on road safety has been studied by a number of authors among with World Bank (2006), Vinand and David (2003), Thomas *et al.* (2004), Hoque *et al.* (2000), Odero *et al.* (1997), Borrell (2001) and Qazi (2000) are important.

4 Actual annual unemployment numbers are not available for every year covered in the study. However, number of monthly unemployed persons and quarterly population figures for Victoria are available since 1982. The conventional large sample *Z-statistic* is used to test the differences of proportions of unemployed persons for the month of August and annual average for each year since 1982, and it shows that there is no significant differences between these two proportions.

5 The compulsory seatbelt (SB) wearing in motor vehicles introduced in December 970, various drink-driving (DD) reduction measures implemented during 1978–1990, recent road safety initiatives (RRSI), and the 1974 and 1980 oil price (OP) rise are used in this category.

6 This was about the time when a new package of road safety measures were undertaken including increased police enforcement with operation '100' and extensive media coverage of road safety issues, and when monthly number of road fatalities began to fall from a very high monthly road fatality number (82 in September 1989).

7 Various statistics and parameter estimates of the dummy variables for the months of year are not presented here. However, these statistics can be obtained from the author on request.

8 Some of the important road safety initiatives implemented and/or announced during 1989/90 in conjunction with an intensive focus on road safety issues reinforced by wide spread media coverage are: (1) increased level of random breath testing; (2) a tough new points demerit system which began in November 1989 and commencement of severe on the spot penalties for drink-driving and speeding offences; (3) commencement of the radar speed camera enforcement program with much higher levels of enforcement preceded by a mass media 'Speed Kills' publicity campaign; (4) commencement of the compulsory bicycle helmet wearing requirement; and (5) commencement of graduated licensing provisions for new probationary licence holders.

9 Evans (1996) examined the influence of crash severity and selective recruitment due to the implementation of seatbelt legislation. While Odero *et al.* (1997), Asian Development Bank (2003), Road Maintenance and Transport Organisation (2006) and Rahman (2004) undertook epidemiological studies to investigate the socio-economic impact on road casualties.

10 A detailed analyses covering a number of years of data of socio-economic, geographical and environmental factors for various road user groups cross-classified by age and sex (in different states of Australia and whole of Australia) is already underway and will be reported in due course. This detailed analysis will be performed by using more sophisticated statistical and econometric techniques.

CHAPTER 13

COST OF ROAD ACCIDENTS

In this chapter, a brief review of the literature on the cost of road accidents is presented. The estimation of the cost of road accidents is important for planning and evaluating implemented road safety countermeasures. Measurement of cost of road accidents encompassing 'tangible and intangible costs' and 'the economic value of life'; are discussed. It is thus hoped that the method of estimating the cost of road accidents presented here will help to take appropriate road safety strategies that will ultimately reduce the road toll.

13.1 Introduction

The estimation of road accident costs is both useful and important in planning and evaluating road safety programs. This is because it can assist policy makers to efficiently allocate resources to projects that reduce the incidence of severity of accidents. It also helps to raise the public awareness of the economic and socials impact of road accidents. However, it is a difficult task to estimate the cost of road accidents, because there are a number of points still unresolved due to a diversity of opinions among authors and to the complexity of the issues involved. In the present chapter, a brief review of the literature on the cost of road traffic accidents is made, and how to measure the 'intangible costs' including 'the value of life' is discussed. An appropriate method of estimating the cost of road accidents is presented in this chapter. It is hoped that this improved method of estimating the cost of road accidents will help to allocate limited road safety funds for the development of the most appropriate road safety strategies.

13.1.1 Some Existing Concepts and Estimation Methods of Road Traffic Accident Costs. 1

(a)   CONCEPTS: There are three broad concepts of costs viz., (i) **financial costs** associated with day-to-day receipts and payments throughout the economy. These are usually referred to as recorded accounting costs; (ii) **real economic costs/opportunity costs** which measure the value of scarce resources produced and consumed in the economy; and (iii) **social costs** which refer to the total loss to the whole society and often cannot be measured in monetary terms. Such costs may not be restricted to producers or consumers.

The costs associated with road traffic accidents clearly belong to the third category, since they include external cost effects upon others such as traffic delay, police and hospital services, etc., covered by public funds. They also include tangible and a significant component of non-market and intangible costs.

(b)   **ESTIMATION METHODS**: There are two major approaches in estimating the cost of road accidents namely (i) the *ex-ante* method and (ii) *ex-post* method.

The *ex-ante* (before the event) method assesses willingness-to-pay to reduce the cost of potential accidents. It is based on the monetary sums that the public would be prepared to pay to offset such costs. This method is more suitable for future policy analysis, since it can establish relationships between risk, expected accident rate and potential costs incurred. However, conceptual problems such as interpersonal comparison utility and valuation of life make this method impractical, although it is consistent with the Pareto principle.2

The *ex-post* (after the event) method measures actual costs and losses after an actual road accident has occurred and it is relatively simple to calculate, inexpensive to perform and free of the conceptual problems, which are associated with the *ex-ante* method. However, the *ex-ante* method theoretically has potential and would be simple to use if it were possible to aggregate individual utilities into a single function. Unfortunately, this operation cannot be performed since interpersonal comparisons of utility are not possible [Vide Henderson and Quant (1971: 255)]. Thus the *ex-ante* method is severely limited in its practical applications and cannot be considered as a viable option in the estimation of road accident costs. In contrast, the *ex-post* method can estimate these costs and losses, and will therefore be adopted in this chapter.

13.2   Brief Review of the Literature

In the past, many attempts have been made to estimate the cost of road accidents in various parts of the world. Some of the early major exponents in this field were Reynolds (1956), Dunman (1958), Twomby (1960), Thedie and Abraham (1961), Mackay (1966), Burton and Ekstien (1967), Dawson (1967, 1971) Troy and Butlin (1971), etc. An excellent review of these studies can be found in Paterson (1973). Recently, Faigin (1976), Sherwin (1977), Japan Research Centre for Transport Policy (1978), Lawson (1,978) and Fox *et al.* (1979)

produced some useful and interesting studies based on the ex-post method, which are summarized by Atkins (1981).

In Australia, the responsibility for project evaluation of the transport sector rests with individual states, although some are allocated to Commonwealth agencies such as the Bureau of Transport Economics (BTE) and the Office of Road Safety of the Department of Transport. Current research methodology is based on techniques used by Troy and Butlin (1971), who adopted the *ex-post* method to derive cost estimates that include vehicle-repair, write-off, injury and 'overhead costs' such as police and legal services. Paterson (1973) subsequently generalized his work and applied it for Australia. He also adopted the *ex-post* cost approach, utilizing the net economic cost of a fatality. Later, Atkins (1981) made a thorough review of the economic and social costs of road accidents to include some recent studies employing this approach. He also suggested estimating the cost of road accidents in Australia by an *ex-post* matrix approach [Faigin (1976)],[3] where a zero cell value indicates that a cost category is excluded due to lack of data. He however admitted that this approach suffers from the deficiencies inherent in these cost formulations and therefore his estimates are subject to criticisms. For example, his social cost estimates represent only minima of the true value society places upon the benefits from accident reductions.[4] Foregone income was calculated by discounting future value and productivity rates which would have accrued in the interval between actual death and normal life expectancy. In order to estimate foregone income, both gross and net income concepts were employed, with costs set equal to both zero and to the average wage (opportunity costs) for employable persons (aged between 17 and 65 years) not in the workforce, such as housewives and the unemployed.

Somerville and McLean (1981) conducted a similar study for the Adelaide inner metropolitan area by adopting an ex-post approach. They identified fourteen major cost parameters under the heading of five primary ex-post consequences of accidents. Societal welfare losses resulting from fatalities and from temporary and permanent disabilities were estimated by valuing the cost of lost production measured in terms of market remuneration. Housewives, students and the unemployed are equated to opportunity costs – which approximate to income foregone in the market. Incomes rather than earnings were considered as the appropriate measures.

Wigan (1982) reviewed the methods and values used to measure road accident costs in Australia and showed that the costs obtained by the *ex-post* method are of the same order of magnitude as road construction and maintenance costs. An additional result was that there was a clear link between the valuation of lost consumption and travel time for unemployed people. He also advocated the use of gross consumption foregone, and a willingness-to-pay (*ex-ante*) approach to measure road accident cost in Australia.

13.3 The Economic Value of Life

The cost of a fatal accident is one of the major components of the total road accident costs and therefore it is important that economic evaluation be undertaken for the value of life. Atkins (1982) showed that the average cost of a fatal accident is more than 60 times greater than the overall average cost per accident. In fact, its share was 37% of the estimated total costs, although this represented less than 1% of the number of reported accidents. While, a study of the Bureau of Transport and Communications Economics (1992) indicated that fatal accidents cost about $1.6 billion, contributing 26% of the total cost of road accidents. The average cost of fatal accidents was $631,000 in 1988 in Australia.

There are six major methods of economic evaluation available, which are briefly summarized below.5

(i) **The gross loss of output (or human capital) approach**: This approach asserts that the cost of a traffic accident to society is the sum of all real resource costs and the victim's future output converted to present market value. A significant contribution to lost output is due to death, pain, grief, suffering of accident victims and those undertaking care.

(ii) **The net loss of output approach:** Here the discounted present value of a victim's future consumption is deduced from the gross output figure derived by the above method.

(iii) **The life-insurance approach:** Value of human life is estimated on the basis of typical individuals' willingness to insure their lives through some formula.

(iv) **The court-award approach:** The value of human life is given by the sum awarded by the courts to the dependents of the accident victims.

(v) **The implicit public sector valuation approach:** Safety legislation is generally based on public sector investment decisions. It is possible to derive the implicit value of a life from prevention measure and investment decisions.

(vi) **The value of risk-change approach:** It is assumed that most road safety measures provide only a small change in perceived accident risk for each person in the community. The value of an accident involving one fatality is measured as the total sum paid by the potentially affected individuals' willingness to reduce the cost of a low risk.

It is important to note that the costs associated with a fatal road accident vary substantially from one approach to another. Such variation is due to their different costing methods as can be seen in Hills and Jones-Lee (1981). Note that only the first four methods are applied in the road safety field. The human capital approach is frequently applied to measure the loss in expected future income. Opinion varies however as to whether gross earnings or net consumption should be used. In the correct sense, net income of accident fatalities foregone should be included in *ex-post* accident costs. This is based on the age-specific actuarial approach, which considers that the loss of any human life is a net loss, to society. However, Atkins (1982) argued that accident victims in the workforce will represent a net loss to society as fatalities, but the loss of infants and elderly may appear as a gain to GNP: a contradictory statement of social loss. Thus, we define an appropriate definition of social cost as:

> 'A society that remains indifferent in terms of cost due to a fatality, if that person can be replaced from the bundle of whole population, to offer exactly the same level of satisfaction to society in all respects'.

It is thus difficult to assess whose death is a gain or loss to the community. However, it is not difficult to show that sometimes a person's death even from the potential workforce group is a net gain to the community. For example, the death of a member of the potential workforce involved in a fatal accident is a net gain to the society if society can replace that individual by another person with a higher performance level.

13.4 New Concepts of Measurement of Intangible Costs

'Intangible' implies incapable of being perceived by the senses. In the road accident field the term identifies those factors which cannot be made concrete and measured by any existing scales, such as grief, pain, suffering and even loss of life. Such items cannot be measured in monetary terms, making the calculation of cost an extremely complex topic.6

VALUE OF LIFE: Strictly, any loss of human life in whole or part is an incalculable loss to the community.7 Thus, it is incorrect as well as inhuman to measure the value of life in simplistic monetary terms. Moreover, if road accidents are considered as a social disease then it can easily be shown as an event taken from a countable infinite set of possible events. This makes the probability of death of an individual in a road accident (one event) essentially negligible. Thus, the value of life in monetary terms is negligible and perhaps shall be accepted as a penalty of nature. However, there is sufficient justification to evaluate the value of accrued monetary benefits lost to dependents due to the death of the road accident victim. In practice this judgment depends on court decisions and therefore, in the real world the cost of a fatal accident has two essential components, viz., (i) the number killed; and (ii) the amount of sum awarded by the courts to the dependents of the victims.

In addition, there is a type of cost categorised as (iii) the 'chain reaction', that society has to bear. This process operates where the fatality is a member of the workforce whose job can be filled by the next best available candidate with the most appropriate skills for that position. There is consequentially a high cost incurred by society in fulfilling the subsequent cascaded series of compensating job positions that arise due to that initial job vacancy. This implies that the chain reaction' social cost equals the monetary sum required to replace the victim throughout the entire job changing process less the value of a lower bound position defined by an entry into the labour market, which might be positive or negative. It should be noted that no 'chain reaction', cost is incurred for certain group of victims such as housewives, the unemployed and people out of the workforce. A low cost is associated with the 'chain reaction' only if the victim's position is replaced by any member of these groups. This argument can be applied in evaluating the costs of grief, pain and suffering. The cost of permanent disability is estimated in the same manner as the cost of life omitting the first component (the number of persons killed). In other cases, costs should be calculated on the basis of the second component only.

13.5 A Proposed Method of Estimating Road Traffic Accident Costs in Victoria

In the earlier sections, it has been seen that the ex-post method of estimation of accident costs is more practically feasible. This method is recommended in estimating the cost of road accidents in Victoria. The next task is to identify all the relevant cost components, and calculate the total road accident cost. Some of the major cost components of road accidents are given below.

13.5.1 Cost Components

1. **Number of persons killed:** Road fatalities represent a substantial component of road accident costs, although it is difficult to put monetary value associated with it.

2. **Total sum of money awarded to the dependents of the victim involving fatal accident:** Courts generally pay large sums to dependents of the victims, although it is not a subject of discussion as to how these decisions on financial compensation are made.8 Sometimes insurance companies compromise with the dependents by agreeing to pay an attractive sum. In this case, the amount should be taken as the compensation money for the victim's death. If no claim is made however, then compensation money is not paid.

3. **Total chain reaction effect:** This is only relevant to killed and permanently disabled persons as members of the workforce. Information should be collected from the administrations of the various employers and employees groups, although it is a very difficult but not impossible task to perform. Such details have been discussed earlier in this paper.

4. **Family and community losses:** This is a direct cost of the victim's contribution to family and social activities. It can be taken as the opportunity cost value of non-work, social and community services previously performed and can be estimated as a replacement cost that allows the performance of these duties by others.

5. **Ambulance:** This is a direct cost covering resources used in the transport of the injured person from the point of accident to hospital.

6. **Hospitals (public and private), medical and private doctor:** These costs can be obtained from the Motor Accident Board of Victoria. This covers the loss of resources for the treatment of the injured person and is divided into various forms of treatment such as on-site treatment, hospital in-patient, out-patient, paramedical (dentistry, physiotherapy, occupational therapy, social work and optical treatment) and medical treatment outside hospitals.

7. **Additional care or rehabilitation:** This includes all sorts of care given by the family or friends to the affected individual during the whole period until the resumption of normal activities. This can again be taken as an opportunity costs to families and friends for their times spent in these activities such as in visiting, transport and home care. Again this may be represented as the replacement cost by another person undertaking the same activity.

8. **Legal and court:** These components are meant to cover the cost of resources used to provide legal and judicial services.

9. **Accident investigations:** This cost should be estimated on the basis of resources used in the police investigation of the specific accident, including traffic supervision, interviewing witnesses and reporting procedures.

10. **Towing:** This component covers the cost of resources to remove the damaged vehicles from the accident location.

11. **Funeral:** An amount of money paid by the Motor Accident Board of Victoria should be considered as an appropriate figure for those applying, otherwise no funeral cost would be included.

12. **Insurance administration:** This component covers the cost of all resources used in administration dealing with third party, personal injury, property damage and comprehensive cover.

13. **Property damage:** This is a direct cost of motor vehicle accidents which consists of all resources used to repair or replace damaged property. Included are property related to accident victim viz., motor vehicle, pedal cycles, goods carried and clothing, road facilities, houses and fences.

14. **Time delay:** The cost of traffic delay is defined by the extra time and fuel used as a result of an accident. These types of costs are determined from accident numbers and characteristics in peak hour traffic flows to compute lost time per accident.

15. **Grief, pain and suffering:** These represent a valid loss of the injured or killed to their relatives and dependants. This loss should again be taken as an acceptable fact of life. The monetary sum awarded by the Court should be taken as the societal value of pain, grief and suffering.

The cost components described above need to be added to give the total cost. An average accident cost figure is useful, in the appraisal of prevention measures. The simple arithmetic mean cost is meaningless because each category of costs is widely scattered around the mean and usually highly positively skewed. A useful analytical device to overcome this problem is to divide accident costs into a number of intervals, each with a known probability of occurrence.9 The injury severity scores [such as Faigin's Abbreviated Injury Scales (AIS)] may be taken as a suitable basis for estimating the costs at various injury severity levels.

13.5.2 Estimation Procedure

The need for various RTA research projects is to update total and average accident cost estimates disaggregated by the following factors:

(1) **Injury severity level:** fatal, hospital admission, medical treatment only, and property damage both reported and not reported to police;

(2 **Accident type:** pedestrian, motorcycle, bicycle, single and multi-vehicle;

(3) **Locality:** MSD and rest of Victoria, and urban and rural defined by speed zone less than 100 km/h and 100 km/h respectively.

It appears that road accident costs can be estimated by a matrix approach. The order of the matrix will be $a \times b$, where a represents accident type (5) and b the injury severity level (5). Further, these costs can be estimated separately for MSD and the rest of Victoria, and urban and rural defined by speed zone. The actual structure of the cost matrix is presented below.

Let C_{ij} represents the cost of ith type of accident and jth level of injury severity. Then $C_{i.} = \sum_j C_{ij}$ = total cost of ith type of accident, and

$C_{.j} = \sum_i C_{ij}$ = total cost of jth level of injury severity. Thus the total cost is estimated by:

$$C = \sum_{i,j} C_{ij} = \sum_i C_{i.} = \sum_j C_{.j} \qquad (13.1)$$

Table 13.1: Cost Matrix by Accident Type and Injury Severity Levels

Accident type	Injury severity level					Total
	Fatality	Hospital admission	Medical treatment	Reported property damage	Non-reported property damage	
Pedestrian	C11	C12	C13	C14	C15	C1.
Motorcycle	C21	C22	C23	C24	C25	C2.
Bicycle	C31	C32	C33	C34	C35	C3.
Single-vehicle	C41	C42	C43	C44	C45	C4.
Multi-vehicle	C51	C52	C53	C54	C55	C5.
Total	C.1	C.2	C.3	C.4	C.5	C

Now if C_m and C_{nm} represent the costs in the Melbourne Statistical Division (MSD) and rest of Victoria respectively, then the total road accident cost for Victoria is given by:

$$C_v = C_m + C_{nm} \qquad (13.2)$$

Similarly, a bi-variate frequency table and an average cost matrix can be constructed respectively by replacing with an appropriate frequency and an average accident cost in the (ij)th cell as follows.

If n_{ij} represents the number of ith type of accident having jth level of injury severity, then the total number of accidents of ith accident type and jth level of injury severity is respectively given by:

$$n_{i.} = \sum_j n_{ij} \text{ and } n_{.j} = \sum_i n_{ij}$$

Thus the total number of accidents is estimated by:

$$n = \sum_{i,j} n_{ij} = \sum_i n_{i.} = \sum_j n_{.j} \qquad (13.3)$$

Further, if n_m and n_{nm} represent the number of accidents in MSD and rest of Victoria, then the total number of road accidents in Victoria is given by:

$$n_v = n_m + n_{nm} \qquad (13.4)$$

Lastly, if $\overline{C}_{ij}$ stands for the average cost of ith type of accident and jth level of injury severity, then the average cost of ith type of accident and jth level of injury severity are respectively defined by:

$$\overline{C}_{i.} = \frac{\sum_j n_{ij} \overline{C}_{ij}}{n_{i.}} \text{ and } \overline{C}_{.j} = \frac{\sum_i n_{ij} \overline{C}_{ij}}{n_{.j}}$$

Consequently the overall average cost of an accident is estimated by:

$$\overline{C} = \frac{\sum_{i,j} n_{ij} \overline{C}_{ij}}{n} = \frac{\sum_i n_{i.} \overline{C}_{i.}}{n} = \frac{\sum_j n_{.j} \overline{C}_{.j}}{n} \qquad (13.5)$$

If $\overline{C}_m$ and $\overline{C}_{nm}$ represent an average cost of an accident for MSD and rest of Victoria, then the overall average cost of an accident in Victoria is given by:

$$\overline{C}_v = \frac{n_m \overline{C}_m + n_{nm} \overline{C}_{nm}}{n_m + n_{nm}} \qquad (13.6)$$

In short, using equations (13.1), (13.2), (13.3), (13.4), (13.5) and (13.6), the information needs of various RTA research projects for total number of accidents, total and average accident cost estimates are summarized in Table 13.2.

COST OR ROAD ACCIDENTS

Table 13.2: Total Number of Accidents Including Total and Average Cost of Accident Types and Injury Severity Levels in MSD and Rest of Victoria

Accident Type		Melbourne Statistical Division					Total	Rest of Victoria					Total
		Injury Severity Level						Injury Severity Level					
		F	HA	MT (j^{th})	PDO			F	HA	MT (j^{th})	PDO		
					Rep	NRep					Rep	NRep	
Pedestrian	Number												
	Average cost												
	Total cost												
Motor-cycle	Number												
	Average cost												
	Total cost												
Bicycle (i^{th})	Number			n_{ij}			$N_{i.}$			–			–
	Average cost			$\overline{C}_{ij}$			$\overline{C}_{i.}$			–			–
	Total cost			C_{ij}			$C_{i.}$			–			–
Single Vehicle	Number												
	Average cost												
	Total cost												
Multi-Vehicle	Number												
	Average cost												
	Total cost												
Total	Number			$n_{.j}$			n_{m}			–			n_{nm}
	Average cost			$\overline{C}_{.j}$			$\overline{C}_{m}$			–			$\overline{C}_{nm}$
	Total cost			$C_{.j}$			C_{m}			–			C_{nm}
Victoria		$n_v = n_m + n_{nm}$ $\overline{C}_v = \overline{C}_m + \overline{C}_{nm}$ $C_v = C_m + C_{nm}$											

Notes: F   = Fatality
        HA   = Hospital admission
        MT   = Medical treatment
        PDO   = Property damage only
        REP   = Reported to police
        NREP   = Not reported to police
        –   = stands for rest of Victoria for the corresponding symbol of MSD.

13.6 Sources of Information

The number of accidents in various injury severity levels with the exception of non-police reported property damage could only be obtained from the RTA casualty accident file (form 513A). The latter information can be collected from the State Insurance Office (SIO) and other private motor insurance companies.

The total and/or the average cost of an accident can be collected from statistical records of a number of organisations such as MAB, SIO, RTA/Police, Courts, private insurance companies, government and non-government employers. In some cases, a survey may be conducted to collect information.

It should be noted that the MAB use an injury classification scale (ICDA-9) and not an injury severity scale as classified for our purposes. Conversion of ICDA-9 classification to our injury severity scale is a difficult but feasible. Similarly, other types of injury classifications used by various organisations can be expressed in our injury severity scales.10

13.7 Conclusions

The recommended method of estimating road traffic accident cost is based on an ex-post method. A new and readily enumerated method of measurement for 'intangible', cost is suggested. Calculations of total and average costs are based on a matrix approach using official statistical records of different organisations. Injury classifications can be converted to our injury severity scales without difficulty. This approach promises to open a new era in research into estimating the cost of road accidents in Victoria, which is followed to estimate road traffic accident cost for Bangladesh (2003) for its future transport planning.

Notes

1 There is a huge literature dealing with cost of road accidents among which Al-Masaeid *et al.* (1999), BRTE(2000), Chin *et al.* (2003, 2006), ICBC (1995), Elvik (1995), Miller et.al (1997), Morden (1989),Todd Litman (2004), Economics Circle (2005), Tervonen (1999) and Sarkar (2006) are important.

2 The Pareto principle asserts that at least one person in the community gains with nobody else losing, so that a social gain is assured.

3 Faigin formed an ex-post cost matrix of order 11 x 7, consisting of eleven categories of social and economic costs attributed to road accidents, where each category is decomposed into seven classes according to the Abbreviated Injury Scale (AIS), 6 and Property Damage Only.

4 Richardson (1983) however argued through the zero-sum-game that the total value of social cost of accidents is not necessarily higher than the ex-post: cost as presently calculated for Australia.

5 See Johnes Jones-Lee (1976), and Hills (1981) for more details of these methods.

6 Putignano and Pennisi (1999) estimated social costs of road accidents for Italy. Hijar *et al.* (2004) undertook an epidemiological cost analysis for urban areas of Mexico.

7 Social satisfaction is multidimensional and there is a 'trade-off', between human loss and monetary gain. Their well-being is a set of items which do not trade off each other since there ... is no functional relationship between them. Collard also expressed a similar view in a review of Pearce (1978).

8 The Court's decision may be based on ad-hoc or any one of the above methods to evaluate the compensation for the dependents of the victim.

9 Arkins (1982) mentioned that separate accident costs could be modelled by different versions of the gamma distribution.

10 A number of experts (including Atkins) indicated that the conversion of ICDA – 9 and other injury classification used by MAB and other organizations to our injury severity scale would not be difficult.

CHAPTER 14

RISK ANALYSIS IN ROAD SAFETY

At a time of strict budget constraint, the government and the road safety administrators are faced with complex and controversial decisions, requiring the assessment of various road safety programs and balancing of imperfectly known/unknown risks, costs and benefits. This chapter shows how the quantitative decision-making approaches can be used to choose the 'best' option among various alternatives. The definition and the underlying concepts of risk, cost and benefit are also presented in reasonably non-technical terms so that decision-makers and government officials can understand the merits of such approaches in any decision-making process.

14.1 Introduction

As time passes, mobility increases with the rising standard of living due to economic development. In many respects, this rising mobility creates an unprecedented magnitude of man-made catastrophes on roads due to accidents. Moreover, we now want to drive more and want to make our lives even safer on our roads. Many road accidents are now considered to be under our control rather than an accident which is purely based on a chance factor. An accident is an unfortunate event that might occur to anyone at any time.

In order to measure the risk of accident, many recent attempts have been made to express risk in quantitative terms, which are not known to many decision makers and politicians of our society. As a result, some of our valuable road safety programs are wiped out by this lack of understanding.

The main objective of this chapter is to discuss the role of risk analysis in order to assess the various road safety programs, so that the most beneficial road safety programs to society are selected as opposed to various alternatives. However, for the sake of clarification, the definition and underlying concepts of risk analysis are discussed first.

14.2 Risk Analysis

In 1901, Willet defined risk as the objectified uncertainty regarding the occurrence of an undesirable event. More recently, Rowe (1988) defined risk as the potential for realization of unwanted negative consequences of an event. Risk aversion is an action taken to control risk. Risk can be minimised either by direct reduction of uncertainty or by intuitive perception of risk takers. Risk occurs under uncertainty.1 However, costs and benefits are certain and can be traded off against each other. Risk can be considered as a subset of cost, because risk adds a new dimension to the cost function.

14.2.1 Steps in Evaluating Risk

When a new project is undertaken to achieve some particular benefits to the society, a process to establish an acceptable level of risk is necessary. It involves four steps, which are given below.

(a) **Acceptable Risk Level:** An acceptable level of risk should be established for different types of risk consequences. An acceptable risk level should be determined independently irrespective of the activity to be evaluated.

(b) **Evaluation of Risk Associated with the New Program and Alternatives:** Identification and estimation of the overall risk involved in the new program and possible alternatives should be undertaken.

(c) **Compare the Overall Risk of the New Program and Various Alternatives:** In order to find the best option, it is necessary to find the risk of the new program and various alternative programs. Cost-benefit analyses should then be undertaken for those alternatives whose risks are within the acceptable range. On the basis of these cost-benefit results, it is then be decided which alternative should be selected. If the estimated risk is greater than the acceptable level of risk, then either abandon the program or follow risk aversive action.

(d) **Risk Aversive Action:** If risk is unacceptable, then alternative programs of lower level of risk should be sought. These alternatives may include increased safety, decreased exposure or other means of road accident risk reduction.

Further reduction of risk to a level as low as practicable can be sought, if the risk is acceptable. Many methods are available to follow the above steps, which are not discussed here as they are discussed elsewhere such as Rowe (1988).

14.2.2 Components of Risk

There are two major components in risk analysis, viz.: (i) the existence of possible unwanted consequences; and (ii) an uncertainty in the occurrence of that consequence, which can be expressed in the form of a probability. The probability may be derived from the probable behaviour of opponents and/or nature. The magnitude of a probability depends on the magnitude of a consequential effect. It is the latter topic, which is selected here for discussion in order to make decision for any road safety program.

14.3 Test of Hypothesis

In order to compare the risk with the referent within the limits of errors of the estimate and referent, statistical hypothesis testing is essential, which is a key element in Statistics. It concerns with the behaviour of observable random variables. There are two types of hypotheses, viz., *Null Hypothesis* (H_0) is that hypothesis which is to be tested for all possible rejection under the assumption that the hypothesis is true, or in other words, it is a statement of no difference or improvement; and *Alternative Hypothesis* (H_1) is any hypothesis other than the *Null Hypothesis*. The problem of constructing a test of Null Hypothesis for the problem under discussion is really the problem of choosing a critical region for the test.

14.3.1 Critical Region

To test any hypothesis, on the basis of a random sample of observations, we must divide the sample space (W) into two regions, viz., (i) critical region (c) and (ii) non-critical region (W-c). If the observation sample point X falls into one of these regions, say 'c' we will reject the hypothesis. On the other hand if X falls into the complementary region (W-c), we will not reject the null hypothesis. In this case 'c' is called the *critical region* of the test, and (W-c) is called the *non-critical region*.

14.3.2 Type I and Type II Errors

As a result of testing certain hypothesis on the basis of sample values, two kinds of errors may occur. In statistics, these are popularly known as *Type I* and *Type II* error. There are four possible situations, which usually arise in any test procedure and these are shown below.

Hypothesis	Decision	
	Accept	Reject
H_0 is true	Correct	Wrong (*Type I* error)
H_0 is false	Wrong (*Type II* error)	Correct

In the above illustration, a decision-maker makes a correct decision if one (i) accepts H_0 when H_0 is true, and (ii) rejects H_0 when H_0 is false. The person commits (iii) Type I error if he rejects H_0 when H_0 is true, and (iv) Type II error if he accepts H_0 when H_0 is false. This distinction is very important, because the importance of the two errors is different, and this difference must be taken into consideration when selecting the appropriate test.

In the road safety field, the probabilities of Type 1 (α) and Type II (β) errors can be called as decision-maker's risk and road-users risk respectively. This is because, suppose a road safety administrator has implemented a certain road safety program, which reduces a desirable number of road casualty, but if the sample information shows that there is no road casualty reduction then he may abandon the project. By abandoning the project, he is putting himself into a great loss. Hence, this is a risk to him and he will always try to put his risk as low as possible.

On the contrary, suppose that a road safety administrator implemented a bad road safety countermeasure program, which increases the road toll but the sample observations may indicate that it reduces road casualty substantially. By continuing this project the road users would be put into a great loss. Hence, the probability of Type II error (β) represents the road user's risk.

An inverse relationship between the probabilities of *Type I error* (α) and *Type II error* (β) error exists, i.e. probability of *Type I error* (α) can be reduced by increasing the probability of *Type II error* (β) and vice-versa. The following figure can illustrate the situation more clearly.

Figure 14.1: Construction of Decision Rule to Control α and β Risks, Large Sample, One-sided Upper Tail Test

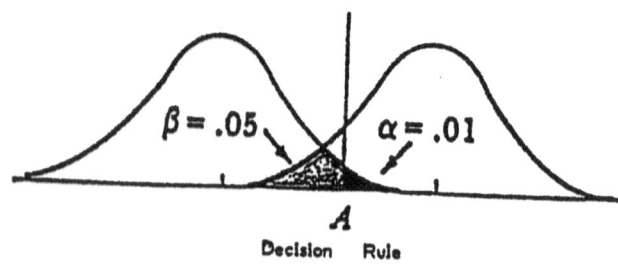

Most road safety administrators are more worried about the Type I error and try to ignore *Type II error*. Campbell (1974) mentioned that the probability of *Type II error* (β) error is rather high for most highway safety program evaluation. Hence many effective programs are disbanded due to lack of statistical significance observed from sample data. In the opinion of the author of this book, it

RISK ANALYSIS IN ROAD SAFETY

is essential to follow the principle of minimising the probabilities of both types of errors before any decision is made about the fate of a given road safety program.

Principle: 'The principle of minimising the probabilities of both types of errors should be considered to evaluate the effectiveness of any road safety program'.

Dietz (1967) has demonstrated how the expected cost varies with the *Type I* and *Type II* errors. For example, he first searched the probability of *Type II error* for various values of probability of *Type I error* and find the most optimum value for the probability of *Type II error* (i.e. $\beta = 0.20$). He then obtained various expected costs for different values of α.

$$\begin{aligned}\text{Cost} &= \$192 \text{ when } \alpha = 0.01; \\ &= \$182 \text{ when } \alpha = 0.05; \text{ and} \\ &= \$210 \text{ when } \alpha = 0.10.\end{aligned}$$

Thus, $\alpha = 0.05$ would be preferred over $\alpha = 0.01$ or 0.10.

He however admitted that the values of (α, β) that minimizes expected errors and costs could be quite different for other values of costs, prior success probabilities, and initial number of accidents, etc. He then advocated to using the utility theory approach in any decision-making process. It is essential to gain government support to use 'utility theory approach', for risk analysis in road safety areas.

14.4 Utility Theory and Decision-Making Process 2

Many important decisions involve risks to the road safety of the public. It is very useful to analyse explicitly the alternatives in terms of their risks and other implications. In order to do this, one needs to quantify and evaluate the possible risks for each separate alternative. The focus of this section is on the evaluation of such risks.

The main purpose of any analysis of road accident risk is to provide better advice to various decision-making authorities. In the long-term, better decision means fewer lives being lost on the road, the quality of life being improved, and a lessening of the economic and social justice to the citizens of the country. Analysis affects decision making in the short-run, but it is assumed that better informed decision-making in the short run would ultimately lead to better results in the long run.

The overall interest of any road safety research is to assist in identifying appropriate actions given the risks and costs of various alternatives. Thus, the risk analysis is concerned with the relative desirability of spending different sums of money to reduce road casualty risk. This kind of analysis requires indices of costs and risks as arguments. Thus, the process necessarily involves value judgments. In this respect, the author proposes to consider a number of value judgment options that fit the situation. The implication for various alternative assumptions would then be examined on the basis of the resulting indices.

The ex-anti approach would be an appropriate method of estimating risks where numerous individuals are at risk. This means we have to estimate risks before any casualty occurs. Our main interest is in casualty risk, which may happen because of road accidents. Hence the problem may be expressed as:

$$P = (p_1, p_2, \ldots\ldots\ldots\ldots, p_N),$$

where p_i is the risk to individual i, and N is the total number of individuals who are at risk.

It is noted that p_i will be the probability if individual i is a casualty in the time period of concern due to the cause of concern. This probability is independent of all the other probabilities in the risk profile. A risk profile can characterise a situation before the accident in which casualties could occur. At the end of the period, each individual will either be or not be a casualty due to the cause of concern. Thus, we will define attribute X_i to take on levels X_i and equal to 1 or 0 depending on whether ith individual was or was not a casualty. Then a casualty profile can be written by:

$$X = (X_1, X_2, \ldots\ldots\ldots\ldots, X_N)$$

From time to time, it is good to record the information about how many casualties occur. Let us denote the attribute A to be the number of casualties and 'a' to be a specific level of A. Then clearly:

$$a = X_1 + X_2 + \ldots\ldots\ldots\ldots + X_N$$

Now let us suppose that C would denote the cost that one might wish to spend to reduce casualty risk. Thus, overall the situation could be expressed as:

$$(P, C) = (p_1, p_2, \ldots\ldots, p_N, C)$$

Thus, the main problem for estimating casualty risk is to find an appropriate utility function U, which assigns the utility U (P; C) to each possible consequence (P; C). On the basis of the utility theory, outcomes of higher utilities should be preferred over the lower utilities and when uncertainty is involved, higher expected utilities should be preferred over the lower expected utilities.

Now suppose that our utility function is separable i.e.:

$$U(P; C) = G[U_r(P), U_c(C)] \qquad (14.1)$$

where G is any function, U_r is the utility function for casualty risks and U_c is the utility function for costs. For simplicity, let us assume the above utility function (14.1) for risks and costs is additive, i.e.:

$$U(P, C) = U_r(P) + \lambda U_c(C) \qquad (14.2)$$

where λ is the Lagrange multiplier to make sure that U_r and Uc are consistently scaled, and C is evaluated in millions of dollars.

Therefore, the aim should be to minimise the above utility function (14.2) in order to attain maximum satisfaction subject to the budget constraint.

14.5 Conclusions

Use of the models requires careful deliberation of several value judgments. First, the general structure of the problem should be appropriately identified. Second, one must incorporate the appropriate value judgments necessary to structure the utility function U. For example, in this chapter we assume that the utility function (14.1) is additive for casualty risks and costs. This assumption could easily be relaxed without loosing any generality of the idea. Third, even if a particular functional form is found to be appropriate, parameters for that utility function or value function must be assessed in the light of reality.

It is evident from the discussion that seemingly reasonable assumptions can lead to a compatible utility function for casualty risks.

It should be noted that the utility function (14.1) described above contains many objective functions, such as: (i) to minimise casualty; (ii) to avoid fatalities; (iii) to maximise ex-post equality; and many others. A multi-attribute utility function could be constructed to reflect concern for each of these objectives. Among the individual components, there might be inconsistencies, but collectively the resultant utility function could represent an overall value and include the appropriate value trade-offs to address the inconsistencies.

14.5.1 Recommendations

It is recommended that the road safety decision-makers, government officials and politicians should adopt the quantitative decision-making approaches in order to choose the 'best' programs to be implemented before any public funds are allocated for road safety programs. Also, the principle of minimising the probability of both *Type I error* (α) and *Type II error* (β) should be considered before any decision being made about the fate of a given road safety program.

Notes

1 Schagen and Janssen (2000) discussed how to manage road transport risks in a sustainable society such as the Netherlands, while Haque et al. (2006) estimated the risk of children in road traffic accidents in Bangladesh. Peden et al. (20002) reviewed the global burden of injuries from back injuries.

2 Note that Keeney (1986) had adopted similar approach for the analysis of risks of fatalities.

CHAPTER 15

CONCLUSIONS

In this chapter, we summarise the main findings and make some concluding remarks about the contributions of this book. Here we discuss and develop a number of statistical techniques and methods which can be used to collect, monitor, evaluate and analyse road accident data. These methods are then applied to the Victorian road accident data to illustrate the usefulness of these methods, showing how to reduce the number of road casualties and cost of road accidents. It is argued here that many countries can save many lives and road casualties with associated costs by following the road safety techniques and methods provided in this book.

15.1 Introduction

This book is mainly concerned with road accident data collection, analysis, monitoring and evaluating implemented road safety legislations. As such it is shown here how to collect, analyse, monitor and evaluate implemented road safety laws, using Victorian (Australian) data. First, we have shown that collecting road casualty data is a difficult task and as such it is discussed here how to collect accurate and complete road casualty data for developing road safety initiatives for certain target group drivers and motor cyclists, and these are presented in Section 15.2. Section 15.3 is mainly concerned with how to monitor short-term road casualty data in order to determine any deviation from its regular patterns, so that quick remedial actions can be taken if the situation deteriorates. Section 15.4 deals with the evaluations of some implemented road safety legislations. It also discusses if any implemented legislation fails to reduce road casualties, and investigates the causes for such failures and tries to make recommendations on what actions can be further taken to make these laws work to reduce the road toll. Casual relationships of road accidents and economic activities together with costs of road accidents are presented in Section 15.5. Finally, a few concluding remarks of the book are given in Section 15.6.

15.2. Road Safety Data Collection

Accurate and complete road accident data collection is very important for proper planning and making strategies to reduce road toll. Many organizations collect road casualty data such as the Road Traffic Authority, Transport Accident Commission, Hospitals, Ambulances, Tow-truck Allocation organizations, etc., for their own uses. However, data collected by these organizations are not only different in magnitude, but they also differ in direction, even though they all should coincide with each other. It is extensively discussed here how one can produce accurate and complete road casualty data, using various sources of road accident data to make proper road safety strategies to reduce road casualties.

This book also deals with how to collect population and road casualty data for a small geographical area, where certain categories of people (old, young or poor) live. This will enable researchers to analyse the incidence of road accidents for small geographical areas, and can be used to compare with the national average to find any significant differences and can take necessary actions if it exists.

A simple model of estimating sample size is an important part of collecting transport exposure and road accident data, which is presented in Chapter 4. It provides statistical formulas for estimating sample size based on various levels of differences between the mean accident-rates of two types of motorcycle engines expressed as a percentage of overall average accidents, using exposure data. It shows that reduced sample size is required if the difference between accident rates of two types of engines is large when expressed as percentage of overall accidents. It also provides techniques to compare the differences of two sample proportions and estimating sample size related to the power of a test, which are important to detect any significant difference of the performances of two types of cars, modes and/or road user types.

15.3 Short-term Road Accident Monitoring System

Short-term accident monitoring provides a timely and accurate picture of any changes in levels rather than the level *per se* of road safety. In this book we have shown how to monitor the road accident situation, using monthly road fatality data. Here, we compare the current month's total road fatalities with the same month's figure of last year and/or the average figure of the last five years of certain road user types according to various age and sex groups. We also developed a technique to see whether the current month's road fatality trend deviates from the expected trend based on historical data, which is bounded by the 95% confidence limits. If any current month's road fatality number exceeds the upper limit then the causes of such behaviour will immediately be investigated and remedial actions are taken to bring the road toll within tolerable limits. Further, this book also developed a new technique of road accident monitoring system by plotting the actual number of monthly road casualty numbers of certain type against expected numbers based on historical data bounded by 95% upper and lower limits, using tow-truck data. This will enable policy makers to see whether the current trend of road casualties differs from the expected trends and to find out whether the current road casualty numbers are within the tolerable limits or not. This will help to know the current road accident situation, if it goes beyond the tolerable limits.

15.4 Evaluation of Road Safety Legislations

Road safety initiatives can be taken based on the findings of these monitoring system for certain events, timing and road user types. Based on such a monitoring system, Victorian police initiated reducing the road toll at the time of Christmas, Easter, the Queen's Birthday and other public events when historically road casualties are high, by showing their presence on the roads. The analysis shows that this extra measure, i.e., their presence during these events, could reduce road casualties significantly compared to no police presence on the road. Therefore regular monitoring of road accidents and taking remedial actions in the appropriate ways does help to reduce road accidents.

Governments often introduce road safety legislations to reduce road casualties. However, introducing legislation in papers does not always work, and for that reason it is essential to evaluate implemented road safety legislations. Evaluating the effect of such implemented legislations needs special methods. These are many methods to measure the effect of implemented laws among which the pre-post method and the intervention time series analysis are important. These methods are used to evaluate the Victorian Motorcycle Rider Training and License scheme, Random Breath Testing Campaign and Zero BAC legislations. It is shown that these road safety legislations have significant effect in reducing road accidents in Victoria. It can thus be concluded that the implementation of these laws in other countries can significantly reduce the road toll. Sometimes it is not possible to find any significant effect due to lack of information and low power of the test. In those cases we have to investigate the matter further and try to find out the causes for such insignificant results. The absence of any significant effect may be caused due to the lack of specific enforcement, on-going mass media publicity campaigns supporting the legislation and the pre existing decreasing trend involving target groups. All these are analysed and discussed extensively in this book to measure the effect of implemented road safety legislations, which can be used to make proper transport exposure and traffic safety laws for the future development of any country.

The demerit points system (DPS) is another popular way to reduce road casualties. In this book we develop a statistical model to measure the effect of the DPS in Victoria. It is shown in this book that most of the deterrent effect reflected in the increased mean time until the third offence subsequent to the first and second offences detected was less than three years apart. This technique can also be used by many countries to reduce traffic offences which ultimately decreases the number of road accidents.

15.5 Casual Relationships between Road Accidents and Economic Activities and Costs of Road Accidents

Many road safety experts such as Partyka (1984), Evans and Graham (1988 and Legget (1990) have shown that these exists a relationship between business activity and road fatalities. It is also demonstrated in Chapter 12 that the effect of unemployment has a strong negative relationship with road fatalities even after controlling fuel sales and road safety countermeasure initiatives. A statistical model has been developed which can forecast the road toll for future years based on predicted change in the economy, and social and other factors, assuming the road safety activity would remain constant. Thus it can assist road safety policy makers to make decisions about how to use limited funds to achieve maximum benefit by targeting more risky road user groups in the event of economic growth. It is clear from our analysis that the performance of the economy exerts a powerful influence on traffic casualties.

Accurate costing of road accidents is important for appropriate road safety planning and using limited road safety money appropriately. There are several methods to estimate the cost of road accidents all of which are subject to criticisms. We have surveyed the literature on the cost of road accidents and developed a framework in estimating these costs, encompassing all costs associated with 'tangible, intangible and the value of life', which is presented in Chapter 13. It is thus expected to produce a more accurate cost of road accidents, because it is based on actual observations which were actually costed after the road accident. This estimated cost of road accidents will help to improve road safety strategies that will ultimately reduce road toll.

15.6 Concluding Remarks

In this book we have demonstrated that there are several organizations collecting road casualty data, none of which are correct and complete. In fact they not only differ in magnitude but also differ in direction. For that reason, in this book we have demonstrated how to collect accurate and complete road casualty data which are important to make necessary road safety laws, improving vehicle safety and designing better roads, all of which can reduce road accidents.

A short-term accident monitoring system is another mechanism often used by road safety administrators in order to detect any deviation of the current road accident trend from the established trend based on historical data. If the current trend of road accidents differs from that of the historical trend, then remedial

CONCLUSIONS

actions are taken quickly in order to bring the road casualty numbers within limits. Thus a new short-term road accident monitoring system is developed in this book based on monthly tow-truck allocation data which can provide an actual situation of road accidents in Victoria. In addition to this technique, monthly road fatality numbers are also used to monitor the road casualty situation by comparing the current month's road fatalities with the same month's road fatalities of the previous year and an average figure based on the last five years for various road user types. These are important to develop various road safety initiatives in order to reduce road accidents. It is better to mention that these techniques can also be used to monitor other socio-economic determinants to develop social and economic conditions of people in the society.

In this book we have evaluated several important road safety legislations using sophisticated intervention time series analysis in addition to the widely used pre-post method. The intervention time series method is more appropriate when there does exist any pre-legislation trend similar to the expected direction of the outcome resulted from the implemented legislation. Three most important Victorian legislations, Victorian Motorcycle Rider Training and License Scheme, Random Breath Testing Campaign and Zero BAC legislations are evaluated by using time series methods. The first two showed significant reduction of traffic accidents, but the zero BAC legislation showed a smaller non-significant effect due to lack of power of the test caused by the absence of media campaigns and other factors. Evaluation of the implemented road safety laws are important to know whether the laws are working or not, if not then proper investigations need to be made to find out the causes of the laws not working. These are important to make proper safety strategies in order to reduce the road toll.

We have also evaluated the DPS system by using a newly developed statistical model, showing that the deterrent effect reflected in the increased mean time until the third offence subsequent to the first and second offences detected was less than three years apart. This technique can also be used by many other countries to reduce traffic offences which ultimately decrease the number of road accidents.

A statistical model is also developed in this book which showed that there is a strong negative relationship between road casualties and unemployment. This can forecast the road toll for future years based on predicted change in the economy, social and other factors. Thus, it can assist road safety policy makers to take decisions about how to use limited road safety funds to reduce road accidents by targeting more risky road users in the event of economic growth.

A review of literature on the cost of road accidents is also presented in this book. It is expected to give an accurate cost of road accidents, which may help to improve and target appropriate road safety strategies that might ultimately reduce the road toll.

Finally, risk analysis in road safety is discussed in Chapter 14. It is written with the aim to show how the quantitative decision making approaches can be used to choose the 'best' road safety strategy among various alternatives.

CONCLUSIONS

The research which was undertaken as a contribution to our knowledge of an important sector of transport system has special practical aims in mind. It is hoped that the findings will be of interest to many whose concerns are not only road accident data collection, analyses, monitoring and countermeasure evaluation but also academic. It is also hoped that much of the materials presented in this book should not only be of interest to road safety administrators, community and political leaders and academicians but also should be of interest from market research point of view, while the evaluation of various road safety legislations and risks in road safety are important for making proper road safety strategies in order to save lives and injuries of our people.

The present book should be regarded as indicative of the type of problem that may be solved in road safety discipline, using statistical methods for road casualty data. The results presented in this book are thus in the nature of a series of pieces of research, which are based on Victorian data, but attempts to add bricks here and there and end with the hope that other road safety researchers will undertake further research to complete the rest of the tasks. More importantly, many statistical/econometric techniques developed and presented in this book can also be used in health, market research, humanities, social, business, engineering and many other disciplines.

APPENDICES

Appendix 1A: Road Safety Legislations Introduced in Victoria

Many road safety countermeasures have been introduced in Victoria since 1960 in order to reduce Victorian road toll among which the following are important.

1A.1 Countermeasures Based on Legislations and Its Enforcement, and Education and Engineering Improvements with Date of Commencement of Legislations

- Roadworthiness of motor vehicles (October 1968)

- Points Demerit System (April 1969)

- Compulsory breath tests for motorcar drivers suspected of having a blood alcohol content in excess of 0.05 per cent (September 1970)

- Permits for Learner Drivers (April 1970)

- Absolute Speed Limits and Speed Zones (December 1971)

- Visual Average Speed Computer and Recorder (April 1972)

- Age of Driver Licensing (October 1972)

- Pedestrians and Street Lighting (March 1972)

- Fatalities and injuries involving children under eight who are unrestrained in motorcars (October 1975)

- Identification of motor vehicle drivers with blood alcohol levels in excess of 0.05 per cent (June 1976)

- Education, Training and Assessment of Motorcycle Learner Riders (October 1977)

- Restraint of children under eight in the rear seats of motorcars (April 1981)

- Alcohol prohibition for First-Year Drivers (May 1981)

- Compulsory motorcycle rider helmet wearing legislation (January 1961)

- Minimum penalties for drink-driving offences (1963)

APPENDICES

- Compulsory roadworthiness tests on resale (March 1964)

- Probationary License System includes automatic license cancellations for various offences during the first 3 years of licensing

- Seat belt anchorage requirement (October 1964)

- On the spot Traffic Infringement Notices (August 1965)

- Blood Alcohol limit of 0.05%

- Australian Design Rules (ADRs) for Motor Vehicle Safety (January 1969)

- Safety Glass (ADR8) (July 1971)

- P-plate and speed Limit for First year probationary license holders (March 1969)

- Points Demerit System includes license suspension at 12 points and warning letter sent to motorists who accumulated 6 points (May 1970)

- Compulsory Seat belt wearing legislation (December 1970)

- Absolute Speed Limit (70 mph) (January 1972)

- Reduced Absolute Speed limit (60 mph/ 100 km/h) (January 1974)

- Compulsory blood alcohol testing of road accident victims attending hospitals (April 1974)

- School crossing Supervisor Scheme (December 1974)

- Roundabout sign regulation (January 1976)

- Random Breath Testing Legislation (July 1976)

- Increased Penalties for Drink-Driving Offences (December 1978)

- Rader Speed detector (December 1981)

- Random checks (mid 1982)

- Motorcycle learner permit training and testing program (June 1983)

- Mandatory disqualification for exceeding speed limit by 30 km/h (December 1983)

- Zero BAC for novice drivers, and mandatory alcohol education course (May 1984)

- Red Light Cameras (August 1983)

- Power of court to cancel, suspend or vary license or permit for speeding offences [over 130 km/hr or 30 km/hr over the limit], (November 1989)

- Cancellation of license or permit for drink driving offences (May 1991)

- Speed cameras introduced (December 1989)

- Bicycle helmet wearing law (July 1990)

- Introduce new breath analyzing instrument, alcotest 7110 (August 1994)

- Zero BAC for taxi drivers (July 1995)

- Enable 40 or 50 km/hr speed limits in local traffic precincts (December 1995)

- Adopt regime for management of fatigue among drivers of commercial buses and trucks (February 1996)

- Provide for the mandatory suspension of the registration of speeding heavy vehicles as part of an agreed national uniform scheme (June 1998)

- Introduces 3 new speed measuring devices: the DCD ROBOT Digital Smart Camera, the Poltech Safe-Cam Red Light/Speed Mk 1, and the REDFLEX red-speed system, and provides regulations relating to their use and testing (July 2003)

1A.2 Non-legislative Countermeasures

- Pre-Driver Education (1967)

- Media Campaigns: Motorcycle Conspicuity, Drink-driving, child restrain (1977-1979)

- Bicycle helmet Promotion (November 1982)

- Driver Improvement Program (March 1982)

Appendix 3A: Emergency Road Trauma Admissions Public Hospital Morbidity Data

3A.1 Public Hospital Morbidity Data

Includes: Any person processed through the formal admission procedures of the hospital, which is recorded as an emergency admission resulting from injuries received in a road accident

Excludes: Any person attending the casualty or accident and emergency department of a hospital who is not admitted (i.e. sent home after treatment); People who die at the scene of accident; People who die prior to arrival at hospital (i.e. in ambulance); Planned admissions to hospitals

Appendix 4A: Comparison of Two Sample Proportion and Estimation of Sample Size for Road Accident Data Analysis

This appendix provides a technique to compare the differences of two sample proportions. It also shows how to estimate required sample sizes and in estimating the power of a test associated with a study involving pre-specified sample size.

In the past, a number of authors such as Transport Research Laboratory (1999), Wilde (1984), Hauer (1995), Li *et al.* (2001), West (1997), Levitt and Porter (2001), Scheers *et al.* (1991), Redondo-Calderon *et al.* (2001), Chipman *et al.* (1993), Massie *et al.* (1995) and Van and Martin (1993) have estimated traffic accident involvement rates by road user types, age, gender and vehicle types. Some of them also estimated the required sample sizes to undertake a valid statistical test for the differences of two sample means and proportions.1

The present study however goes beyond the boundaries of the existing methods and develops a technique to compare the differences of two sample proportions, as well as showing how to calculate the required sample size when the power of the test is incorporated.

Suppose that the proportions found in two samples are p_1 and p_2. The statistic used for testing the significance of difference for large samples of equal sizes is given below (ignoring the continuity correction):

$$Z = \frac{p_1 - p_2}{\sqrt{\left(2\bar{p}\bar{q}/n\right)}} \qquad (4A.1)$$

where $\bar{p} = 1/2\,(p_1 + p_2)$ and

$\bar{q} = 1 - \bar{p}$

From equation (4A.1), we can write the following expression:

$$Z^2 = \frac{n\,(p_1 - p_2)^2}{2\bar{p}\bar{q}}$$

$$= \frac{n(p_1 - p_2)^2}{(p_1+p_2)\left(1 - \frac{p_1+p_2}{2}\right)} \qquad (4A.2)$$

for small proportions (4A.2) can be approximated as:

$$Z^2 = \frac{n(p_1 - p_2)^2}{(p_1+p_2)} \quad \text{if the proportions are negligible.}$$

$$Z = \frac{\sqrt{n}(p_1 - p_2)}{\sqrt{(p_1+p_2)}} \qquad (4A.3)$$

To assure that the probability of a type I error is α, the difference between p_1 and p_2 will be declared significant only if:

$$|Z| > C\alpha/2 \qquad (4A.4)$$

where $C\alpha/2$ denotes the value cutting off the proportion $\alpha/2$ in the upper tail of the standard normal curve and $|Z|$ is the absolute value of Z, which is always ≥ 0. For example if $\alpha = 0.05$ then $C_{0.05/2} = C_{0.025} = 1.96$.

If the difference between the underlying proportions is actually P_1 and P_2. We wish the chances to be $1 - \beta$ of rejecting the hypothesis, i.e., of having the outcome in (4A.4) actually occur. Thus we must find the value of n such that $P_1 - P_2$ is the difference between the proportions.

$$\Pr\left(\frac{|p_1 - p_2|}{\sqrt{2\bar{p}\bar{q}/n}} > C\alpha/2\right) = 1 - \beta \qquad (4A.5)$$

The probability in (4A.5) is the sum of two probabilities.

$$1-\beta = \Pr\left(\frac{p_1 - p_2}{\sqrt{(2\bar{p}\bar{q}/n)}} > C_{\alpha/2}\right) + \Pr\left(\frac{p_1 - p_2}{\sqrt{(2\bar{p}\bar{q}/n)}} < -C_{\alpha/2}\right) \quad (4A.6)$$

If P_1 is hypothesized to be greater than P_2 then the 2nd probability on the R.H.S. of (4A.6), representing the event that P_1 is appreciably less than P_2 is near zero. Thus we need only to find the value of n such that $P_1 - P_2$ is the actual difference:

$$1-\beta = \Pr\left(\frac{p_1 - p_2}{\sqrt{(2\bar{p}\bar{q}/n)}} > C_{\alpha/2}\right) \quad (4A.7)$$

The probability in (4A.7) cannot yet be evaluated because the mean and the standard error of $p_1 - p_2$ appropriate when $P_1 - P_2$ is the actual difference have not yet been taken into account. The mean of $(p_1 - p_2)$ is $(P_1 - P_2)$ and the standard error (S.E.) is given by:

$$S.E(p_1 - p_2) = \sqrt{\left(\frac{P_1 Q_1 + P_2 Q_2}{n}\right)} \quad (4A.8)$$

Where: $Q_1 = 1 - P_1$

and $Q_2 = 1 - P_2$

From (4A.7) we have:

$$1-\beta = \Pr\left((p_1 - p_2) > C_{\alpha/2}\sqrt{(2\bar{p}\bar{q}/n)}\right)$$

$$= \Pr\left((p_1 - p_2) - (P_1 - P_2) > C_{\alpha/2}\sqrt{(2\bar{p}\bar{q}/n)} - (P_1 - P_2)\right)$$

$$= \left[\frac{(p_1 - p_2) - (P_1 - P_2)}{\sqrt{\left(\frac{P_1 Q_1 + P_2 Q_2}{n}\right)}}\right] > C_{\alpha/2} \frac{\sqrt{(2\bar{p}\bar{q}/n)} - (P_1 - P_2)}{\sqrt{\left(\frac{P_1 Q_1 + P_2 Q_2}{n}\right)}} \quad (4A.9)$$

The final probability of (4A.9) can be evaluated using tables of normal distribution because:

$$Z = \frac{(p_1 - p_2) - (P_1 - P_2)}{\sqrt{\left(\frac{P_1 Q_1 + P_2 Q_2}{n}\right)}} \cong \text{normal distribution for large n.} \quad (4A.10)$$

Let $C_{1-\beta}$ denotes the value cutting off the proportion $1 - \beta$ in the upper tail and β in the lower tail of the standard normal curve. Then by definition:

$$1 - \beta = \Pr(Z > C_{1-\beta}) \qquad (4A.11)$$

By matching (4A.11) with the last probability of (4A. 9), we find that the value of "n" we seek is the one that satisfies:

$$C_{1-\beta} = \frac{C_{\alpha/2}\sqrt{(2\,\bar{p}\,\bar{q}/n)} - (P_1 - P_2)}{\sqrt{\left(\dfrac{P_1 Q_1 + P_2 Q_2}{n}\right)}}$$

$$= \frac{C_{\alpha/2}\sqrt{(2\,\bar{p}\,\bar{q})} - (P_1 - P_2)\sqrt{n}}{\sqrt{(P_1 Q_1 + P_2 Q_2)}} \qquad (4A.12)$$

It is noted that (4A.12) is a function not only of P_1 and P_2, which may be hypothesized by the investigator, but also of $\bar{p}\,\bar{q}$, which is observable only after the study is complete. If "n" is large $\bar{p}$ will be close to:

$$\bar{P} = \frac{P_1 + P_2}{2} \qquad (4A.13)$$

and similarly $\bar{p}\,\bar{q}$ will be close to $\bar{P}\bar{Q}$, where $\bar{Q} = 1 - \bar{P}$. Therefore, replacing $\sqrt{(2\,\bar{p}\,\bar{q})}$ in (4A.12) by $\sqrt{(2\,\bar{P}\,\bar{Q})}$ and solving for n we get:

$$n = \frac{\left(C_{\alpha/2}\sqrt{2\bar{P}\bar{Q}} - C_{1-\beta}\sqrt{P_1 Q_1 + P_2 Q_2}\right)^2}{(P_1 - P_2)^2} \qquad (4A.14)$$

to be the required sample size for each of two populations being compared when the continuity correction is not employed.

By incorporating the continuity correction only in the statistic (4A.3), Casagrande, Pike and Smith (1978) derived:

$$n^0 = \frac{n}{4}\left(1 + \sqrt{1 + \frac{4}{n\,|P_1 - P_2|}}\right)^2 \qquad (4A.15)$$

To a remarkable degree of accuracy (especially when n and $|P_1 - P_2|$ are such that $n |P_1 - P_2| \geq 4$; then

$$n^0 = n + \frac{2}{|P_1 - P_2|} \qquad (4A.16)$$

This result provided by Fleiss, Tytun and Ury (1980) is useful to estimate the required sample sizes and in estimating the power associated with a study involving prespecified sample sizes. Suppose that one can study no more than a total of 2n subjects. If the significance level is α and if the two underlying proportions are P_1 and P_2, then one can invert (4A.16) and (4A.14) to obtain:

$$C_{1-\beta} = \frac{C_{\alpha/2} \sqrt{2 \bar{P} \bar{Q}} - |P_1 - P_2| \sqrt{n_0 - \frac{2}{|P_1 - P_2|}}}{\sqrt{P_1 Q_1 + P_2 Q_2}} \qquad (4A.17)$$

As the equation defining the normal curve deviates corresponding to the power associated with the proposed sample sizes. Power can be taken from any available power table, which can be found in many statistical textbooks such as Cohen (1977).

Appendix 5A: Effects of Road Safety Campaigns on Road Fatalities

Figure 5A.1: Victorian Road Fatalities, Monthly Data Moving 12 Month Average

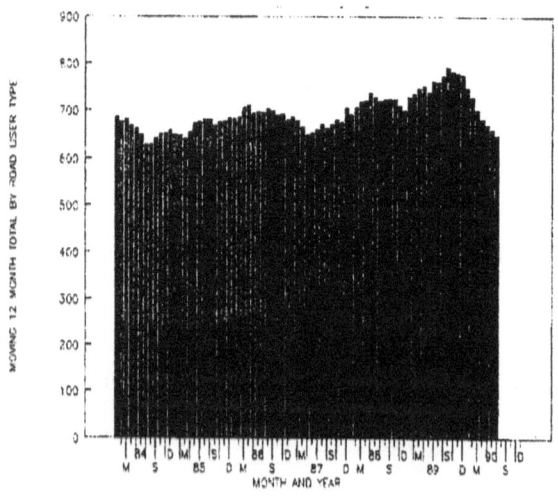

APPENDICES

Figure 5A.2: Speed Offences, Victorian Police Data Total Victoria, 1986 – 1990

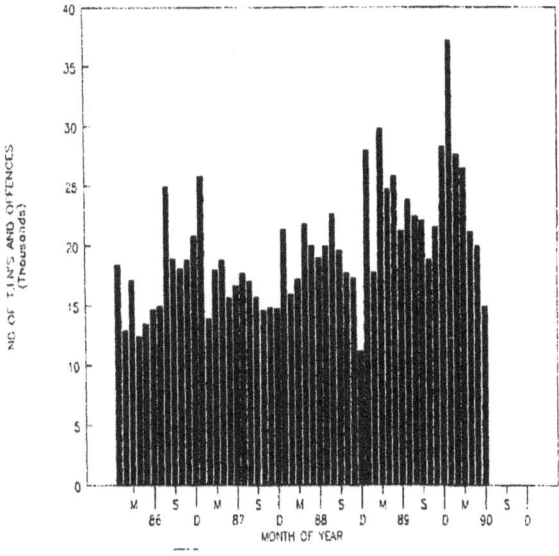

Figure 5A.3: Random Breath Testing, Monthly Data Total Victoria, 1984 – 1990

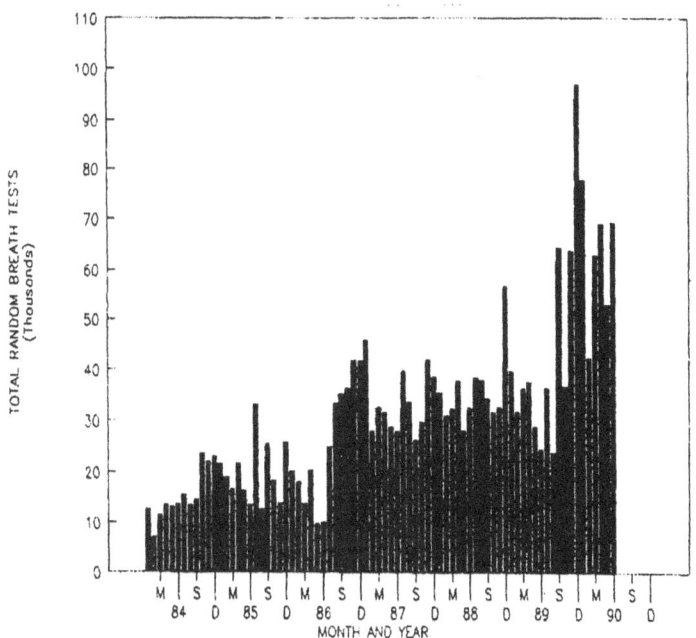

Figure 5A.4: Random Breath Tests, 12 Months Moving Average, 1984 – 1990

Appendix 6A: Forecasting Models

Raw data are not suitable to make an accurate forecast, because these data are highly variable. For that reason, we have to smooth the raw data in order to eliminate the variation from the raw data. There are many methods to smooth the data, viz., (i) Moving average smoothing, (ii) Exponential smoothing, and (iii) differencing the raw data. Smoothed data are then used to make accurate forecast. There are several classical forecasting methods, which are discussed below. Besides these methods there are some sophisticated modern forecasting methods such as the Box-Jinkins Univariate Forecasting Method, which will not be discussed here due to the scope of this book.

6A.1   Classical Forecasting Methods

The following classical forecasting methods are discussed here.

6A.1.1   Moving Average Forecasting Models

When a time series pattern does not exhibit rapid growth or seasonal characteristics, calculation of Moving Average may be useful in canceling out random fluctuations, so that reliable short-term forecasts can be generated. The method consists of averaging the available observations over a fixed period of time (period of repetition) and then using the calculated average as the forecast for the next observation. The formula of the Moving Average Forecasting Model is complex to express in symbol, but easy to demonstrate. For example, if the moving average period M = 5, the moving average forecasting formulae for one, two and three period lead forecast can be expressed below.

(i)   One-period Lead Forecast

$$\hat{Y}_{t+1} = \frac{Y_t + Y_{t-1} + Y_{t-2} + Y_{t-3} + Y_{t-4}}{5} \qquad (6A.1)$$

(ii) Two-period Lead Forecast

$$\hat{Y}_{t+2} = \frac{\hat{Y}_{t+1} + Y_t + Y_{t-1} + Y_{t-2} + Y_{t-3}}{5} \qquad (6A.2)$$

(iii) Three-period Lead Forecast

$$\hat{Y}_{t+3} = \frac{\hat{Y}_{t+2} + \hat{Y}_{t+1} + Y_t + Y_{t-1} + Y_{t-2}}{5} \qquad (6A.3)$$

Note that the two-period and three-period forecasts use prior forecasted values for calculation.

6A.2   Exponential Smoothing Forecasting Models

R. G. Brown developed the Exponential Smoothing Forecasting model. It is a popular forecasting procedure that offers two basic advantages, viz., (i) it provides forecasting values, and (ii) its data store requirements are small. There are three types of exponential smoothing forecasting models, which are given below.

6A.2.1   Single Parameter Exponential Forecasting Model

This basic exponential forecasting model provides the next period's forecast value from the current period's actual, and forecasted values based on the following formula:

$$F_{t+1} = \alpha Y_t + (1 - \alpha) F_t \qquad (6A.4)$$

where F_{t+1} is the forecast value for time (t + 1)

F_t is the forecast value for time t

Y_t is the actual value for time t

α is called the smoothing parameter, $0 \leq \alpha \leq 1$.

This procedure is usually applied when the time series data is constant over time. This method gives more and more weights to the more recent values, and gives less and less weights to the more and more remote values. This method can be modified at any time by changing the value of α.

6A.2.2 Two Parameter Exponential Smoothing Forecasting Model

The single parameter Exponential Smoothing Forecasting method fails to provide accurate forecast when there is a pronounced linear trend in the data. In that case, the two parameter exponential smoothing forecasting models should be used, which requires three equations given below. This method is popularly known as the Holt-Winters Forecasting Model.

$$T_t = \alpha Y_t + (1-\alpha)(T_{t-1} + b_{t-1}) \quad \text{(Getting trend by smoothing data)} \quad (6A.5)$$

$$b_t = \gamma(T_t - T_{t-1}) + (1-\gamma)b_{t-1} \quad \text{(Smoothing the slope in the trend)} \quad (6A.6)$$

$$F_{t+1} = T_t + b_t \quad \text{(Forecast)} \quad (6A.7)$$

where T_t = the smoothed value for period t
$T_t - T_{t-1}$ = the current slope in the trend
γ = Slope-smoothing constant; $0 \leq \gamma \leq 1$.

6A.2.3 Three Parameter Exponential Forecasting Model

The single and two parameter exponential forecasting models cannot handle data which has a seasonal component. In that case three parameter exponential forecasting model should be used, which requires the following four formulae.

$$T_t = \alpha\left(\frac{Y_t}{S_{t-p}}\right) + (1-\alpha)(T_{t-1} + b_t) \quad \text{(Getting trend by smoothing the data)} \quad (6A.8)$$

$$b_t = \gamma(T_t - T_{t-1}) + (1-\gamma)b_{t-1} \quad \text{(Smoothing the slope in the trend)} \quad (6A.9)$$

$$S_t = \beta\left(\frac{Y_t}{T_t}\right) + (1-\beta)S_{t-p} \quad \text{(Smooth the seasonal factor)} \quad (6A.10)$$

$$F_{t+1} = (T_t + b_t)S_{t-p+1} \quad \text{(Forecast)} \quad (6A.11)$$

Trend values can be obtained from equation (6A.8) which smoothes the past data. Here the current value Y_t is first deseasonalized by dividing Y_t by S_{t-p}, which implies that the seasonal factor is taken from p periods earlier. The letter p denotes the number of periods in a cycle, i.e., for monthly data p = 12 in a year; p = 7 in a weekly data, etc. The equation (6A.9) smoothes the slope in trend, while the equation (6A.10) smoothes the seasonal factor. Finally equation (6A.11) provides the forecasting values.

Knowledge of the types of sub patterns included in the data is important in selecting the most appropriate forecasting method, since different methods vary in their ability to cope with different types of patterns.

If the data are stationary, then moving average and/or simple exponential smoothing methods are appropriate. If the data exhibits a linear trend then the two-parameter exponential smoothing method is appropriate. If a seasonal pattern emerges from the data, then the three-parameter exponential forecasting method would be appropriate. Our present study of the tow-truck allocation data indicated a strong seasonal pattern. Hence the three-parameter exponential forecasting method should be fitted to our data.

In order to find the best forecasting model, one should calculate the Mean Sum Squares of Error (MSE), which is defined as follows:

$$MSE = \frac{\sum_{i=1}^{n}(X_i - F_i)^2}{n} \qquad (6A.12)$$

where: X_i is the actual data for time period i,

F_i is the forecast value for the period i, and

and n is the number of observations.

The model that gives minimum MSE should be considered as the best forecasting model among the alternatives. One should then start to forecast for future values based on the best forecasting model.

Appendix 8A: Surrogate Measure of Alcohol Related Accidents 2

An examination of the extent to which alcohol is known to be involved in SCAs at different times of the week was carried out to determine a surrogate measure of alcohol related accidents.

Time of day/ day of week combinations during which the percentage of accidents known to involve a driver with BAC in excess of 0.05g/100ml equals or exceeds 9% are as follows.

Sunday	4pm – 4pm Monday
Monday	6pm – 6am Tuesday
Tuesday	6pm – 6am Wednesday
Wednesday	6pm – 6am Thursday
Thursday	6pm – 6am Friday
Friday	6pm – 8am Saturday
Saturday	2pm – 8am Sunday

If the combination of these time periods is considered as the "alcohol" period, then during this time period there was an average of 3,657 SCAs per year, of which 896 (24.5%) were known to involve alcohol over the years 1977–1982. In the "non-alcohol" period, there was an average of 3,646 SCAs per year, of which 117 (3.3%) were known to involve alcohol.

It is suggested that these time periods be used in studies that require a surrogate measure of alcohol involvement in accidents. The 9% figure is arbitrary, but can be justified on the grounds that:

It leads to two groups of accidents with approximately equal numbers in each;

For Monday to Thursday nights, it leads to a 6pm – 6am period, which accords with the conventional "night" period;

The periods designated seem sensible;

The difference between 24.5% and 3.3% is impressive. If we are under-estimating alcohol involvement by 100%, then a measure that affected alcohol related accidents only could affect 49% of SCAs in the designated alcohol period, and 7% of SCAs in the "non-alcohol" period. That should give reasonable power in detecting an effect of alcohol related measures.

Appendix 8B: Alternative Target and Control Group Drivers

Here, we have evaluated the Victorian Zero BAC legislation, using learner and first year probationary drivers as "target group", and second and third year probationary drivers as "Control group". The results obtained from the intervention-time series analyses, and the pre-post methods are presented in the following tables 8B1 and 8B2 respectively.

Table 8B1: Drivers Involved in Serious Casualty Accidents During July 1984 – December 1984 (6 Months Post-legislation)

Driver Groups	ARIMA Forecasts*	Actual numbers	Difference (%)
Learner and First year probationary drivers	184.41 (172.36)	164	– 11.07
Second and third year probationary drivers	304.32 (315.23)	312	+ 2.52
Learner and first year probationary (Target group) net difference relative to second and third year probationary (Control group) net Difference			– 13.59

* Intervention model forecasts are presented in parentheses.

Source: Road Traffic Accident Data File of the RTA of Victoria extracted from the Victorian Police Road Accident Report Form.

Table 8B1 indicates a reduction of 13.6% in SCAs for target group drivers compared to control group drivers at alcohol times. Similar to Table 8.1 in the main text, a negative intervention coefficient (– 6.5%) was observed for target group drivers when the step function was estimated for alcohol times. This was statistically insignificant since its t-value = – 0. 22. The intervention coefficient (+ 3.6%) was positive for second and third year probationary drivers at alcohol times, although not statistically significant (t-value = 0.49). Further, the difference between these two standardized coefficients was not statistically significant since its t-value = 0.22. Thus the estimated net reduction 13.6% in the target group SCA involvements during alcohol times relative to control group drivers cannot be separated from chance variation.

Table 8B2: Drivers Involved in Serious Casualty Accidents During Six Month Pre- and Post-legislation Periods.

Driver Groups	July 1983 – December 1983	July 1984 – December 1984	Change (%)
Learner and first year probationary drivers	192.5	164	– 14.81
Second and third year probationary drivers	308.5	312	+ 1.13
Learner and first year probationary (Target group) net difference relative to second and third year probationary (Control group) net difference			– 15.94

Source: Road Traffic Accident Data File of the RTA of Victoria extracted from the Victorian Police Road Accident Report Form.

Results of Table 8B2 can be interpreted exactly in the same way as described for the results of Table 8.2 in the main text. The directions of the changes for the two groups of drivers at alcohol times are very similar to that of Table 8.2. The magnitudes of the change are also very similar for both target and control group drivers during alcohol times. In addition to that it is also observed from both Tables 8B1 and 8B2 that both methods of evaluation indicate that there was an insignificant reduction of SCA for target group drivers compared to control group drivers at alcohol times.

Appendix 10A: Target and Control Group Drivers

This appendix deals with results based on alternative target and control group drivers. The target group consisted of learner and first year probationary drivers only, while the control group was comprised of second and third year probationary drivers. This is a parallel study of the original work with new definitions of target and control group drivers involved in serious casualty accidents. Similar to the main study, four separate series of drivers involved in SCA's were used for both time series and pre-post analyses to examine the effectiveness of the zero BAC legislation in the first six and eighteen months of its implementations.

10A.1 First Eighteen Months of Legislation

As discussed in Section 8.3.2.2, the usual ARIMA and Intervention techniques were applied to each of the four separate series of drivers involved in serious casualty accidents. The results of the ARIMA and intervention models together with the actual number of drivers involved in SCA's for target and control groups in the alcohol and non-alcohol times are given in Table 10A.1

The results of this table can similarly be interpreted as the results of Table 10.6 in the text. A negative intervention coefficient (-8.2%) was observed for target group drivers when the step function was estimated for alcohol times. This coefficient was not statistically significant since its t-value = -0.27. In contrast, a positive intervention coefficient (+12.7%) was observed for target group drivers when a step function was estimated at non-alcohol time. This coefficient was statistically significant since its t-value = 2.13. This means that there was a significant increase for target group drivers involved in SCA's at non-alcohol times above that expected from the ARIMA forecasts. However, the difference between these two standarised intervention coefficients was not statistically significant (t-value = -0. 66).

The results of the table can be interpreted as the results of Table 10.6 of section 10.6. It should be noted that the magnitude and direction of the changes are similar to that of Table 10.6 for target group drivers both at alcohol and non-alcohol times. This is in contrast to the Table 10.6 which shows that there were increases in SCA involvements for the standard drivers both at alcohol and non-alcohol times.

The results of the pre-post method are presented in Table 10A.2 which shows that there were increases of SCAs for learner and first year probationary drivers at both alcohol and non-alcohol times, but the increase was much higher during non-alcohol times. This indicates the net reduction of SCAs for learner and first year probationary drivers at alcohol times relative to non-alcohol times. Similar net reduction of SCAs for second and third year probationary drivers was observed at alcohol times relative to non-alcohol times. But this reduction is slightly less than the reduction observed for learner and first year probationary drivers. As a result, the net reduction for learner and first year probationary drivers compared to second and third year probationary drivers was only 1.03%, which is statistically insignificant.

10.A.2 First Six Months of Legislation

In order to match the analyses of the main report, the first six months of the legislations data were analysed for the alternative target and control group drivers by the time-series and pre-post methods. The results of the time series and pre-post analyses are presented in Tables 10A.3 and Table 10A.4 respectively.

For second and third year probationary drivers during alcohol times, the intervention coefficient was negative (-6.3%) and was not statistically significant since its t-value = -1.07. However, the intervention coefficient was +3.1% with t-value = 0.66 for second and third year probationary drivers at non-alcohol times.

When the adjusted net difference of the four estimated intervention coefficients was calculated, it was found to be statistically insignificant since its t-value = -0.36. Thus, the observed net increase (10.6%) in the target group SCA involvements during alcohol times relative to second and third year probationary drivers, can not be separated from chance variation.

Table 10A.3 indicates a reduction of 5.9% in SCA's for target group drivers at alcohol times compared to non-alcohol times and parallel changes of the control group. Similar to Table 10A.3 in the main text, a negative intervention coefficient (-6.5%) was observed for target group drivers when the step function was estimated for alcohol times. This was statistically insignificant since its t-value = -0.22. On the other hand, a positive intervention coefficient (+2.0%) was observed for target group drivers at non-alcohol times. This was also statistically insignificant since its t-value = +0.22. Further, the difference between these two standardized coefficients was not statistically significant (t-value = 0.28). The intervention coefficient (+3.6%) was positive for second and third year probationary drivers at alcohol times, although not statistically significant (t-value=0.49). Also, a positive intervention coefficient (+13.9%) was observed for the second and third year probationary drivers at non-alcohol times. This was not statistically significant.

A test of statistical significance of the adjusted net intervention coefficient based on the four standarised intervention coefficients was carried out (refer Section 10.5.1.2) and was found statistically insignificant since its t-value = 0.05. Thus, the observed net reduction (5.9%) in the target group SCA involvements during alcohol times, relative to second and third year probationary drivers cannot be separated from chance variation.

The results of Table 10A.4 can be interpreted exactly in the same way as described for the results of Table 10.2 in the main text. The directions of the changes for the two groups of drivers at alcohol and non-alcohol times are very similar to that of Table 10.2. The magnitudes of the change are also very similar for both target and control group drivers during alcohol times.

Table 10A.1: Drivers Involved in Serious Casualty Accidents During July 1984 – December 1985 (18 Months Post-legislation): Intervention Method

Driver Groups	ARIMA Forecasts*	Actual numbers	Difference (%)
Learner and first year probationary drivers			
Alcohol times	528.40 (429.0)	603.00	+ 14.12
Non-alcohol times	481.70 (542.84)	549.00	+ 13.97
Net difference: alcohol times relative to non-alcohol times			+ 0.001
Second and third year probationary drivers			
Alcohol times	912.95 (853.54)	844.00	
Non-alcohol times	672.75 (693.47)	687.00	
Net differences: alcohol times relative to non-alcohol times			-9.47
Learner and first year probationary net difference relative to second and third year probationary net difference			+10.59

* Intervention model forecasts are presented in parentheses.

Source: Road Traffic Accident Data File of the RTA of Victoria extracted from the Victorian Police Road Accident Report Form.

Table 10A.2: Drivers Involved in Serious Casualty Accidents During July 1984 – December 1985 (18 Months Post-legislation Period): Pre-post Method

Driver Groups	July 1982 –31 December 1983 (Six Moths pre-legislation)	July 1984 – December 1985 (18 Months Post Legislations	Change (%)
Learner and first year probationary drivers			
Alcohol times	563	603	+7.10
Non-alcohol times	484	549	+13.43
Net difference: alcohol relative to non-alcohol times			- 5.58
Second and third year probationary drivers			
Alcohol times	886	844	-4.74
Non-alcohol times	688	687	-0.15
Net differences: alcohol relative to non-alcohol times			-4.60
Learner and first year probationary net difference relative to second and third year probationary net difference			-1.03

Source: Road Traffic Accident Data File of the RTA of Victoria extracted from the Victorian Police Road Accident Report Form.

Table 10A.3: Drivers Involved in Serious Casualty Accidents During July 1984 – December 1984 (6 Months Post-legislation): Intervention Method

Driver Groups	ARIMA Forecasts*	Actual numbers	Difference (%)
Learner and first year Probationary drivers			
Alcohol times	184.41(172.36)	164	- 11.07
Non-alcohol times	160.57 (163.71)	167	+ 4.01
Net difference: alcohol relative to Non-alcohol times			- 14.49
Second and third year Probationary drivers			
Alcohol times	304.32 (315.23)	312	+ 2.52
Non-alcohol times	224.25 (255.43)	253	+ 12.82
Net differences: alcohol relative to non-alcohol times			- 9.13
Learner and first year probationary net difference relative to second and third year probationary net difference			- 5..90

*   Intervention model forecasts are presented in parentheses.

Source: Road Traffic Accident Data File of the RTA of Victoria extracted from the Victorian Police Road Accident Report Form..

Table 10A.4: Drivers Involved in Serious Casualty Accidents During July 1984 – December 1984 (6 Months Post-legislation Period): Pre-post Method

Driver Groups	July 1983 – December 1983	July 1984 – December 1984	Change (%)
Learner and first year probationary drivers			
Alcohol times	192.5	164	-14.81
Non-alcohol times	154.0	167	+8.44
Net difference: alcohol relative to non-alcohol times			-21.44
Second and third year probationary drivers			
Alcohol times	308.5	312	+1.13
Non-alcohol times	232.0	253	+9.05
Net differences: alcohol relative to non-alcohol times			-7.26
Learner and first year probationary net difference relative to second and third year probationary net difference			-15.29

Source: Road Traffic Accident Data File of the RTA of Victoria extracted from the Victorian Police Road Accident Report Form.

Appendix 11A: Sampling from a Censored Exponential Distribution

The exponential distribution of the type (11.1) has been considered in this study. The method of Maximum Likelihood (ML) is used to estimate the mean waiting time Parameter θ for an offense.

The likelihood of the data is the product of contributions from each driver, assuming they are independent to each other. The form of the contributing factor for the i-th driver depends upon whether or not the driver has committed an offense.
The contribution to the likelihood is:

$$\left(\frac{1}{\theta}\right) e^{(-t_i/\theta)}$$

if the driver is involved in an offense during the study with a survival time t_i or:

$$e^{\left(-u_i/\theta\right)}$$

if the driver survives an exposure time u_i without an offense. This factor is the probability of surviving the exposure time u_i, assuming the exponential model (11.1).

For a group of n drivers the likelihood is the product of n terms either of those terms for each driver. The likelihood function for these densities can be written as:

$$L(\theta) = \theta^{-m} \exp\left[-\left(\Sigma_{oi} t_i + \Sigma_{noi} u_i\right)/\theta\right]$$

where m = number of drivers who committed an offense during the study period:

$$\sum_{oi=1}^{m} t_i = \text{Total survival time for those drivers who committed an offense,}$$

$$\sum_{noi=m+1}^{n} u_i = \text{Total exposure for those drivers without offenses.}$$

The ML estimate for θ is given by:

$$\hat{\theta} = \left(\frac{1}{m}\right)\left(\Sigma_{oi} t_i + \Sigma_{noi} u_i\right) + \bar{t} + \frac{n-m}{m}\bar{u} \qquad (11A.1)$$

where $\bar{t}$ is the average survival time of the drivers who committed an offense and $\bar{u}$ is the average exposure time of the (n-m) offense free drivers. It is interesting to note that if all vehicles survive until the end of study period without an offense then m = 0 and θ becomes unbounded. It is worthwhile to mention that Symons and Reinfurt (1975) have used the same formula to evaluate the effectiveness of motor vehicle inspection program in reducing highway crashes using Florida accident data. The variance of the estimate $\hat{\theta}$ can be approximated by:

$$\hat{\theta}^2/m \qquad (11A.2)$$

11A.1 Estimation of the Mean Time Interval between First and Second Offenses

All drivers considered in this study have had a second demerit point offense within three years (i.e., 1,095 days) of the first offense after the implementation of the DIP program and up to the end of February 1985. This implies that any distribution of the time interval between the first and the second offense obtained here is conditional. We have seen that the occurrence of traffic offenses followed an exponential distribution. Therefore, the conditional distribution between the first and second is given by:

$$f\left(t, \theta / t < 1{,}095 \text{ days}\right) = \frac{f(t, \theta)}{g(t \leq 1095)} = \frac{f(t, \theta)}{\int_0^{1095} f(t, \theta)\, dt}$$

$$= \frac{(1/\theta) e^{(-t_i/\theta)}}{1 - e^{(-1{,}095/\theta)}}$$

$$= \left[(1/\theta) e^{(-t_i/\theta)}\right]\left[1 - e^{(-1{,}095/\theta)}\right]^{-1}$$

The likelihood function can be written as:

$$L(t, \theta) = \left[\theta\left(1 - e^{(-1{,}095/\theta)}\right)\right]^{-n} e^{(-\Sigma t_i/\theta)}$$

The log likelihood is given by:

$$\log L = -n\left[\log \theta + \log\left(1 - e^{(-1{,}095/\theta)}\right)\right] - \left(\Sigma t_i/\theta\right)$$

The maximum likelihood estimate of $\hat{\theta}$ can be obtained by solving:

$$\frac{\partial \log L}{\partial \hat{\theta}} = 0$$

Therefore, the maximum likelihood estimate of $\hat{\theta}$ given by:

$$\hat{\theta} - 1{,}095\, e^{(-1{,}095/\hat{\theta})} \left(1 - e^{(-1{,}095/\hat{\theta})}\right)^{-1} = \bar{t} \qquad (11A.3)$$

Analytical solution for $\hat{\theta}$ might be difficult, but the numerical estimation for $\hat{\theta}$ by direct search method by computer, is a relatively easy task.

The variance of the estimate $\hat{\theta}$ can be estimated either by:

$$\frac{1}{\text{Var }\hat{\theta}} = n E \left(\frac{\partial}{\partial \hat{\theta}} \log f\right)^2$$

or

$$\frac{1}{\text{Var }\hat{\theta}} = - n E \left(\frac{\partial^2}{\partial \hat{\theta}^2} \log f\right)$$

After tedious calculation, we have derived the variance formula for the estimate of θ, that is, $\text{Var }\hat{\theta}$ as follows:

$$\text{Var}\left(\hat{\theta}\right) = \left[n\left(\frac{1}{\hat{\theta}^2} - \frac{1,095^2 \, e^{\left(-1,095/\hat{\theta}\right)}}{\hat{\theta}^4 \left(1 - e^{\left(\frac{-1,095}{\theta}\right)}\right)^2}\right)\right]^{-1} \qquad (11\text{A}.4)$$

This variance formula can then be used to test the interoffense time interval between second and third offense, and that of the first and second offenses to show the effectiveness of the DPS in reducing traffic offenses.

11A.2 Hypothesis Testing

In a comparison of the DIP and MRB drivers of similar type, one test of interest is to test the hypothesis that the weighted mean interoffense time interval (θ*) of the DIP drivers equals that (θ) of the MRB drivers with the alternative hypothesis that θ* exceeds θ; that is,

$$H_0 : \theta^* = \theta$$
$$H_1 : \theta^* > \theta$$

The approximate large sample test statistic can be given by:

$$Z = \frac{\hat{\theta}^* - \hat{\theta}}{\sqrt{\left(\frac{\hat{\theta}^{*2}}{m_1} + \frac{\hat{\theta}^2}{m}\right)}}$$

where m_1 and m are the number of drivers who committed a third offense for the DIP and MRB groups respectively.

APPENDICES

Z is approximately distributed as a standard normal variate. An observed value of Z would be significant at the α level if it exceeds $(1 - \alpha)$ 100 percentile of the standard normal distribution. In such a situation the data would reject the hypothesis that the weighted average time interval for the DIP drivers equals that for the MRB drivers. Similarly, if the test of interest is to test the hypothesis that the weighted mean time interval (θ') between second and third offenses equals that of the time (θ'') between first and second offense for all drivers with the alternative hypothesis that θ' exceeds θ'' that is:

$$H_0 : \theta' = \theta''$$
$$H_1 : \theta' > \theta''$$

Then the approximate large sample test statistic:

$$Z = \frac{\hat{\theta}' - \hat{\theta}''}{\sqrt{Var(\hat{\theta}') + Var(\hat{\theta}'')}}$$

can be used to verify the hypothesis. $Var(\hat{\theta}')$ and $Var(\hat{\theta}'')$ can respectively be calculated by using the formula (11A.2) and (11A.4) of this appendix.

Appendix 12A: Truck fatalities and pair-wise correlation of various variables for long and short-term fatality models

Table 12A.1: Fatalities Involving Trucks: Victoria 1980–1990[*]

Year	Number of trucks registered	Fatalities involving trucks	Fatalities per 100,000 registered trucks
1980	141,000	96	68.08
1981	147,900	110	74.37
1982	161,700	108	66.79
1983	169,700	74	43.6
1984	181,000	101	55.8
1985	194,100	95	48.94
1986	200,300	95	47.42
1987	206,800	115	55.6
1988	215,500	120	55.68
1989	219,600	123	56.01
1990	224,900	102	45.35

* Only rigid and articulated trucks are included.

Source: Road Traffic Accident and Vehicle Registration Data Files of the RTA of Victoria.

This table clearly shows that the numbers of fatality per 100,000 registered trucks are significantly lower in 1983 and 1990 (recession years) compared to other non-recession years.

Table 12A.2(a): Pair-wise Correlations of Various Variables
for Long-term Fatality Model*

Correlation

Variables	Unemployment	Fuel Sales	Alcohol Legislation	Seat-B Legislation	Trend	Oil price	Recent road safety initiatives	Total road Fatalities
	1.0000							
	0.1237	1.0000						
	0.2861	-0.4057	1.0000					
Seat Belt Legislation	0.3369	0.7616*	0.3707	1.0000				
Unemployment	0.0000	0.0000	0.0000	-0.0118	1.0000			
Fuel Sales	-0.0150	0.1204	0.0103	0.3150	-0.0409	1.0000		
Alcohol Legislation	-0.0915	-0.3643	0.0267	-0.2516	0.3397	-0.0602	1.0000	
Total Road Fatalities	-0.1951	0.2846	0.2798	-0.0674	-0.8518	-0.1947	-0.4148	1.0000
Durbin Watson Statistic		2.06						
(for number of observations)		25						
1st Order Autocorrelation		-0.03						

* Step-wise regression also gives the same estimate of this parameter

Source: Fatality, seatbelt wearing and drink driving data are taken from the RTA Accident Data File; unemployment data from the ABS Labour Force Survey; and fuel sales data are taken from the Australian Petroleum Sales Data.

APPENDICES

Table12A. 2(b): Pair-wise Correlation of Various Variable for Short-term Fatality Model**

Correlation

Variable	Unemployment	Fuel sales	Trend	Current road safety initiatives	Monthly road fatalities
Unemployment	1.0000				
Fuel Sales	-0.3969	1.0000			
Trend	0.0037	0.0122	1.0000		
Current Road Safety Initiatives	-0.1943	-0.0971	0.7082**	1.0000	
Monthly Road Fatalities	-0.3130	0.3651	-0.1743	-0.1154	1.0000
Durbin Watson Statistic		1.997			
(for number of observations)		71			
1st Order Autocorrel-ation		0.001			

** In order to save space various statistics and parameter estimates of the Dummy variables for the months of year are not presented here. However, these statistics can be obtained from the author on request.

Source: Fatality, seatbelt wearing and drink driving data are taken from the RTA Accident Data File; unemployment data from the ABS Labour Force Survey; and fuel sales data are taken from the Australian Petroleum Sales Data.

Notes

1 Dutch Ministry of Transport, Public Works and Water Management (1996 a, b) has also put road safety policy into practice, using estimated road accident rates by various road user types. Royal Thai Police (2004) also estimated sample size for road accidental injury rates for Thailand. Elliott and Broughton (2005) have developed methods to estimate the effect of policing for road casualty rates based on the estimation of sample size.

2 This appendix was prepared by David South, Manager of Alcohol, Drugs and Legislative Countermeasures, VicRoads.

BIBLIOGRAPHY

AAAM, (1998), Abbreviated Injury Scale: 1998 version, Association for the Advancement of Automotive Medicine, Chicago, Illinios

Abdel-Aty, M., Keller,J and Brady, P.A. (2005), "Analysis of the types of Crashes at singalized Intersections Using Complete Crash Data and Tree-based Regression", *Transportation Research Board 2005 Annual Meeting*, CD-ROM.

Abdel-Aty, M and Keller. J. (2005), "Exploring the Overall and Specific Crash Severity Levels at Signalized Intersections", *Accident Analysis and Prevention* 37, 417- 425

Abraham, B. (1987), "Application of Intervention Analysis to a Road fatality Series in Ontario", *Journal of Forecasting* 6, 211-219

ABT Associates Inc, (1997), ATV Exposure Survey: Pretest Report, Technical Report CPSC-C-94-1115, No. 4, Cambridge, MA.

Afukaar, F. K., Antwi, P. and Ofosu-Amaah, S. (2003), "Pattern of Road Traffic Injuries in Ghana: Implications for Control", *Injury Control and safety promotion* 10, 69-76.

Akaike, H. (1973)," Maximum likelihood Identifications of Gaussian Auto Regressive Moving Average Models", *Biometrika* 60, 225-265.

Al-Masaeid, Al-Mashakbeh, A. A and Qudah A. M. (1999), "Economic Costs of Traffic Accidents in Jordan" *Accident Analysis and Prevention* 31, 347-357.

Ameratunga, S., Hijar, M and Norton, R. (2006), "Road-traffic Injuries: Confronting Disparities to Address a Global Health Problem", *Lancet* 367, 1533-40.

Anderson, D. (1993), Personal Communication of Results of Analysis Undertaken by J. Cunningham, Road Safety Division, Vic Roads.

Andrews, C. N., Kobusingye, O. C and Lett, R. (1999), "Road Traffic Accident Injuries in Kampala", *East African Medical Journal* 76, 189-94.

ARUP Transportation Planning, (1995)," *The 1994 Exposure Survey"*, Final Report, Prepared for Vic Roads, Melbourne

Asian Development Bank, (2003), *"Road Safety Audit for Road Projects – an operational Tool kit"*, ADB, Manila.

Asogwa, S. E. (1999), *Road Traffic Accident in Nigeria: A Handbook for All Road Users*, pp. 18-19, Nugu:Snaap Press LTD.

Association of National Driver Improvement Scheme Providers (ANDISP), (1998), *National Driver Improvement Scheme Guidelines for Instructors*, ANDISP

Atiyah, P. S. (1975), *Accidents, Compensation and the Law*, (Second edition) Weidenfeld and Nicolson, London

Atkins, A. S. (1981), *The Economic and Social Costs of Road Accidents in Australia: with Preliminary Cost Estimates for Australia 1978*, Office of Road Safety, Department of Transport Australia.

Atkins, A. S. (1982), "The Economic Costs of Road Accidents in Australia: Some Issues in Estimation, Concept and Application", *The Australian Road Research Board Proceedings* 11, Part 5, 206-220.

Attewell, R. G., Glase, K., McFadden, M. (2001), "Bicycle Helmet Efficacy: A Meta-Analysis", *Accident Analysis and Prevention* 33 (3), 345-352.

Australian Bureau of Agricultural and Resource Economics, (1992) *Sales of Petroleum Product by State Marketing Area, January 1985 - December 1990*, Canberra, Australia.

Australian Bureau of Resource Economics, (1987), *Energy Demand and Supply, Australia 1960 - 61 to 1984 – 8*, Australian Government Publishing Services.

Australian Bureau of Statistics, (1988), Estimated Resident population by Age and Sex in Statistical Local Areas, Victoria, 30 June 1988, Catalogue No. 3207.2.

Australian Bureau of Statistics, (1984), The Labour Force, Australia: Historical Summary 1966 to 1984 ,Catalogue No. 6204.0.

Australian Bureau of Statistics, (1990), Time Series Data: Unemployed Persons - Victoria, catalogue no. 1355.0 (Source of original data - ABS CAT (6203.0).

Australian Bureau of Statistics, Survey of Motor Vehicle Use: Twelve Months Ended 30 September; 1976, 1979, 1982, 1985, 1988.

Australian Road Research Board, (1992), Costs for Accidents – Types and Casualty Classes, Research Report 227, Australian Road Research Board, Melbourne.

Australian Transport Council (ATC), (2000), The National Road safety Strategy, 2001-2010, Australian Transport Safety Bureau – *2005*, Fatal Road Crash Database http://www.atsb.gov.au; ATSB.

Australian Transport Safety Bureau, (ATSB), (2002), *Road Crash statistics*, 1996,. http://www.atsb.gov.au/roads/stats/timefatl.cfm, Assessed May 2002.

AUSTROADS, (2000), *Road Facts 2000*, Sydney: Austroads.

AUSTROADS, (2002), *Road Safety Audit* (Second Edition), Sydney, Australia.

AUSTROADS, (2002a), *Evaluation of the Proposed Actions Emanating from Road Safety Audits*, APR209/02, Sydney, Australia.

AUSTROADS, (1999) Guide to Traffic Engineering Practice: Part-15 Motorcycle Safety, Sydney.

Awane, T. (1999), "Integrating Simulators in Motorcycle in Motorcycle Safety Education", *IATSS Research* 23, 26-35.

Baker, J. A and Lambert, J. H. (2001), Information System for Risks, Cost, and Benefits of Infrastructure Improvement Projects, *Journal of Public Works Management and Policy* 5(3), 198-208.

Beesley, M. E. (1965), "The Value of Time Spent Travelling: Some New Evidence", *Economica,* 32, 174-185.

Begg, D. J., Langley, J. D and Stephenson, S. (2003), " Identifying Factors that Predict Persistent Driving after Drinking, Unsafe Driving after Drinking, and Driving after using Cannabis Among Young Adults", *Accident Analysis* and *Prevention* 35, 669-675. (Work package 2) of the ESCAPE project, Espoo: VTT.

Belloti, P. (1997), "Cutting Back on Casualties", (Gloucester safe city initiative), *Surveyor* 17, 4.97, 6-19.

Benjamin, J. R and Coombell, C.A, (1970), *Probability, statistics, and decision for Civil Engineers*, New York: McGraw-Hill.

Bernard, G. S and Matthews, W. A. (2003), "A Contemporary Analysis of Road Traffic Crashes: Fatalities and Injuries in Trinidad and Tobago", *Injury Control and Safety Promotion* 10, 21-27.

Berns, S. (1998), *Definitions and data Availability Compilation and Evaluation of A-Level Roads and Hospitalization in OECD Countries Accident and Injury Definitions*, International Road Traffic and Accident Database Special Report, Bundesanstalt fur Strassenwesen, Germany.

Beroggi, G. E. G and Wallace, W. A. (1995), "Topics in Safety, Risk, Reliability and Quality", Vol. 4, In *Computer Supported Risk Management*, Kluwer Academic Publishers, Dordrecht.

Bhattacharyya, M. N and Layton, A.P. (1979), "Effectiveness of Seat Belt Legislation on the Queensland Road toll--An Australian Case Study in Intervention Analysis", *Journal of the American Statistical Association* 74, 596-603.

Bishop, M.M., Fienberg, S. E and Holland, P.W. (1978), *Discrete Multivariate Analysis: Theory and Practice*, The MIT Press, London.

Bjornskau, T and Elvik, R. (1992), "Can Road Traffic Law Enforcement Permanently Reduce the Number of Accidents", *Accident Analysis and Prevention* 24, 506-520.

Blincoe, L. B. (1995), "Economic Cost of Motor Vehicle Crashes 1994", NHTSA, USDOT, Washington ADC, http://www.nhtsa.doc.gov/people/economic/ecomvc1994.html

Blomberg, R. D. (1992), Lower BAC Limits for Youth: Evaluation of the Maryland 0.02 law, Washington DC: US Department of Transportation, National Highway Traffic Safety Administration, DOT HS 807 860.

Blomquist, G. *(1979)*, "The Value of Life Saving: Implications of Consumption Activity", *Journal of Political Economy* 87, 540-558.

Borkenstein, R. F., Crowther, R. F., Shumate, R. P., Ziel, W. B and Zylman, R. (1974), "The Role of the Drinking Driver in Traffic Accidents", *Blutalkohol* 11, (Supp no. 1).

Borrell, P. A. (2001), "Reducing Socioeconomic Inequalities in Road Traffic Injuries: Time for Policy Agenda", *Journal of Epidermal Community Health* 55, 853-54

Borschos, B, *An Evaluation of the Swedish Drunken Driving Legislation Implemented on February 1*, 1994, Centre for Social Research on Alcohol and Drugs, Stockholm University, S-106 91 Stockholm, Sweden.

Bowen, R. (1985), "The Victorian Zero BAC Legislation Evaluation- Part 1: Surveys of P-plate Usage" (Report No. 6/85), Hawthorn, Victoria: Road Traffic Authority.

Box, G.E.P and Jenkins, G.M. (1976), *Time Series Analysis: Forecasting and Control,* San Francisco: Holden Day.

Box, G.E.P and Tiao, G.C. (1975), "Intervention Analysis with Applications to Economic and Environmental Problems", *Journal of the American Statistical Association 70,* 70-79.

Brindle, R. (1998), "Managing the Impacts of Traffic on local Communities", *Proceedings of the National Road Safety Summit, 16-18 September 1998,* Canberra: Federal Office of Road safety.

Broyles, R. W., Narine, 1., Clarke, S. R and Baker, D. R. (2003), "Factors Associated with the likelihood of Injury Resulting from Collisions between four wheel Driver Vehicles and Passenger Cars", *Accident Analysis and Prevention 35,* 677-681.

Bureau of Regional Transport Economics (BRTE) (2000), "Road Crash Cost in Australia",Bureau of Regional Transport and Economics, Report No. 102. Canberra.

Brude,U.(2005),"Basic Statistics for Accidents and Traffic and Other Background Variables in Sweden", Version 2005-06-30", VTI *notat 27A-2005,* VTI, Linkoping, Sweden.

Brundell-freij, K and Ekman, L. (1990), Safety and Exposure-aspects of the Relationship with Special Attention to Vulnerable Road Users, Research Report, Department of Traffic Planning and Engineering, University of Lund, Sweden.

Bureau of Transport and Communications Economics, (2004), *Costs of Road Crashes in Australia – 1993,* Information Sheet 4, Bureau of Transport and Communications Economics, Canberra.

Bureau of Transport Economics, (2000), Road crash costs in Australia (Report 102), Canberra, Bureau of Transport Economics.

Bureau of Transport Statistics, (2001), *Transportation Data and Risk Measures,* Bureau of Transport Statistics, www.bts.org, USA.

Burgess, C and Webley, P. (1999), *Evaluating the Effectiveness of the United Kingdom's National Driver Improvement Scheme,* School of Psychology, University of Exeter.

Burrow, I. (1999), "Accident will Happen", TRL's New Safe NET Software, *Surveyor,* 15.4.99.

Burton, R. W and Ekstien, R. B. (1967), Unit cost Estimates of Road Accidents in South Africa, South African Council for Scientific and Industrial Research, National Institute for Road Research Section 1, Road Economics.

Calabresi, G. (1970), *The Costs of Accidents: a legal and Economic Analysis,*Yale University Press, New Haven.

Calabresi, G. C and Bobbitt, P. (1978), *Tragic Choices,* W.W. Norton, N.Y, U.S.A.

Caldwell, R. C and Wilson, E. M. (1999), "Starting a Safety Improvement Program for Rural Unpaved Roads", *Transportation Research Record* 1652, 126-130, Transport Research Board, National Research Council, Washington, D.C.

BIBLIOGRAPHY

Cameron, M.H and Strang, P.M. (1982), "Effect of Intensified Random Breath Testing in Melbourne during 1978 and 1979 "(pp. 1-12), In *Proceedings of the 11th ARRB Conference*, Vol II, Part 5.

Cameron, M. H. (1970), "Accident Rate Analysis and Confidence Limits", *Proceedings: Fifth Conference of the Australian Road Research Board*.

Cameron, M. H. and Russell, I. P. (1981), *Victorian Road Accident Toll during 1981*, Royal Automobile Club of Victoria (RACV) Ltd, Melbourne, Australia.

Cameron, M. H. (2000), *Estimation of the Optimum Speed on Urban Residential Streets*, Australian Transport Safety Bureau (ATSB)

Cameron, M. H., Haworth, N., Oxley, J., Newstead, S and Le, T. (1993)," *Evaluation of Transport Accident Commission Road safety Television Advertising"*, Report No. 52, Monash University Accident research Centre, Monash University.

Cameron, N. H., Strang, P.M and Vulcan, P.(1980), "Evaluation of Random Breath Testing in Victoria, Australia: Alcohol, Drugs and Traffic Safety", Vol. III, Proceedings 8th International Conference on Alcohol Drugs and Traffic Safety, Stockholm, Sweden.

Campbell, B. J. (1958), *Driver Improvement: The Points Systems*, Chapel Hill: University of North Carolina, Institute of Government for America, Association of Motor Vehicle Administrators.

Campbell, B. J. (1974), "*Objective Program Evaluation*", 7th Australian Road Research Board Conference, Paper No. A 44,

Carsten, O. M. J., Tight, M. R., Southwell, M. T and Plows, B. (1989), "Urban Accidents: Why Do they Happen?" *Accident Analysis Foundation for Road Safety Research*, Basingstoke, Hampshire.

Carstensen, G. (2002), "The Effect on Accident Risk of a Change in Driver Education in Denmark", *Accident Analysis and Prevention* 34, 111-121.

Carthy, T., Packham, D., Rhodes-Defty, N., Salter, D., Silcock, D and Hills, P. (1993), *Risk and Safety on the Roads: Perceptions and Attitudes*", Accident Analysis Foundation for Road Safety Research, Basingstoke, Hampshire.

Cercarelli, L. R. (1994),"The Adequacy of Existing Driver Training and Education Programmes: A Literature Review", Report to the Traffic Board of Western Australia, RR31.

Cercarelli, L. R. (1998),"The Role of Police and Hospital data in Road Safety Research and Strategy Development", Report to the Road safety Council of Western Australia, RR75.

Cercarelli, L.R., Hendrie, D., Ryan, G, A., Legge, M and Kirov, C. (1998)," Road Safety Risk Factors Survey: Results for the Fourth S", Report to the Western Australian Office of Road Safety, *RR62*

Cercarelli, R. L and Ryan, G. A. (1995), "*Evaluation of the Western Australian 'Driver-Reviver'*", Program, RR37

Cesar, M., Antonio, M. D., Carlos, T and Joao, M. D. (2001), "The Influence of Prehospital Trauma Care on Motor Vehicle Crash Mortality", *The Journal of Trauma, Injury, Infection and Critical Care*, May, 2001.

Chatfield, C. (1980), "Inverse Autocorrelations", *Journal of the Royal Statistical Society*, A, 142, 363-377.

Chen, W., Cooper, P and Pinili, M. (1995), "Driver Accident Risk in Relation to the Penalty Point System in British Columbia", *Journal of Safety Research*, 26, 9-18.

Chesham, D. J., Rutter, D. R and Quine, L. (1993), "Motorcycling Safety Research: A Review of the Social and Behavioural literature", *Social Science Medicine* 37, 419-429.

Chipman, M. L., MacGregor, C. G and Smiley, A. (1993), "The Role of Exposure in Comparisons of Crash Risk among Different Drivers and Driving Environments", *Analysis and Prevention* 25, 207-311.

Chin, H. C., Haque, M. M and Jean, Y. H. (2006), "An Estimate of Road Accident Costs in Singapore", In *International Conference on Road Safety in Developing Countries*, 22-24 August 2006, BUET, Dhaka.

Chin, H. C and Quddus, M. A. (2003), "Applying the Random Effect Negative Binomial Model to Examine Traffic Accident Occurrence at Signalized Intersections", *Accident Analysis & Prevention* 35, 253-259,

Chin H. C., Tan, E., Melhuish, C., Ross, A and Goodge, M. (2003), "Road Accident Cost in Singapore", *ADB- Asean Regional Safety Program, Accident Costing Report*: AC 08.2003, Singapore.

Chin, H. C and Huang, H. (2006), "A Safety Evaluation Procedure on Traffic Treatments Using Modified Empirical Bayesian Approach", In International Conference on Road Safety in Developing Countries, 22-24 August 2006, BUET, Dhaka.

Chipman, M.L. (1982), "The Role of Exposure, Experience and Demerit Point levels in the Risk of Collision", *Accident Analysis and Prevention* 14, 475-83.

Chipman, M.L and Morgan, R.P. (1975), "The Role of Driver Demerit Points and Age in the Prediction of Motor Vehicle Collisions", *British Journal of Preventive Social Medicine* 29, 190-95.

Cleveland, W. S. (1972), "The Inverse Autocorrelations of a Time Series and their Application", *Technometrics*, 14, 277.

Cohen, J. (1977), *Statistical Power Analysis for the Behavioural Sciences*. Revised Edition, Academic Press, New York.

Commandeur, J. J. F. (2002), *General and Periodical Trends in Road Safety Development in Eight Developed Countries*, SWOV, Leidschendam, the Netherlands State Highway Plan short-Term Needs, obtained at http://www2.state.ed.us/itd/planning/reports/shp/shorterm.html

Conley, B. C. (1976), "The Value of Human Life in the Demand for Safety", in *American Economic Review* 61, No. 1, 45-55.

Coppin, R.S., Lew, A and Peck R.C. (1965), *The 1964 California Driver Record Study*, Part 4: *The Relationship between Concurrent Accidents and Citations*. Sacramento, CA: Department of Motor Vehicles.

BIBLIOGRAPHY

Corbett, C., Simon, F and O'Connell, M. (1997), "The Deterrence of High Speed Driving: A Criminological Perspective", TRL Report No. 296, Transport Research Laboratory.

Cox, D.R. *(1972)*, Regression Models and life Tables (with discussion), *Journal of the Royal Statistical Society 34*, Series B, 187-220.

Cramer, J.S. (1973), *Empirical Econometrics,* 3d printing, Amsterdam and London: North Holland

Crampin, J. (1997), "Gloucester's Safer City Project Aims to Show the Ways forward for Road Safety Strategies," *Local Transport Today*, 3.7.97.

Cuthbert, J. R. (1994), "An Extension of the Induced Exposure Method of Estimating Driver Risk", *Journal of the Royal Statistical Society* 157 Series A, 177-190.

Daltrey, R. (1986), *The Application of Time Series and Intervention Analysis to Evaluating the 1983 Random Breath Testing Campaign*, Internal Report, Road Traffic Authority Victoria.

Daltrey, R and Thomspon, B. (1986), "Evaluation of Motorcycle Rider Training and Licensing Scheme: Time Series Analysis", Internal Report, Road Traffic Authority, Victoria.

Dasgupta, A. K and Pearce D. W. (1972), *Cost Benefit Analysis,* Macmillan, London.

Dawson, R. F. F. (1967) *Cost of Road Accidents in Great Britain*, Road Research Laboratory, Crowthorne.

Dee, T. S. (1999), "State Alcohol Policies, Teen Drinking and Traffic Fatalities", *Journal of Public Economics* 72, 289-315.

Dee, T. S. (2001), "Does Setting Limits Save Lives? The Case of 0.08 BAC laws", *Journal of Policy Economics* 72, 289-315.

Delhomme, P. (1999), Evaluation of Road Safety Media Campaigns, Deliverable4, GADGET Project, European Commission/INRETS, France

Delhomme, P. (2002), "Some Criteria for Running Successful Campaigns", PRI Road Safety Forum 2002, PRI, Lisbon.

Delhomme, P., Vaa, T and Meyer, T. (1999), "Evaluated Road Safety Media Campaigns: An Overview of 265 Evaluated Campaigns and Some Meta-Analysis on Accidents", *Report WP4*.

Department of Transport, (1996), "Child Development and the Aims of Road Safety Education: A Review and Analysis", Road Safety Research Report No. 1, DOT, UK.

Despontin, M., Verbeke, A. and Brucker, K. de. (1997), "The Economic Evaluation of Road Safety in the European Union", In Proceedings of the European Seminar of Cost-Effectiveness of Road Safety Work and Measures, Luxembourg

DETR, (2000), *Tomorrow's Roads: Safe for Everyone, The Government's Road Safety Strategy and Casualty Reduction Targets for 2010*, The Department of the Environment, Transport and the Regions, London.

DFID, (2004), "*Guidelines for Conducting Community Road Safety Education Programs in Developing Countries*

Diamantopoulou, K., Cameron, M., Dyte, D and Harrison, W. (1997)," The Relationship between Demerit Points Accrual and Crash Involvement", Report No. 116, Monash University Accident Research Centre.

Dickerson, A., Peirson, J and Vickerman, R. (2000), "Road Accidents and Traffic Flows: An Econometric Investigation", *Economica* 67, 101.

Dickerson, A., Peirson, J and Vickerman, R. (1998), Road Accidents and Traffic Flows: An Econometric Investigation, Department of Economics, Keynes College, University of Kent at Canterbury, E-mail: jdpl@ukc.ac.uk

Dietz, S. K. (1967), "Significance Test for Accident Reductions Based on Classical Statistics and Economic Consequences", *Transportation Science* 1, No. 3.

Donaghey, B and Ram, S. (2000), *"Effective Speed Management 50 km/h Local Street Speed Limit – An Engineer's Perspective"*, paper presented at the public forum on 50/k/h Speed Limit for Local Roads, http://www.transport.wa.gov/roadsafety/issues/donaghey.htm

Douglas, J. B., Dunne, M. C., Griffiths, D. A and Mc Gilchrist, C. A. (1986), *Analysis of Traffic Crash Patterns for Traffic Authority of NSW*, Unisearch Limited Draft Road Safety Goals of Asia and the Pacific: 2007-2015(2006),extracted from www.unescap.org/TTDW/common/TIS/AH/files/egm06/road_safety_goals.pdf

Drummond, A.E and S.E. Torpey. (1985), "Driver Improvement Program Evaluation", *Report No.12/85, Road* Traffic Authority, Melbourne, Victoria, Australia.

Drummond, A.E., Cave, T.C.and Healy. D.J. (1986), "*The Risk of Accident Involvement by time of Week. An Assessment of the Effect of Zero BAC legislation and the Potential of Driving Curfews"*, Paper presented to International Symposium on Young Drivers' Alcohol and Drug Impairment, Amsterda*m*

Dunman, R. (1958)," Economic Cost of Motor Vehicle Accidents", *Highway Research Board,* Bulletin 208, Traffic Accident Studies.

Durbin, J. (1960), "Estimation of Parameters in Time-series Regression Models", *Journal of Royal Statistical Society* 22, Series B, 139-153.

Dutch ministry of Transport, Public works and Water Management, (1996a), *Long-term Programme for Road Safety; Putting Policy into Practice, Ministry of Transport, Public works and water Management*, The Hague

Dutch Ministry of Transport, Public works and Water Management, (1996b), *"Towards Safer Roads; Opportunities for a Policy to Bring About A Sustainable Safe Traffic System", Transport Research Centre (AVV) of the Ministry of Transport, Public works and water Management*, Rotterdam.

Dyson, C. B., Taylor, M. A. P., Woolley. J. E and Zito, R. (2001)," *Lower Urban Speed Limits –Trading off safety, mobility and environmental impact"*, paper presented at the 24th Australian Transport Research forum, 17-20 April, Hobart.

Dyson, R. B. (1975), "Safety Versus Savings: An Essay on the Fallacy of Economic Costs of Accidents" in *Proceedings of 4th I.C.A.S*, pp. 145-153.

Economics Circle, (2005), "*RHD Road User Cost*", Annual Report for 2004-2005, Sarak Bhaban, Ramna, Dhaka.

Economics Circle, (2004) " RHD Road User Cost", Annual Report for 2003-2004. Sarak Bhaban, Ramna, Dhaka.

Elizabeth, K and Maureen, C. (2003),"Traffic Fatalities and Economic Growth", Vol.1, *Policy*, Research Working Paper Series, No. WPS 30351,1-48

Ellard, J. (1970), "Psychological Reactions to Compensible Injury", *Medical Journal of Australia* 1, 349.

Elliott, M and Broughton, J. (2005), "How Methods and Levels of Policing Affect Road Casualty Rates", *TRL Report* TRL 637, Workingham: TRL Limited.

Elvik, R. (1995), "An Analysis of Official Economic Valuations of Traffic Accident Fatalities in 20 Motorized Countries", *Accident Analysis and Prevention* 27, 237-247.

Elvik, R. (1997), *Cost-benefit Analysis o f Road Safety Measures is more Important and Relevant than Ever Before*, In Proceedings of the European Seminar of Cost-Effectiveness of road Safety Work and Measures, Luxembourg.

Elvik, R. (2001), "Cost-benefit Analysis of Police Enforcement", Report ESCAPE project, Working paper, Helsinki, VTT.

Elvik, R and Mysen, A. B. (1999), "Incomplete Accident Reporting", *Transport Research Record*, 1665 (CD-ROM), 133-140.

Elvik, R and Vaa, T. (2004), "*The Handbook of Road Safety Measures*", Amsterdam: Pergamon Press.

Engel, U and Thomsen, L. (1992)," Safety Effects of Speed Reducing Measures in Danish Residential Areas", *Accident Analysis and Prevention* 24, 17-28.

Epstein, B. (1958), "The Exponential Distribution and its role in Life Testing", *Industrial Quality Control* 15, 4 - 9.

Epstein, B. (1960), "Tests for the Validity of the Assumption that the Underlying Distribution of life is Exponential", *Technometrics* 2, 83-101 and 167-83.

Ergun, G and Qayyum, T. (1998), "Investigation of Highway Safety Problems in Saudi Arabia", *Saudi Arabian National Centre for Science and Technology*, Report Grant no: AR3-030.

Erskine, A. (1996), "The Burden of Risk: Who dies Because of Cars?" *Social Policy and Administration* 30, 143-157.

ESCAP SECRETARIAT (2006), "Status of road safety in Asia", Bangkok.

ETSC, (1999), Police Enforcement Strategies to Reduce Traffic Casualties in Europe, Brussels, European Transport Council.

European Road Safety Action Program (2003), "Halving the Number of Road Accident Victims in the European Union by 2010: A Shared responsibility", Brussels.European.

Transport Safety council, (1999), *Exposure Data for Travel Risk Assessment: Current Practice and Future needs in the EU*, European Transport Safety Council, Brussels, Belgium.

Evans, L. (1986), "Risk Homeostasis Theory and Traffic data", *Risk Analysis* 6, 81-94.

Evens, L. (1991), *Traffic Safety and Driver*, New York: Van No Strand Reinhold.

Evens, L. (1996), "Safety Belt Effectiveness: the Influence of Crash Severity and Selective Recruitment", *Accident Analysis and Prevention* 28, 423-433.

Evans, W and Graham, J. D. (1988), "Traffic Safety and Business Cycle", *Alcohol, Drugs and Driving* 4, No. 1, 31-38.

Expert Group on Road Safety, (1975)," The Road Accident Situation in Australia in 1975", (A report to the Australian Minister for Transport by the Expert Group on Road Safety); Parliamentary Paper No 274, Canberra.

Faigin, B. M. (1975), "Societal Costs of Motor Vehicle Accidents for Benefit-Cost Analysis: A Perspective on the Major Issues and Some Recent Findings" in Proceedings of the Fourth International Congress on Automotive Safety, July 14-16 1975, U.S. Department of Transportation, National Highway Traffic Safety Administration, Washington D.C., pp.155-172.

Faigin, B. M. (1976), *1975 Societal Costs of Motor Vehicle Accidents*, U.S. D.O.T. NHTSA, Washington, D.C., December 1976.

Falconer, W. (1996), "Road Safety: the Challenge", *The Evening Post*, January 31, p. 5.

Federal Office of Road Safety, (1998), *Road Injury Australia: Crashes Resulting in Hospitalisation in 1996*, Federal Office of Road Safety, Canberra.

Federal office of Road Safety, (1999), "Road Risk for Sober, Licensed Motorcyclists", *Monograph* 27, Canberra: Commonwealth of Australia.

Federal office of Road Safety, (2000), *Ride on: Survival Skills the Novice Rider Must Have*, Canberra: Commonwealth of Australia

Federal Road Safety Commission (FRSC) (2006), "Road Traffic Accident Trends: 1960-2002", retrieved from www.frscnigeria.org/currentevents.htm

Federation of Road Traffic Victims, (1997), "Impact of Death and Injury on the Roads", *Road Peace*, London.

Fisher, G. H. (1973), *Cost Considerations in System Analysis*, Elsevier, New York (Especially Chapter 3: 'Concept of Economic Cost', pp. 24-62.

Fitzpatrick, J. L. (1992), "Problems in the Evaluation of Treatment Programs for Drunk Drivers: Goals and Outcomes", *The Journal of Drug Issues* 22, 155-167.

Fitzpatrick, J. (2002), "*Too High a Price: Injuries and Accidents in London*", London Health Observatory (LHO), October, http://www.lho.org.uk

Fleischer, G. A. (1981), *Contingency Table Analysis of Road Safety Studies*, Sijthoff and Noordhoff Int. Pub.

Fleiss, J.L., Tytun, A and Ury, H.K. (1980)," A Simple Approximation for Calculating Sample sizes for Comparing independent Proportions", *Biometrica* 36, 343-346.

Forjuoh, S., Mock, C. N and Freidman, D. (1999), "Transport of the Injured to Hospitals in Ghana: the Need to Strengthen the Practice of Trauma Care", *Pre-hospital Immediate Care* 3, 66-70.

Fox, J. C., Good, M.C and Joubert, P. N. (1979), *Collisions with Utility Poles*, University of Melbourne for Office of Road Safety, Dept. of Transport (CR1).

Frame, G. (1999), "Traffic Management and Road Safety in World Bank Projects in Chinese Cities: A Review", World Bank, Washington DC.

Fridstrom, L., Ifver, J., Ingebrigtsen, S., Kulmala, R. and Thomsen, L. K. (1995), "Measuring the Contribution of Randomness, Exposure, Weather and Daylight to the Variation in Road Accident Counts" *Accident Analysis and Prevention* 27, 1-20.

Fukuda, A and Fukuda, T. (2006), "Current Situation of Road Traffic Accidents and Traffic Safety Education in Japan", In International Conference on Road Safety in Developing Countries, 22-24 August 2006, BUET, Dhaka.

Fukuda, T. (2006), "Motorcycle Accidents and its Countermeasures in Thailand", In International Conference on Road Safety in Developing Countries, 22-24 August 2006, BUET, Dhaka

Gelau, C., Gitelman, V., Jayet, M.C and Heidstra, J. (2004), "Development of Guidelines for Monitoring Routine Enforcement", *ESCAPE* Working Paper 12, available at http://www.vtt.fi/rte/projects/escape/escapewp12.htm

Gelman, A., Carlin, J. B and Stern, H. S. (2003), *Bayesian Data Analysis*, 2nd edition, Chapman and Hall, New York.

Ghaffar, A., Hyder, A. A., Bishai, D and Morrow, R. H. (2002), "Interventions for Control of Road Traffic Injuries: Review of Effectiveness Literature", *Journal of Pakistan Medical Association* 52, 69-73.

Ghaffar, A., Hyder, A. A., Veloshnee, G and David, B. (2004), "Road Crashes: A Modern Plague on South Asia's Poor", *Journal of College of Physical Surgeon - Pakistan* 14, 739-41.

Glass, G. V., Wilson V.L and Gottman, J.M. (1975), *Design and Analysis of Time-Series Experiments*; Colorado Associated University, Press.

Glejser, H. (1969), "A New Test for Heteroscedasticity", *Journal of the American Statistical Association* 64, March, 316-323.

Global Road Safety Partnership (GRSP), (2000), GRSP News and Brochure (1st Edition), January 2000, Geneva.

Goldenbeld, C., Gelau, C., Heidstra, J., Jayet, M., C., Nilsson, G., Papaioannou, P., Rothengatter, T., Quimby, A., Rehnova, V. and Vaa, T. (2003), "Traffic Enforcement in Europe: Effects, Measures, Needs and Future", Final Report of *ESCAPE*, Espoo: VTT.

Granau, R. (1973), *"The Measurement of Output of the Non-Market Sector: The Evaluation of Housewife's Time" The Measurement of Economic and Social Performance*, National Bureau of Economic Research, New York.

Gregg, S. (1996), Victorian Shock Tactics Drive Home Message, *The Sunday Star Times,* July 7, p. C3.

Griffin, L and Flower, R. (1997), "A Discussion of Six Procedures for Evaluating Highway Safety Projects", Draft Report for the Federal Highway Administration, Washington, D. C.

Griffith, M. S., Hayden, C and Kalla H. (2003), "Data is Key to Understanding and Improving Safety", In Public Roads, US Department of Transportation Federal Highway Administration, available in http://www.tfhrc.gov/pubrds/03jan/09.htm

Gururaj, G., Thomas, A. A., Reddi, M. N. (2000), *Under Reporting on Road Traffic Injuries in Bangalore: Implications for Road Safety Policies and Programmes*, pp. 54-55, Macmillan India Ltd., Delhi.

Gustafson, K. (2006), "Road Safety Development and the *"* Vision Zero*"* in Sweden *"* in International Conference on Road safety in developing Countries, 22-24 August 2006 BUET, Dhaka.

Haight, F. A. (1986), "Risk, Especially Risk of Traffic Accidents", *Accident Analysis and Prevention* 18, 359-366.

Haimes, Y. (1998), *Risk Modeling, Assessment, and Management*, New York; John Wiley and Sons.

Hakkert, A. S and Braimaister, L. (2002), *The Uses of Exposure and Risk in Road Safety Studies*, SWOV Institute for Road Safety Research, Leidschendam, The Netherlands.

Hakkert, S and Hauer, E. (1988), "The Extent and Implications of Incomplete and Inaccurate Road Accident" Reporting, in J. A. Rothengatter and R. A. de Bruin, *Road User Behaviour Theory and Research,* Assen, The Netherlands, Van Gorcum .

Hall, J. W., Turner, D S. and Hall, L. E. (1994), "Concerns About Use of Severity Indexes in Roadside Safety Evaluations", Transportation Research Record No. 1468, pp. 54-59, TRB, National Research Council, Washington D. C.

Haque, M.O. (1987)," Evaluation of the Demerit Points System in Deterring Traffic Offences*",* Report No.GR/87/21, Road Traffic Authority, Melbourne, Victoria, Australia.

Haque, M .O. (1988), "Estimation of Future Population for Community Facilities in New Housing Estates*"*, A Paper presented at the 5th National Evaluation Conference, Melbourne, July 27-29, 1988.

Haque, M. O. (2006), "Developing Road Safety Countermeasure Initiatives Using Monthly Road Fatalities", In International Conference on Road Safety in Developing Countries, 22-24 August 2006, BUET, Dhaka.

Haque, M. O. (2006), "A Short Term Serious Road Casualty Monitoring System: A case Study for Victoria", In International Conference on Road Safety in Developing Countries, 22-24 August 2006, BUET, Dhaka.

Haque, M. O and Cameron, M.H. (1987), "Evaluation of the Effect of the Victorian Zero BAC legislation: July 1984-December 1985*"* (Report No. G11/187/11*).* Hawthorn, Victoria: Road Traffic Authority.

Haque, M. O and Cameron, M. H. (1987)," Evaluation of the Effect of the Victorian Zero BAC Legislation: July 1984 - December 1985 ", Report No. GR/87/I 1, Road Traffic Authority, Victoria.

Haque, M. O and Le, H. H. (1988), "A Short-term Accident Monitoring System: A case study for Victoria", *Proceeding 14th ARRB Conference*, part 4, pp.234-243.

Haque, M. O., Strang, P.M and Crabb, M. (1986), "Evaluation of the Victorian Zero BAC legislation" *Interim Report* (Research Note No. RN/86/5). Hawthorn Victoria: Road Traffic Authority.

Harris, A. H., Giles, M. J., Hendrie, D and Kroll, L. (1992)," The Property Damage Costs of Road Accidents in Western Australia", Report to the Australian Road Research Board, RR20.

Harrison, A. H. (1974), *The Economics of Transport Appraisal*, Croom Helm, London.

Harrison, W. (1987), "An Examination of penalties Imposed by Courts for Speeding Offences", Report no. RN/87/11, Road Traffic Authority: Melbourne, Australia.

Harrison, W., South, D., Portans, I., Armour. M., Lau, H and Haque, O. (1987)," *An Evaluation of the Effects of the Motor Car (Photographic Detection Devices) Act 1986 on Police Costa and Efficiency and Road Safety"*, Road Traffic Authority, Melbourne.

Hartunian, N. S., Smart, C. N and Thompson, M. S. (1980), "The Incidence and Economic Costs of Cancer, Motor Vehicle, Injuries, Coronary Heart Disease and Stroke", *American Journal of Comparative Public Health* 70 No. 12, 1249-1260.

Harvey, A. C and Durbin, J. (1986) "The Effects of Seat Belt Legislation on British Road Casualties: A Case Study in Structural Time Series Modeling", *Journal of the Royal Statistical Society* A, 149, 187-227.

Hauer, E. (1995), "On Exposure and Accident Rate", *Traffic Engineering Control* 36, 134-138.

Hauer, E. (1997), *Observational Before-After Studies in Road Safety*, Pergamon/Elsevier Science, Inc., Terrytown, New York.

Hauer, E and Persaud, B. N. (1983), "A Common Bias in Before and After Comparisons and its Eliminations", *Transportation Research Record* 905, 164-174, Transportation Research Board, National Research Council, Washington DC.

Haworth, N and Symmons, M. (2002), *Local Government Road Safety Survey 2000*, MUARC Roport No. 189.

Haworth, N and Smith, R. (1999), *Single Training Course and Test for the Motorcycle license*, Melbourne: Monash University Accident Research Centre.

Haworth, N., Smith, R., Brumen, I and Pronk, N. (1997), *Case Control Study of Motorcycle Crashes* (CR174), Canberra: Commonwealth of Australia.

Haworth, N., Tingvall, C., Vulcan, P and Cameron, M. (1999), "Future Directions: Safety First", 2000-2005, Development of Road Safety Initiatives, Report Prepared for Vic Roads.

Hazen, A and Ehiri, J. E. (2006), "Road Traffic Injuries: Hidden Epidemic in Less Developed Countries", Journal of *Natl Medical Association* 98, 73-82.

Heidi, W. (2006), *"Road Traffic Accidents Increase Dramatically Worldwide"*, Population Reference Bureau, Washington DC, USA.

Heidstra, J., Goldenbeld, C., Gelau, C., Makinen, T., Jayet, M and Evers, C. (2000), "Traffic Law Enforcement by Non-Police Bodies", The *ESCAPE* Project Contract No. RO-98-RS.3047, Project funded by the European Commission under the Transport RTD Programme of the 4th Framework Programme.

Henderson, M. (1978), "The Value of Human Life : Cost Benefit Considerations in Traffic Safety", *Search* 6, 19-23.

Henderson, M. (1991), "Education, Publicity and Training in Road Safety: A Literature Review", Report No. 22, Monash University Accident Research Centre, Clayton. Road Safety Publicity Campaigns, In Safer Road Users, Available in http://www.i-connect.ch/grsp/grspdev/campaign.htm

Henderson, M. and Quandt, R. E. (1971), *Microeconomic Theory: A Mathematical Approach,* McGraw-Hill, Kogakusha, Ltd., Tokyo.

*Hendrie, D., Legge, M.(Date) (Interim Report on the Costs of Injury Database for Western Australia, Report to the Department of Health, Western Australia, RR138.

Hijar, M., Arredondo, A., Carrillo, C and Solorzano, L. (2004), "Road Traffic Injuries in an urban area in Mexico: An Epidemiological and Cost Analysis", *Accident Analysis and Prevention* 36, 37-42.

Hills, P. J and Jones-Lee, M. W. (1981), "The Costs of Traffic Accidents and the Valuation of Accident Prevention in Developing Countries", *Seminar G: PTRC Annual Summer Meeting*, pp.113-32.

Hingson, R., Heeren, T and Winter, M. (1994)," Lower legal blood alcohol limits for young Drivers", *Public Health Rep* 109, 738-44.

Hobley, M. (2002), "Rating Risk", (the value of rating roads for safety)", *Surveyor* 21.3.02, pp. 12-14

Holmes, R.A. (1970), "On the Economic Welfare of Victims of Automobile Accidents", *American Economic Review* 60, 143-152.

Hopkins, M and O'Reilly, D. (1993), "Revaluation of the Cost and Road Accident Casualties: 1992 Revision", TRL RR378, Transport Research Laboratory, Crowthorne.

HOPS, (1992), "Framework for Prospective Traffic Safety Analysis", *DRIVE* Project V2002.

HOPS, (1993), "Guidelines for Planning Safety Evaluation", *DRIVE* Project V2002.

Hoque, M. M. (1989), "Road Accident Prevention", *Journal of the Institution of Engineers* 17, 19-34. Bangladesh.

BIBLIOGRAPHY

Hoque, M. M. (2001), "Road Safety Improvements in Developing Countries: Priority Issues and Options", Proceedings of 20th Australian Road Research Board (ARRB) Conference.

Hoque, M, M. (2004), "The Road to Road Safety: Issues and Initiatives in Bangladesh", Proceedings of the 2nd Asian Regional Conference on Safe Community and 1st Bangladesh Conference on Injury Prevention, 15-17 February, 2004, Dhaka.

Hoque, M. M. (2006), "Road Safety in Bangladesh: The Contemporary Issues and Priorities", In International Conference on Road Safety in Developing Countries, 22-24 August 2006, BUET, Dhaka

Hoque, M. M., Mahmud, M. I., Azad, A. K and Sarkar, S. (2006), "The Risk of Children in Road Traffic Accidents in Bangladesh", In International Conference on Road Safety in Developing Countries, 22-24 August 2006, BUET, Dhaka.

Hoque, M. M., McDonald, M and Hall, R. D. (2000), "Road Safety Improvements in Developing Countries: Priority Issues and Options", Proceedings of 20th Australian Road Research Board (ARRB) Conference, 2000.

Hoque, M. M., Solaiman, T. A., Khondaker, B. and Sarkar, S. (2004),"Road Safety in Bangladesh: Overview of Problems, Progress, Priorities and Options", ARC, BUET, Dhaka.

Hossain, M. (2006a), "Application of Data Mining in Road Safety", Masters Thesis, Asian Institute of Echnology, 2000, Bangkok.

Hossain, M. (2006b), "A Study on Pedestrian Accidents Based on the Injury Surveillance (IS) Data: Thailand's Case", In International Conference on Road Safety in Developing Countries, 22-24 August 2006, BUET, Dhaka.

Hurt, H.H., Ouellet, J. V and Thom, D. R. (1981), "Motorcycle Accident Cause Factors and Identifications of Countermeasures", Technical Report, Vol. 1, Traffic Safety Centre, University of Southern California, California.

Hutchinson, T. P. (1987), *Road Accident Statistics*, Rumsby Scientific Publishing, Adelaide, Australia.

Hvoslef, H. (1994), "Under-Reporting of Road Traffic Accidents Recorded by the Police, at the International Level", International Road Traffic and Accident Database Special Report, Norway: Public Roads Administration, November Statistical Summary, Canberra.

Hyden, C., Nilsson, A and Risser, R. (1998), *Relation Between the Numbers of Cyclists and the Number of Casualties Among Cyclists in a Road Accident* Lund, Sweden.

Hyden, C. (2003), "Theories on Traffic Safety Evaluation Connected to New Road Transport Informatics (RTI)", 6th ICTCT Workshop Salzburg Proceedings, Department of Traffic Planning and Engineering, Lund Institute of Technology, Lund, Sweden.INRETS, Paris,http://www.kfv.or.at/gadget/wp4/index.htm

ICBC, (1995), "The Economic Cost of Society of Motor Vehicle Accidents", Insurance of corporation of British Columbia, Vancouver.

Iamtrakul, P., Sattayaprasert, W., Hossain, M and Charankol, T. (2006), "Probability of Survival (PS): An Alternative Severity Assessment Approach in Road Safety", In International Conference on Road Safety in Developing Countries, 22-24 August 2006, BUET, Dhaka.

Iamtrakul P., Tanaboriboon, Y and Hokao, K. (2003), "Analysis of Motorcycle Accidents in Developing Countries: A Case Study on Khon Kaen Thailand ", *Journal of Eastern Asia Society for Transportation Studies* 5, 147-162.

Institute for Public Policy Research and Imperial College, (2002), *Street Ahead*, Institute for Public Policy Research, London.

Institute of Civil Engineering, (1996), *A Vision for Road Safety Beyond 2000*, Oversize Pamphlet HD7333.A3.M8, London.

Institute of Highways and Transportation, (1999), *Guidelines for Rural Safety Management*, Oversize HE336.R85, London.

Johnston, I. (1980), "Alcohol Related Accidents: Characteristics, "Causes" and Countermeasure Implications," Road Safety Initiatives Conference, Melbourne.

Jacobs, G. D. (1983), "Road Accidents in Developing Countries", *Accident Analysis and Prevention* 15, 337-353.

Jacobs, G. D. (1996), "Road Safety in Emerging Nations", Inter-Traffic Middle East '96 Safety Symposium,24-26 November,1996, Dubai.

Jacobs, G.D. (2000), "Road Safety as a Global Problem", 65th Road Safety Congress, 6-8 March, UK.

Jackobs, G. D. (2006), "*Road Safety: The Global Problem*", In International Conference on Road Safety in Developing Countries, 22-24 August 2006, BUET, Dhaka.

Jacobs, G., Aeron-Thomas, A and Astrop, A. (2000), "Estimating Global Road Fatalities", *Transport Research Laboratory Report* 445, Crowthorne.

Janke, M. L. (1991), "Accidents, Mileage and the Exaggeration of Risk", *Analysis and Prevention* 23, 183-188.

Janssen, W. (1994), "Seatbelt Wearing and Driving Behaviour: An Instrumented-Vehicle Study", *Accident Analysis and Prevention* 26, 249-261.

Japan Research Centre for Transport Policy, (1978), *Social Losses from Road Accidents*, p.55

Japan Statistics of Road Accidents, (2004), Abridged Edition, Traffic Bureau, National Policy Agency, International Association of Traffic and Safety Sciences, Tokyo.

Joksch, H. C. (1975), "A Critical Appraisal of the Applicability of Benefit Cost Analysis to Highway Traffic Safety", *Accidents Analysis Prevention* 7, 133-153.

Joksch, H. C. (1984), "The Relation Between Motor Vehicle Accident Deaths and Economic Activity", *Accident Analysis and Prevention* 16, No. 3, 207 - 210.

Joly, P., Joly, M. F.,Desjardins, D., Messier, S., Maag,U., Ghadirian, P and Laberge-Nadeau, C. (1993),"Exposure for Different License Categories

Through a Phone Survey: Validity and Feasibility Studies", *Analysis and Prevention* 25, 529-536.

Jones, J. (2003), "Speed Cameras and in-vehicle Speed Limits Represent the future for Urban Speed Control", *Local Transport Today* 373, p. 12, 21.8.03.

Jones-Lee, M. W. (1969) "Valuation of Reduction in Probability of Death by Road Accident", *Journal of Transport Economics and Policy* 3, 37-47.

Jones-Lee, M. W. (1976), *The Value of Life An Economic Analysis*, Robertson, London.

Jones-Lee, M. W. (1979a), "Trying to Value a Life: Why Broome Does not Sweep Clean", *Journal of Public Economics* 12, 249-256.

Jones-Lee, M.W. (1979b) "Trying to Value a Life: A Reply", *Journal of Public Economics* 12, 259-262.

Jones-Lee, M. W. (1990), "The value of Transport Safety", *Oxford Review of Economic Policy* 6, 39-60.

Jones-Lee, M. W., Loomes, G., O'Reilly, D and Philips, P. (1993), "The Value of preventing Non-Fatal Road Injuries: Findings of a Willingness-To-Pay National Sample Survey", TRL Working Paper WP/SRC/2.

Jordan, P. (2006), "The Benefits of Road Safety Audit to the Rapidly Motorising World", In International Conference on Road Safety in Developing Countries, 22-24 August 2006, BUET, Dhaka.

Kalbfleisch, J.D and Prentice, R.L (1980), *The Statistical Analysis of Failure Time Data*, New York: John Wiley.

Karim, M. R. (1995), "A Macro Analysis of Road Accident Trends in Malaysia", *Journal of the Eastern Asia Society for Transportation Studies* 1, 941-950.

Karlstrom, U. (2005), "Swedish Development in Road Safety", Proceedings from 13th Road safety on Four Continents, VTI, Linkoping, Sweden.

Keeney, R. L. (1986), "The Analysis of Risks Fatalities", in *Risk Evaluation and Management* (Edited by V T. Covello, J. Menkes and J. Man Power), Plenum Press, New York.

Keeping Children Safe in Traffic – ISBN – 92-64-10629-4 © OECD, (2004), extracted from http://www.cemt.org/JTRC/Children-Policy-brief.pdf

Kendall, M. G and Stuart, A. (1969), *The Advanced Theory of Statistics* 1, Griffin, London.

Keskinern, E and Pasanen, A. (1990), "Self-destruction in Motor Vehicle Accidents: The Proportion of Suicides and Negligent Drivers in Fatal Motor Vehicle Accidents in 1974-75 and 1984-85 in Finland", *Journal of Traffic Medicine* 18, No. 4, 179-185.

Kidd, B. (2000), "50 km/h Urban Speed Limits: The Western Australian Approach," Paper presented at the public forum on the 50 k/h Speed limit for Local Roads, http://www.transport.wa.gov/roadsafety/issues/norwell.htm.

Kloeden, C. N., McLean, A. J., Moore, V. N and Ponte, G. (1997), *Travelling Speed and the Risk of Crash Involvement* (CR 172), Canberra: Office of Road Safety.

Kloeden, C. N., McLean, A. J., Moore, V. M and Ponte, G. (1998), *Travelling Speed and the Risk of Crash Involvement*, NHMRC, Adelaide, Federal Office of Road safety, CR172 (2 volumes), Canberra and c.f: http://plato.raru.adelaide.edu/au/speed/index.htm.

Knox, D and Silcock, B, R. (2002), "International Review of Driver Improvement Schemes, and Evaluation of the UK", 67th Road Safety Congress, 4th – 6th March 2002, Road Driving – The Road to Success.

Kobusingye, O. C and Lett, R. R. (2000), "Hospital-Based Trauma Registers in Uganda", *Journal of Trauma* 48, 498-502.

Krupp, R and McMahon, K. (1993), "Cost-Transport: Completed Actions: Socio-Economic Cost of Road Accidents", *CORDIS*, Report No. COST 313, available in http://www.cordis.lu/cost-transport/src/cost-313.htm

Kulanthayan, S., Radin, U. R., Ahmad, H. H., Mohd, N. M. and Harwant, S. (2000), "Compliance of Proper Safety Helmet Usage in Motorcyclists", *Malaysian Medical Journal* 55, 1

Kyle, S. B. (1998), *Preliminary Results 1997 ATV Injury Survey*, Washington, DC: U. S. Consumer Product Safety Commission.

Lane, J. C. (1964), " The Money Value of a Man", Paper to section J Australian and New Zealand Association for the Advancement of Science, 37th Congress, Canberra, A.C. T.

Lawson, J. J. (1978), "The Costs of Road Accidents and their Application in Economic Evaluation of Safety Programs", *Proceedings of Annual Conference of Roads and Transportation Association of Canada*, (Sept. 18-2, Ottawa, (pp.30).

Leaf, W. A and Preusser, D. F. (1998), *Literature Review on Vehicle Travel Speeds and Pedestrian Injuries*, National Highway Traffic Safety Administration, United States Department of Transport, http://www.nhtsa.gov/people/injury/research/pub/hs809012.html

Lee, Hoe C., Cameron, D and Lee, A. H. (2003), "Assessing the Driving Performance of Older Adult Drivers: On-Road versus Simulated Driving", *Accident Analysis and Prevention* 35, 797-803.

Leggett, L. M. W. (1985), "Monitoring Road System Safety Performance by Quality Control Charting", An Abstract Presented to the Road Safety Researcher's Conference, Melbourne, Australia.

Leggett, M. (1991), "Figure 1: Relative Trends in Fatalities in Economy", *Annualised Per Capita Road Fatality Trends 3*, No. 1.

Levitt, S. D and Porter, J. (2001), "Sample Selection and the Measurement of Seat Belt and Air Bag Effectiveness", *Review of Economics and Statistics* 83, 603-612.

Li, G., Braver, E. R and Chen, L. H. (2001), "Exploring the High Driver Death Rates Per Vehicle-Mile of Travel in Older Drivers: Fragility Versus

BIBLIOGRAPHY

Excessive Crash Involvement", IIHS Research Report, The Insurance Institute for Highway Safety, Arlington, USA.

Lin, M. (1998), "Risk Factors for Motorcycle Crashes in an Urban and Rural Area: A cohort study", *Dissertation Abstracts International: Section B: The science and Engineering* 59, 5-B, 2155.

Lind, B. (1982), *The Effects of Sunday Trading on Traffic Crashes* (Special Report SR 82/112), Melbourne: Traffic Accident Research Unit, Traffic Authority of New South Wales.

Little, A. D. (1968), *Cost Effectiveness in Traffic Safety*, Praeger.

Ljung, G. M and Box, G. E. P. (1978): On a Measure of Lack of Fit in Time Series Models, *Biometrica* 65, 297-303.

Loeb, P. D. (1987), "The Determinants of Automobile Fatalities: With Special Consideration of Policy Variable", *Journal of Transport Economics and Policy* 21, 279-287.

London Health Observatory (Author: Justine Fitzpatrick), (2002), *Too High a Price: Injuries and Accidents in London*, London Health Observatory (LHO), London, October, http://www.lho.org.uk

Lowdell, C. (2002), *Too High a Price: Injuries and Accidents in London, Health of Londoners Programme*, London.

Luby, S., Hassan, I., Jahangir, N., Rizvi, N., Farooqi, M., Ubaid, S and Sadrudin, S. (1997), "Road Traffic Injuries in Karachi: the Disproportionate Roles of Buses and Trucks", *Southeast Asian Journal of Tropical Medicine and Public Health* 28, 395-398.

Ludwig, B. (1985), "Rating Accident Models and Investigations Methodologies", *Journal of Safety Research* 16, 105-126.

Lum, K. M. and Wong, Y. D. (2003), "A Before-and-After Study of Driver Stopping Propensity at Red Light Camera Intersections", *Accident Analysis and Prevention* 35, 111-120.

Lumley, M. (1998), "Australian Child Restrains Lead the World", Proceedings of the Developments in Safer Motor Vehicles Seminar, Parliament House, Sydney, March 1998.

Lyman, S and Braver, E. R. (2001), "Occupational Deaths in Large Truck Crashes in the United States: 25 Years Experience", IIHS Research Report, The Insurance Institute for Highway Safety, Arlington, USA.

Mackay, M. (2003), Global Road Traffic Injuries: An Overview of the Problem, UN Technical Briefings on the Global Road Safety Crisis – May 29, 2003.

MacKenzie, G. (1986), "A Proportional Hazard Model for Accident Data", *Journal of the Royal Statistical Society* 149, Series A, 366-75.

Macpherson, T and Lewis, T. (1998), New Zealand Drink-Driving Statistics: The Effectiveness of Road safety Television Advertising, Marketing Bulletin No. 9, pp. 40-51, available in http://marketing-bulletin.massey.ac.nz/article9/article4b.asp.

Maddison, D., Pearce, D., Johansson, O., Calthrop, E., Litman, T and Verhoef, E. (1996), *Blueprint 5: The True Costs of Road Transport*, Earthscan, London.

Maguire, B.A., Pearson.,E.S and Wynn, A.H.A. (1952), "The Time Intervals Between Industrial Accidents", *Biometrika* 39, 168-80.

Maisey, G. E. (1984), "The Effect of Lowering the Statutory Alcohol Limit for First Year Drivers from 0.08 to gm/100ml (monograph)", Perth, Western Australia: Western Australia Police Department, Research and Statistics Section, Research report No. 84/2.

Makridakis, S., Wheelwright, S.C and Mc Gee, V. E. (1983), *Forecasting Methods and Applications* 2nd *edition*, Willey, New York.

Maniruzzaman, K. M and Mitra, R. (2005), "Road Accidents in Bangladesh", *IATSS Research* 29.

Manual of Road Safety Audit, (1997), Roads Directorate, Ministry of Transport, Denmark.

Manual of Road Safety Improvement by Use of Low Cost Engineering Countermeasures for Pakistan, (1999), Finnroad O. Y, Finland.

Maheshwari, J and Mohan, D. (1989)"Road Traffic Injury in Delhi, a Hospital Based Study", *Traffic Medicine* 17, 23-27.

Mahmud, S. M. S., Rahman, M. F., Hoque, S and Hoque, M. M. (2006), "A Preliminary Comparison of Road Safety Situation in Selected Countries", In International Conference on Road Safety in Developing Countries, 22-24 August 2006, BUET, Dhaka.

Marsh, J. C., Kaplan, R. J and Kornfield, S. M. (1977), *Financial Consequences of Serious Injury*, Highway Safety Research Institute, University of Michigan, (final report) Ann Arbor, UM-HSRI-77-27.

Massie, D. L., Campbell, K. L and Williams A. F. (1995), "Traffic Accident Involvement Rates by Driver Age and Gender", *Analysis and Prevention* 27, 73-87.

Maycock, G. (1996), "Sleepless and Driving: The Experience of UK Car Drivers", *Journal of Sleep Research* 5, 229-237.

Mayhew, D. R and Simpson, H. M. (1983), "Alcohol, Age and Risk of Road Accident Involvement", *Proceedings, Nineth International Conference on Alcohol, Drugs and Traffic Safety*, U.S Department of Transportation.

Mayhew, D. R., Donelson, A. C., Beirness, D. J and Simson, H.M (1986), "Youth, Alcohol and Relative Risk of Crash Involvement ", *Analysis and Prevention* 18, 273-287.

Mayhew, D. R., Simpson, H. M and Pak, A. (2003), "Changes in Collision Rates among Novice Drivers during the First Months of Driving", *Accident Analysis and Prevention* 35, 741-748.

Metzner, G and Brinkmann, B. (1993), "Inaccuracies in the Official Accident Statistics of Fatal Traffic Accidents: Comparative Studies in West Germany During two time Periods", *Journal of Traffic Medicine* 21, 165-169.

Miller, T. R., Lestina, D. and Galbraith, M. (1997), "United States Passenger-Vehicle Crashes by Crasheometry:Direct Costs and Other Losses", *Accident Analysis and Prevention* 29, 343-352.

Ministry of Surface Transport, (2003), *Road Safety Audit Manual*, CRRI, New Delhi.

Ministry of Transport, (2003), *Thailand Road Safety Audit Manual*, Thailand.

.Mishan, E. J. (1971a), *Cost Benefit Analysis,* Unwin University Books, London.

Mishan, E. J. (1971b), "Evaluation of Life and Lim: A theoretical Approach", *Journal of Political Economy* 79, 687-705.

Mitchell-Taverner, P. (2000*), Community Attitudes to Road Safety: Community Attitudes Survey Wave* 13, Canberra: Australian Transport Safety Bureau.

Mittal, N and Sarin, S. M. (2001), "Cost Effective Road Safety Counter-Measures for Metropolitan Cities of India", *Indian Highways*, August 2001, pp. 5-22.

Mohan, D. (2002), "Road Safety in less Motorized Environments: Future Concerns", *InternationalJournal of Epidemiology* 31, 527-532.

Mohan, D. (2004), The Road Ahead: Traffic Injuries and Fatalities in India, NewDelhi,*Transportation Research and Injury Prevention Programme*, pp.1-30, Indian Institute of Technology, Delhi.

Mohan, D. (2004), "Evidence-Based Interventions for Road Traffic Injuries in South Asia", *Journal of the College for Physicians and Surgeons, Pakistan* 14, 746-747.

Mohan, D. (2006), "Road Traffic Injuries and Fatalities in Asia – A Modern Epidemic", In International Conference on Road Safety in Developing Countries, 22-24 August 2006, BUET, Dhaka.

Montgomery, D.C and Johnston, L.A. (1976), *Forecasting and theTime Series Analysis*, Mcgraw Hill, USA.

Mooney, G. H. (1977), *The Valuation of Human Life*, Macmillan, London.

Morden, C. H. (1989), "An Estimate of the Cost of Road Traffic Collisions in South Africa for 1998", *Strategic Management of Infrastructure*, Division of Road and Transport Technology, South Africa.

Morris, A., Begbie, J., Fildes, B., Barnes, J and Claessens, M. (2000), ANCIS-In-Depth Crash Injury Research in Australia, Road Safety Research, Policing and Education Conference.

Morris, A. P., Fildes, B. N., Deery, H., Kenny, D., Bentivegna, F and Edwards-Coghill, K. (1997), The Value of Real-World Crash Injury Data Collection: Methodology of an In-Depth Crash-Injury Study in Australia.

Mountain, L., Maher, M and Fawaz, B. (1998)," Improved Estimates of the Safety Effects of Accidents Remedial Schemes", *Traffic Engineering and Control*, October 1998.

Murphy, J. and Delucchi, M. (1998), "A Review of the Literature on the Social Costs of Motor Vehicle use in the United States", *Journal of Transportation and Statistics* 1, 16-42.

Mussone, L., Ferrari, A and Oneta, M. (1999), "An Analysis of Urban Collisions Using an Artifical Intelligence Model", *Accident Analysis and Prevention* 31, 705-718.

Myers, D. (2000)," The KwaZulu Natal Road Safety Project – Enforcement, Technology and the Community*",* Proceeding of Road Safety Research, Policing & Education Conference, November 2000, Brisbane, Australia, Sponsored by RACQ and CARRSQ.

Nagai, Y and Fukuda, A. (2005), "Research on Traffic Safety Education and Evaluation of its Effects in Chiba Prefecture", Japan, Proceedings of the Sixth International Conference of Eastern Asia Society for Transportation Studies (EASTS), Bangkok, Thailand.

Nancy, L. (2004), "A New Accident Model for Engineering Safer Systems", *Safety Science* 42, 247-270.

Nantulya, V. M. (2002), "The Neglected Epidemic: Road Traffic Injuries in Developing Countries", *British Medical Journal* 324, 1139-41.

Nantulya, V. M., Sleet, D. A., Reich, M. R., Rosenberg, M., Peden, M and Waxwiler, R. (2003), "The Global Challenge of Road Traffic Injuries", *Injury Control and safety Promotion* 10, 3-7.

N.H.T.S.A. (1972), Societal Costs of Motor Vehicle Accidents: Preliminary Report, U. S. DOT, Washington D.C.

National Highway Traffic Safety Administration, (2002), Traffic Safety Facts, Retrieved from www.nhtsa.dot.gov on January 20, 2006.

National Highway Traffic Administration (NHTSA), (2004), "Traffic Safety Facts 2003: Pedestrians", US Department of Transport, Washington D. C.: http://www-nrd.nhtsa.dot.gov/pdf/nrd-30NCSA/TSF2003/809769.pdf

National Occupational Health and Safety Commission, (1999), "Evaluation of Road Transport OHS Prevention Initiatives", *Sharing Practical Solutions to OHS Problems*, National Occupational Health and Safety Commission.

National Road Traffic Accident Report, (2001), "Road Safety Cell", BRTA, Bangladesh, Dhaka National Road Safety Strategy 2001 - 2010 Progress Report, available on-line at http://www.aaa.asn.au/directions/directions%20103/NRSS.htm

National Road Traffic Accident Report, (2001), "2001-Road Safety Cell", BRTA, Bangladesh.

Newstead, S. V., Cameron, M. H and Narayan, S. (1998), "Further Modeling of Some Major Factors Influencing Road Trauma Trends in Victoria: 1990-1996", *MUARC*, Report No. 129.

Newstead, S. V., Cameron, M. H., Watson, L. M and Delaney, A. K. (2003), *Vehicle Crashworthiness and Aggressively Ratings and Crashworthiness by Year of Vehicle Manufacture: Victoria and NSW Crashes during 1987-2000, Queensland and Western Australia Crashes During1991-2000*, Report No. 196, Monash University Accident Research Centre.

New Zealand Road Safety Strategy (2000), Road Safety Strategy 2010, National Road Safety Committee, Land Transport Safety Authority, New Zealand.

NFO Donovan Research (2000a), "Attitudes to the Proposed 50 km/h Speed limits on local area Roads", Report to Office of Road Safety, WA.

NFO Donovan Research (2000b), "Community Attitude Monitor", Report to Office of Road safety, WA.

NFO Donovan Research (2000c), *Community Attitudes Survey –Speed Limits on Local area roads,* Report to office of Road safety, WA.

Nilsson, G. (1997), "Methods and Necessity of Exposure Data in Relation to Accidents and Injury Statistics", IRTAD Special Report, Swedish Road and Transport Research Institute, Linkoping, Sweden

Northern Ireland Office, (2003), "Road Traffic Penalties in Northern Ireland – a Consultation Document", Northern Ireland Office, Belfast, April. http://www.nio.gov.uk/pdf/rtraff.pdf

Odero, W., Garner, P and Zwi, A. (1997), "Road Traffic Injuries in Developing Countries: A Comprehensive Review of Epidemiological Studies", *Topical Medicine and International Health* 2, 445-460.

Odero, W., Khayesi, M and Heda, P. M. (2003), "Road Traffic Injuries in Kenya: Magnitude, Causes and Status of Intervention", *Injury Control and Safety Promotion* 10, 53-61.

OECD Road Transport Research (2005), "International Road Traffic and Accident database (IRTAD)", *Accident Statistics*, OECD/BAST.

OECD Scientific Expert Report (1994), "Targeted Road Safety Programmes", Organisation for Economic Co-Operation and Development, Paris, France.

O'Neill B., Mohan, D., Breen, J., Koonstra, M.J., Mackay, M., Roberts, I and Ryan, G.N. (2002), "The World Banks Global Road Safety Partnership", *Traffic Injury Prevention* 3, 190-94.

Palutikof, J. P. (1991), "Road Accidents and Weather", In A. H. Perry and L. J. Symons (Eds.), *Highway Meteorology*, London: E and F. N. Spon.

Panda, J. (2001), *ORFRTD Bulletin: Orissa Regional Forum for Rural Transport & Development* (IFRTD Regional Forum Group), Bhubaneswar 751015, Orissa, India.

Parker, D., Manstead, A., Stradling, S. and Senior, V. (1998), "The Development of Remedial Strategies for Driving violations", TRL Report No. 300, Transport Research Laboratory, Crowthorne.

Parliamentary Advisory Council for Transport Safety (PACTS) St. Thomas' Hospital, (2003), Best Value, Local Transport Plans and Road Safety, available from: Claire.maltby@pacts.org.uk.

Partyka, S. C. (1984), Simple Models of Fatality Trends Using Employment and Population Data, *Accident Analysis and Prevention* 16, 211-222.

Parzen, E. (1962), *Stochastic Processes,* San Francisco: Holden-Day.

Paterson, J. (John Paterson Urban Systems 1973), "The Cost of Road Accident in Relation to Road Safety", Report No. NR/23 for the Dept of Transport, Govt. Printer, Canberra.

Pearce, D. W. (ed) (1978), *The Valuation of Social Cost,* George Allen and Unwin, London.

Peck, R.C and J, Kuan. (1982), *A statistical Model of Individual Accident Risk Prediction Using Driver Record, Territory and other Biographical Factors;* CAL-DMV-RSS-82-84, Sacramento: State of California Business, Transportation and Housing Agency's Department of Motor Vehicles.

Peden, M., McGee, K and Sharma, G. (2002), The Injury Chart Book: A Graphical overview of the Global Burden of Injuries, World Health Organisation, Geneva.

Peek-Asa, C. (1999), "The Effects of Random Alcohol Screening in Reducing Motor Vehicle Crash Injuries", *American Journal of Preventative Medicine* 16, 57-67.

Peirson, J., Skinner, I. and Vickerman, R. (1998), "The Microeconomic Analysis of the External Costs of Road Accidents", *Economica*, 65 (259), 429-440.

Persaud, B. N. (2001), "Statistical Method in Highway Safety Analysis, a Synthesis of Highway Practice", NCHRP Synthesis 295, Transportation Research Board, National Research Council.

Persson, U and Odegaard, K. (1995), "External Cost Estimates of Road Traffic Accidents: An International Comparison", *Journal of Transport Economics and Policy* 29, 291-304.

Peter Bacon & Associates Economic Consultants, (1999), "Benefits and Costs of the (Irish) Government Road Safety Strategy 1998-2002", (Irish) National Safety Council, The Irish Times on the Web.

Poch, M and Mannering, F. (1996), "Negative Binomial Analysis of Intersection Accident Frequencies", *Journal of Transportation Engineering* 122, 105-113.

Ponboon, T. (2005), "Development of Road Accident Reporting Computerized System in Thailand", *Journal of Eastern Asia Society for Transportation Studies* 6, 3453-3466.

Priestley, M. B. (1981) *Spectral Analysis and Time Series,* Vol. 1, Univariate Series, New York, Academic Press.

Proceedings of the International Conference on Road Safety in Developing Countries, (2006), Edited by M. M. Hoque, Accident Research Centre, Bangladesh University of Engineering and Technology (BUET), Dhaka.

Putignano, C and Pennisi, L. (1999), "Social Costs of Road Accidents (Italian case study)", *Transport Statistics Unit, National Institute of statistics*, Italy.

Qazi, S, A. (2000), "Impact of Road Traffic Accident on Our Social System", *The journal of Bangladesh Orthopaedic Society* 15, No. 1, January 2000.

Quazi, S. H., Sajal, K, A., Wan, H. W. I and Rezaur, R. B. (2005), "Road Traffic Accident Situation in Khulna City, Bangladesh", *Proceedings of the Eastern Asia Society for Transportation Studies* 5, 65-74.

Radin, U. R. (1994), "Analysis of Traffic Accidents in Malaysia", *Journal of International Association of Traffic and Safety Science* (IATSS) 18, 82-83.

Rahman, F. (2004), "Road Traffic Injuries the Burden of Road Traffic Injuries in South Asia: a Commentary", *JCPSP* 14, 707-708.

Razzak, J. A and Luby, S. P. (1998), "Estimating Deaths and Injuries Due to Road Traffic Accidents in Karachi, Pakistan through the Capture-Recapture Method", *International Journal of Epidemiology*, 27, 866-570.

Redondo-Calderon, J. L., Luna-del-Castillo, J.D., Jimenez-Moleon, J. J., Garcia-Martin, M., Lardelli-Claret, P and Galvez-Vargas, R. (2001), "Application of the Induced Exposure Method to Compare Risks of Traffic Crashes among Different Types of Drivers Under Different Environmental Conditions", *American Journal of Epidemiology* 153, 882-891.

Regan, M. A., Triggs, T. J and Godley, S. T. (2000), "Evaluation of a Novice Driver CD-ROM Based Training Program; A Simulator Study", *Proceedings of the International Ergonomics Association/Human Factors and Ergonomics Society Conference*, 2000.

Ribeiro, S. F and Goes, J. R. R. (2005),"Road Accidents in Brazil", *IATSS Research* 29.

Richardson, A. J. (1983), "The Economic Evaluation of Traffic Accidents", *ESSO- Monash Workshop on Traffic Accident Evaluation*, Paper No. 15.

Road Maintenance and Transportation Organisation, (2006), *Road Safety Audit Manual for the Islamic Republic of Iran*, Prepared by Rahan Pooyesh Consultants, Teheran.

Road Safety Committee. (2004), Inquiry in to the Demerit Points Scheme November 1994, Parliament of Victoria: Road Safety Committee Report upon the Inquiry into the Demerit Points Scheme, Melbourne.

Road Safety Guidelines for Asian and Pacific Region, (2003), Asian Development Bank, Manila. Philippines.

Road Safety in Victoria, (1988), *New Strategic Directions and Implementation plan*, Road Traffic Authority and Road Construction Authority, December 1988.

Road Safety Initiatives Recognised through Awards (2001), RACQ News, available at http://www.racq.com.au/13_news/articles/20010731_Road_safety_ini.htm

Road Safety Manual on Low-cost Engineering Countermeasures, (1998), UN Economic Commission for Africa.

Road Safety Strategy 2010, "A Consultation Document, National Road safety Committee, New Zealand", extracted from www.itsa.govt.nz/strategy-2010/docs/summar-of-submissions-final.pdf

Road safety Vision 2010, (2002), 2002 Annual Report, Extracted from: http://www.tc.gc.ca/roadsafety/vision.htm

Road Traffic Authority of NSW, (2003), *Road traffic accidents in New South Wales 2001, Statistical Statement: Year ended 31 December 2001*, Road Traffic Authority: Road Safety Strategic Branch.

Road Traffic Accident Cost Study for Bangladesh, (2003), TRL, UK.

Road Traffic Authority of NSW, *Preliminary Traffic Accident Data: Monthly Bulletin January 2004*, Road Traffic Authority of NSW, Sydney.

Road Transport Research -Targeted Road Safety Programs, (1993), OECD, Paris, France.

Robert, I., Mohan, D and Abbisi, K. (2002)," War on Road", *British Medical Journal*, No 7346.

Roberts, I., Hosford, T and Edwards, P. (2001), "The World Health Organisation and the Prevention of Road Injuries Phone Book Analysis", *British Medical Journal* 323, 1485. http://bmj.com/cgi/content/full/323/7327/1485

Roberts, I., Norton, R. and Taua, B. (1996), "Child Pedestrian Exposure Rates: The Importance of Exposure to Risk Relating to Socio-Economic and

Ethnic Differences in Auckland", New Zealand, *Journal of Epidemiology Community Health* 50, 162-165.

Rodgers, G. B. (1998), *Results of the 1997 ATV Exposure Survey*, Washington DC: U. S. Consumer Product Safety Commission.

Romão, F., Nizamo, H., Mapasse, D., Rafico, M. M., José, J., Mataruca, S., Efron, M. L., Omondi, L. O., Leifert, T and Bicho, J. M. L. M. (2003), "Road Traffic Injuries in Mozambique", *Injury Control and Safety Promotion* 10, 63-67.

Romina Factbook, (2005), "2005 – by Investors – Estimating Global Road Fatalities", extracted from http://www.factbook.net/EGRF_Regional_analysis_HMCs.htm

Rosman, D. L. (1995), "Linkage of Hospital and Police Road Crash Data, An Investigation of Alternative Methods", National Injury Surveillance Unit, RIIP-7, RR 27.

Rosman, D. L. (2000), Uniform Definition of 'Serious 'injury for Road Crash Casualties in Australia, Report to ARRB Transport Research, RR98.

Rosman, D. (2001), "The Western Australian Road Injury Database (1987-1996): Ten Years of Linked Police, Hospital and Death Records of Road Crashes and Injuries", *Accident Analysis and Prevention* 33, 81-88.

Ross, A. (1998), "Road Safety in Developing Countries", *Highways and Transportation*, April 1998, pp. 26-28.

Rowe, W. D. (1988), *An Anatomy of Risk*, Robert E. Krieger Publishing Company, Mallbar, Florida.

Royal Automobile Club of Victoria (RACV), (1983), *Inquiry into road safety in Victoria* (submission to the Social Development Committee of the Parliament of Victoria).

Royal Malaysian Police ((PDRM) (2001), Statistical Report: Road Accidents Malaysia – Traffic Branch, Bukit Aman, Kuala Lumpur.

Royal Thai Police, (2004), Accidental Rate, Death Rate, Injury Rate during 1995-2004, Data available on line at http://www.royalthaipolice.go.th

Ruengsorn, D., Tanaboriboon, Y., Chadbunchachai, W and Teekayuphun, P. (2003), "Development of GIS Based Traffic Accident Database Through Trauma Management System: A Case study of Khon Kaen", Report No. 84-2003-5, ISBN: 974-9593-08-1, Thailand.

Ryan, G. A. (1993), "Road Traffic Accident Prevention Workshop, Hanoi, Vietnam", Report to the World Health Organisation, Western Pacific Regional Office.

Ryan G. A. (1998), "Motorcycle Crashes in Western Australia 1987-1997", Report to Main Roads W. A, RR66.

Ryan, G. A and Hendrix, D. (1995), Review of Road Safety Programs in Victoria, New South Wales, and Western Australia, Report sponsored by the Traffic Board of Western Australia, RR34.

Ryan, G. A., Hendrie, D., Mullan, N and Lyle, G. (1998), Application of the Road Injury Cost Database, ANCAP Testing, Report to ANCAP Panel, RR73.

Saema, M., Muneeza, M., Chtani, H and Luby, S. (1999), "Risky Behaviour of Bus Commuters and Bus Drivers in Karachi, Pakistan", *Accident Analysis and Prevention* 31, 329-333.
Safety Audit of Road Designs, (2002), FINNRA, Finland.
Saffer, H and Chaloupka, F. J. (1989), "Breath Testing and Highway Fatality Rates", *Applied Economics*, 21, 901-912.
Salifu, M. (2004), "Accidents Prediction Models for unsignalised Urban Junctions in Ghana", *IATSS Research*, 28.
Saloniemi, A and Oksanen, H. (1998), "Accidents and fatal Accidents: Some Paradoxes", *Safety Science* 29, 59-66.
Sangowawa, A. O., Ekanem, S.E.U., Alagh B. T., Faseru, B and Ebong, I.P . (2006), "Helmet Use Among Motorcyclists in Ibadan, North West Local Government Area, Oyo State, Nigeria", In Proceedings of the Public Health Association of Southern Africa (PHASA) 3rd Public Health Conference, Johannesburg, South Africa, 16-17 May 2006, Conference Proceeding, 125.
Sarkar, A. A. (2006), "Accident Cost and Benefit Analyses in the Evaluation of Road Projects in Bangladesh", In International Conference on Road Safety in Developing Countries, 22-24 August 2006, BUET, Dhaka
SAS Institute Inc. (1982): *SAS/ETS User's Guide: Econometrics and Time Series Library*, Cary, North Carolina.
SAS Institute Inc. 1990, *SAS/STAT User's Guide*, Version 6, 4th Edition, vol. 2, Cary, North Carolina.
SAS/ETS. (1984), *SAS/ ETS Users guide version 5 Edition*, SAS Institute Inc CARY, NC. USA.
Sass, T. R and Zimmerman, P. R. (2000), "Motorcycle Helmet laws and Motorcyclist Fatalities", *Journal of Regulatory Economics* 18, 195-215.
Sayer, I. A. (1994), Road Accident Data Recording, International Course on Prevention and Control of Traffic Accidents and Injuries, New Delhi, India, 8-16 December 1994.
Schagen, I. V and Janssen, T. (2000), "Managing Road Transport Risks, Sustainable Safety in the Netherlands", *IATSS Research* 24, 18-27.
Scheers, N. J., Newman, R., Polen, C and Fulcher, D. (1991), *The Risk of Riding ATVs: A Comparison from 1985 to 1989*, Washington, DC: U. S. Consumer Product Safety Commission.
Schelling, T. C. (1968), "The Life You Save May be Your Own", (pp 127-176), in *Problems in Public Expenditure Analysis* (ed) S. B. Chase, Brookings Institution, Washington D.C.
Schwarz, G. (1978), "Estimating the Dimension of a Model", *Annals of Statistics* 6, 461-464.
Scottish Executive, (2004), Road Accidents and Children Living in Disadvantaged Areas: A Literature Review, Chapter Three – Factors Associated with Road Accidents and Disadvantaged Areas, available in http://www.scotland.gov.uk/cru/kd01/blue/r-acc07.htm

Servadel, F., Begliomini ,C., Gardini,E., Giustini, M., Taggi, F and Kraus, J. (2003), "Effect of Italy's Motorcycle Helmet Law on Traumatic Brain Injuries", *Injury Prevention* 9, 257-260.

Shannon, H. S. (1986), "Road Accident data: Interpreting the British Experience with particular Reference to Risk Homeostasis Theory, *Ergonomics* 29, 1005-101.

Sherwin, M. A. (1976), "Road Accident Costs" in the *Cost of Road Accidents: Papers and Reports from a Workshop on Cost of Road Accidents*, March, 1977, Wellington, New Zealand, (National Roads Board) 1978), pp.7-31.

Shields, B., Morris, A., Barnes, J and Fildes, B. (2001), Australia's National Crash In-depth Study Progress Report, Monash University Accident Research Centre, Clayton.

Sidi, H. S and Kahoro, P. (2001), "Experience with Road Traffic Accident Victims at the Nairobi Hospital", *East African Medical Journal* 78, 441-44.

Siegrist, S. (2003), *Drivers Training and Licensing- The European Perspective, Forum on Driver Education and Training*, NTSB, Washington, 28/29 October 2003.

Simpson, H. F. (1997), "*National Hospital Study of Road Accident Casualties*", Transport Research Laboratory (TRL) Report No. 272, Transport Research Laboratory, Crowthorne, Berkshire.

Sloane, H. R and South, D.R. (1985), *The Characteristics of Accidents Involving Alcohol in Victoria 1977-1982,* Road Traffic Authority, Victoria.

Smeed, R.J.(1964), "Methods Available to Reduce the Number of Road Casualties", Paper Presented at the 7th International Study Week in Traffic Engineering, OTA, 32 Chesham Place, London.

Smeed, R. J. (1972), "The Usefulness of Formulae in Traffic Engineering and Road Safety", *Accident Analysis and Prevention* 4, 303-312, Pergamon Press.

Smith, D.I. (1980), The Introduction of Sunday Alcohol Sales in Perth: Some Methodological Observations, *Community Health Studies* 4, 289-2113.

Smith, D. I., Jacobs, I and Ferrante, A. M. (1989), *Proposal for the Creation of a Road Injury Database,* Injury Research Centre, School of Population Health, The University of Western Australia.

Social Development Committee, (1984), *Final Report on Road Safety in Victoria*: *Parliament of Victoria*, Melbourne, Australia.

Somasundaraswaran, A. K. (2006), "Accident Statistics in Sri Lanka", *IATSS Research* 30, No. 1.

Somerville, C. J. and McLean, A. J. (1981), *The Cost of Road Accidents*, The University of Adelaide, Road Accident Research Unit.

South African Department of Transport. (2000), *An Estimate of Unit Cost of Road Traffic Collisions in South Africa for 1999*, Draft Report, South African Department of Transport.

South, D.R. (1986), *Surrogate Measure of Alcohol Related. Accidents,* Internal Memorandum, Road Traffic Authority, Victoria.

South, D.R., Swan, E.D and Vulcan, A. P. (1983), Review of Alcohol Countermeasures in Victoria, In *Proceedings of the Ninth International Conference on Alcohol, Drugs and Traffic Safety*, San Juan, Puerto Rico.
SPSSX, (1986), *SPSSX Users Guide*, 2nd Edition, SPSS Inc., Mcgraw Hill, USA.
Stamatiadis, N and Deacon, J. A. (1997), "Quasi-induced Exposure: Methodology and Insight", *Accident Analysis and Prevention* 29, 37-52.
Stone, M and Broughton, J. (2003), "Getting off your Bike: Cycling Accidents in Grate Britain 1990-1999", *Accident Analysis and Prevention* 25, 549-556.
Stoner, D and Srinath, K. P. (1998), *All-Terrain Vehicle Exposure Survey*, Contact CPSC-C-94-1115, Task 004, Cambridge, MA: ABT Associates, Inc.
Struble, D., Paterson, R., Wilcox, B and Friedman, D. (1975), "Societal Costs and their Reduction by Safety Systems" in *Proceedings of 4th I C A S*, pp. 695-779.
Supramaniam, V., Belle, V and Sung. J. (1984), "Fatal Motorcycle Accidents and Helmet laws in Peninsular Malaysia", *Accident Analysis and Prevention* 16, 157-162.
Suriyawongpaisal, P. and Kanchanasut, S. (2003),"Road Traffic Injuries in Thailand: Trends, Selected Underlying Determinants and Status of Intervention", *Injury Control and Safety Promotion* 10, 95-104.
Symons, M.J. and D.W. Reinfurt. (1975), "A Model for Evaluating the Effectiveness of Motor Vehicle Inspection Programs", *Accident Analysis and Prevention* 7, 281-88.
Tanaboriboon, Y. (2004), "The Status of Road Safety in Thailand", ADB, ASEAN Regional Safety Program, Country Report: CR09, Final Report, Thailand.
Tanaboriboon, Y., Ruengsorn, D., Chadbunchachai, W and Suriyawongpaisal, P. (1999), "Analysis of traffic Accidents through Hospital's Trauma Registry Records", *Journal of International Association of Traffic and Safety Sciences*, 23, 117-119.
Tanaboribbon, Y and Santiennam, T. (2005), "Traffic Accidents in Thailand", *Journal of International Association of Traffic Safety Sciences (IATSS) Research*" 29, 88-100.
Tandukar, K. P. (2004), "Traffic Fatalities in Nepal", *JAMA* 291, 2542
Thailand Transport Safety Bureau, (2004), Thailand Road Safety Action Plan: 2004-2008, Office of Transport and Traffic Policy and Planning, Ministry of Transport, Bangkok.
Tervonen, J. (1999), Accident Costing Using Value Transfers, New Unit Costs for personal Injuries in Finland, Technical Research Centre of Finland, ESPOO.
The Guide to Community Preventative Services: Studies Evaluating the Effects of lower blood alcohol Concentration laws for young or Inexperienced Drivers: evidence Summary Table (2002), obtained from www.thecommunityguide.org/mvoi/.

The Home Office. (2000), "Road Traffic Penalties", *a consultation Paper*, the Home Office Communication Directorate.

The Home Office, (2002), "Report on the Review of Road Traffic Penalties", July 2002, http://www.homeoffice.gov.uk/ppd/oppu/traffic.pdf

The Official website for the International Hospital Federation, (2002), "22 October – Accidents Cost NHS£2Billion", *INFORMER*, Available in http://www.hospitalmanagement.net/informer/breakthroughs/break189/

Thedie, J and Abraham, C. (1961), "Economic Aspect of Road Accidents", *Traffic Engineering and Control* 2, PP. 589-595.

Thom, H. C. S. (1958), "A Note on the Gamma Distribution", *Monthly Weather Review*, U. S. Department of Commerce, pp. 117-122

Thomas, A. A., Jacobs G. D., Sexton, B., Gururaj, G and Rahman, F. (2004), "The Involvement and Impact of Road Crashes on the Poor: Bangladesh and India Case Studies", Transport Research Laboratory, USA.

Thomas, R. (2004), "Will Rise in Speeding Prosecutions Force Safety Camera Rethink?", *Local Transport Today*, 383, pp. 9, 15.01.04.

Thompson, S. (2002), "Safety in Numbers?", (Traffic Accident Statistics in Nottingham), *Surveyor* 189, pp. 19 20, 24.10. 02.

Thomson, J. M. (1974), *Modern Transport Economics*, Penguin, Harmondsworth.

Thoresen, T., Fry, T., Heiman, L and Cameron, M. (1992), *Linking Economic Activity, Road Safety Countermeasures and Other Factors with the Victorian Road Toll*, Monash University Accident Research Centre, Clayton.

Thorpe, J. P. (1970), "Estimated Cost of Road Accidents in Victoria, 1966-67" *Australian Road Research* 4, No. 3, (March 1970) 55-70.

Tindall, J. I. (1974), "Economic Analysis of Accidents for Traffic Engineers", Paper Presented at 7th Australian Road Research Board Conference, Adelaide."Tire Safety-everything Rides on it", extracted from www.nhtsa.dot.gov/cars/rules/TireSafety/ridesonit/takeone.html

Todd Litman. (2004a), "Transportation Cost and Benefit Analysis Guidebook", *VTPI*: www.vtpi.org

Todd Litman.(2004b),"Safe Travels: Evaluating Mobility Management Traffic Safety Impacts", *VTPI*, www.vtpi.org.(put

Traffic Authority of New South Wales. (1987), *Monthly Bulletin of Preliminary Traffic Accident Data for April 1987*, Sydney, Australia.

Traffic Authority of NSW, (2005), Monthly Bulletin of Preliminary Traffic Accident Data for April 2005, Sydney.

Transport New Zealand, Project Evaluation Manual, (1997) ISBN 0 478 105681Transport New Zealand, Wellington, New Zealand.

Transport Research Circular (2006), *Safety Data Analysis and Evaluation*, Transport Research Board, USA.

Transport Research Laboratory, (1999), "Accident Rates and Behavioural characteristics of Novice Drivers in the TRL Cohort Study", TRL Report No. 293, Transport Research Laboratory, Crowthorne, Berkshire.

BIBLIOGRAPHY

Transport Research Laboratory, (2000a), "The Effects of Drivers' Speed on the Frequency of Road. Accidents", TRL Report No. 421, March 2000, Transport Research Laboratory, Crowthorne, Berkshire.

Transport Research Laboratory, (2000b), "Estimating Global Road Fatalities", *TRL Report* No. 444, May 2000, Transport Research Laboratory, Crowthorne, Berkshire.

Transport Research Laboratory, (2001), "Monitoring Local Authority Road Safety Schemes Using MOLASSES", *TRL* Report No. 512, December 2001, Transport Research Laboratory, Crowthorne, Berkshire.

Transport Research Laboratory, (2002), "Linkage of Hospital Trauma Data and Road Accident Data", TRL Report No. 518, Transport Research Laboratory, Crowthorne, Berkshire.

Transport Research Laboratory, (2003a), "Road safety publicity campaigns update (2000-2002)", Ct107.2, Transport Research Laboratory, Crowthorne, Berkshire National Safety Council, (Various years), *Accident Facts,* Chicago, Illinois.

Transport Research Laboratory, (2003b), "Risk Hazard Perception and Perceived Control", TRL Report No. 560, Transport Research Laboratory, Crowthorne, Berkshire.

Trinca G. W., Johnston, I.R. and Cambell, B.J. (1988), "Reducing Traffic Injury: the Global Challenge", Royal Australian College of surgeons, Melbourne, AH Massina &co

Troy, P. N and Butlin, N. G. (1971), *The Cost of Collisions*, Cheshire, Melbourne pp. 292.

Tsuang, M. B .M and Fleming J. (1985), "Psychiatric Aspects of Traffic Accidents", *American Journal of Psychiatry* 142, 538-546.

Twisk, D. A. M. (2000)," Why did the Accident Involvement of Young (male) Drivers Drop by about 50 Percent?" In: Proceedings of the 10th Seminar on Behavioural Research in Road Safety, Esher, Surrey, 3-5 April 2000, pp. 109-117.

Twomby, B. B. (1960), "Economic Costs of Road Accidents", in relation to the *Highway Research Board Bulletin* 263.

Taylor, M., Lynam, D. and Baruya, A. (2000), The Effects of Drivers' Speed on the Frequency of Road Accidents, TRL Report No. 421, Transport Research Laboratory, Crowthorne, Berkshire.

Ugar, B. and Erden, O. (1990), "Regression Procedures in SAS: Problems?", *The American Statistician* 44, No. 4, 296 - 301.

Union International des Chemains des Fers (UIC), (2000), "External Costs of Transport: Accident, Environmental and Congestion Costs in Western Europe", UIC, Paris, Fax. +33 1 4449 2029, &# 128;   200- summary at **http://www.uic.asso.fr** (click on 'Environment").

United Nations, (2003), "Global Road Safety Crisis", Resolution Adopted by General Assembly, New York.

University College London (Centre for Transport Studies) & the Babtie Group, (2003), *A Review of the Delivery of the Road Safety Strategy"?* December, 2003.

Utzelman, H. D and Jacobshagen, W. (1996), Validation of the German System of Diagnosis and Rehabilitation of Traffic Offenders, *Traffic and Transport Psychology, Ed.*, T. Rothengatter and E. Carbonell Vaya, Pergamon.

Van, B.G and Martin, D. C. (1993), "Sample Size as a Function of Coefficient of Variation and Ratio of Means", *American Statistician* 47, 165-167.

Vasil, A. (1996), "Road Injuries Rise – Research", *The Dominion*, November 4, p. 3 South African Department of Transport, (1999), Cape Metropolitan Area: Road Traffic Accident Statistics, South African Department of Transport.

Vic Roads, (2000), *"Regulatory Impact Statement for Proposed Road Safety (Road Rules)*, (Amendment) Regulations 2000", Road Corporation of Victoria.

Victor, D. J. (1980), "Priorities in Road Safety Research in Developing Countries", *Proceedings of World Conference on Transport Research* 4, 2464-2472.

Vinand, M. N. and David A. S. (2003), "Introduction: The Global Challenge of Road Traffic Injuries: Can We Achieve Equity in Safety"? *Proceedings of International Conferences on Injury Control and Safety Promotion*, April 10-12, 2003, Cambridge, Massachusetts, USA.

Vingilis, E., Blefgen, H., Lei, H., Sykora, K and Mann, R. (1988)," An Evaluation of the Deterrent Impact of Ontario's 12-hour Licence Suspension Law", *Accident Analysis and Prevention* 20, 9-17.

Voas R. B., Lange, J. E. and Tippetts, A. S. (1998)," Enforcement of the Zero Tolerance Law in California: A Missed Opportunity?", 42nd *Annual Proceedings: Association for the Advancement of Automotive Medicine*, October 5-7, Charlottesville, Virginia, pp. 369-83.

Voas R. B., Tippetts, A. S and Fell J. (1999), "The United States Limits Drinking by Youth Under 21: Does this Reduce Fatal Crash Involvements?" 43nd *annual Proceedings: Association for the Advancement of Automotive Medicine*, September 20-21, Barcelona (Sitges), Spain, pp. 265-78.

Vulcan, P., Cameron, M and Newstead, S. (1995), "Road Trauma in Perspective", *Paper Presented to Vehicle Accidents Their Causes – Reconstruction – Law Conference*, Melbourne, July 28 – 29, 1995, Department of Civil Engineering, Monash University.

Wachtel, A and Lewiston, D. (1994), "Risk Factors for Bicycle Motor Vehicle Collisions at Intersections", *ITE Journal*, September, pp. 30-35, http://www.bicyclinglife.com/Library/riskfactors.htm

Wagenaar, A. C. (1984), "Effects of Macro Economic Conditions on the Incidence of Motor Vehicle Accidents", *Accident Analysis and Prevention* 16, No. 3, pp. 191-205.

Waller, J. A. (1994), "Reflection on a Half Century of Injury Control", *American Journal of Public Health* 84, 664.

Walsh, D. and Smith, M. (1999), "Effective Speed Management the Next Step Forward: Saving lives by Decreasing Speeds in Local Streets", paper presented to *1999 Research, Policing, Education Road Safety Conference*, pp. 685-694.

Wegman, F. and Aarts, L. (Eds). (2006), "Advancing Sustainable Safety; National Road Safety Exploration for 2005-2020", Forthcoming, *SWOV Institute for Road Safety Research*, Leidschendam, The Netherlands.

Wegman, F., Dijkstra, A., Schermers, G and Vliet, P. V. (2006), "Sustainable Safety in the Netherlands: the Vision, the Implementation and the Safety Effects", Contribution to the *85th Annual Meeting of the Transportation Research Board*, 22-26 January 2006, Transport Research Board, Washington.

West, R. (1997)," Accident Rates and Behavioural Characteristics of Novice Drivers: A Study of Data Obtained from the TRL cohort Study", *TRL Report No. 293*.

Whelan, M., Diamantopoulou, K., Senserrick, T and Cameron, M. (2003)," Establishing Benchmark of Safety on Melbourne Roads", report No. 198, Monash University Accident Research Centre.

White Paper on Traffic Safety in Japan, (2005), Abridged Edition, Cabinet Office, International Association of Traffic and Safety Sciences, Tokyo.

Wigan, M. R. (1982), "Accidents Valuation: Induction Options", *The Australian Road Research Board Proceedings* 11, Part 5.

Wilde, G. J. S. (1982), "The Theory of Risk Homeostasis: Implications for Safety and Health", *Risk Analysis* 2, 209-225.

Wilde, G. S. J. (1984), "On the Choice of Denominator for the Calculation of Accident Rates", In S. Yagar (Ed), *Transport Risk Assessment*, pp. 139-154, Waterloo, Ontario, University of waterloo Press.

Wilde, G. J. S. (1989), "Accident Countermeasures and Behavioural Compensation: the Position of Risk Homeostasis", *Journal of Occupational Accidents* 10, 267-292.

Wilde, G. J. S. (1991), "Economics and Accidents: A Commentary", *Journal of Applied Behaviour Analysis* 24, 81-84.

Wilde, G. J. S. (1994), Risk Homeostasis Theory and Its Promise for Improved Safety, In R. M. Trimpop and G. J. S. Wilde (eds.), *Challenges to Accident Prevention: the issue of risk compensation processes*, Styx Publications, Groningen, The Netherlands.

Wilde, G. J. S., Robertson, L. S. and Pless, I. B. (2002), "Does Risk Homoeostasis Theory have Implications for Road Safety?", *British Medical Journal* 324, 1149-1152.

Willet, A. (1951), *The Economic Theory of Risk and Insurance*, Philadelphia:University of Pennsylvania Press, 1951, P. 6 (first published 1901), cited by Herbert S. Denenburg, Robert D. Eilers, Joseph J. Melone, and Robert A. Zelten, *Risk and Insurance* 2nd Ed. Englewood Cliffs, N. J.: Prentice-Hall; 1974, p. 4.

Williams, A. (1979), "A note on Trying to Value Life", *Journal of Public Economics* 12, 257-158.

Williams, A. F. (1994), "The Contribution of Education and Publicity to Reducing Alcohol-Impaired Driving", *Alcohol, Drugs and Driving* 10, 197-205.

Wilson, R. (1979) "Analysing the Daily Risks of Life", Technology Review, Massachusetts Institute of Technology, February 1979, (pp.41-45).

Wiorkowski, J.J and Heckard, R. F. (1977a), "The Use of Time Series Analysis and Intervention Analysis to Assess the Effects of External Factors on Traffic Indices: A Case Study of the Effects of the Speed Limit Reduction and Energy Crisis in the State of Texas", *Accident Analysis and Prevention* 9, pp. 229-247.

Wiorkowksi, J.J and Heckard, R.F. (1977b), The Use of Time Series Analysis to Assess the Effects of External Factors on Traffic Indices: A case study of the effects of the speed limit reduction and energy Crisis in the State of Texas, *Accident Analysis and Prevention* 9, p. 229.

Wood, T and Bowen, R. (1987), *Evaluation of the Revised Motorcycle Learner Permit Scheme: July 1983 to December 1985*, RN/87/15, Road Traffic Authority - Victoria.

World Bank, (2006), Transport and Social Responsibility, Information Available at internet.worldbank.org

World Health Organisation –Regional Office for Africa, (2003), R*oad Accidents Soar in Africa, Cost the Region $7.3 Billion*, Public Information and Communication Unit, World Health Organisation-Regional Office for Africa, Brazzaville, Congo.

World Health Organisation, (2004), *World Report on Road Traffic Injury Prevention : Summary*, Geneva.

World Health Organisation (WHO), (2004), "Road Safety is no Accident", *A brochure for World Health Day 7 April 2004*, Geneva.

Yeates, M. (2002), "More about twisted logic' ... the position of 'soft people' from an upside-down world of 'Road Safety Ideology", World Transport Policy and Practice 8, available at http://wTransport.org

Zaal, D. (1997), Traffic Law Enforcement: A Review of the Literature, Monash University Accident Research Centre, Report No. 53, Available at http://www.general.monash.edu.au/muarc/rptsum/es53.htm, maintained by MUARC Webmaster.

Zaidel, D. (2002), "The Impact of Enforcement on Accidents", Deliverable 3 (Work package 2) of the ESCAPE project, Espoo: VTT

www.ingramcontent.com/pod-product-compliance
Lightning Source LLC
Chambersburg PA
CBHW021358290426
44108CB00010B/295